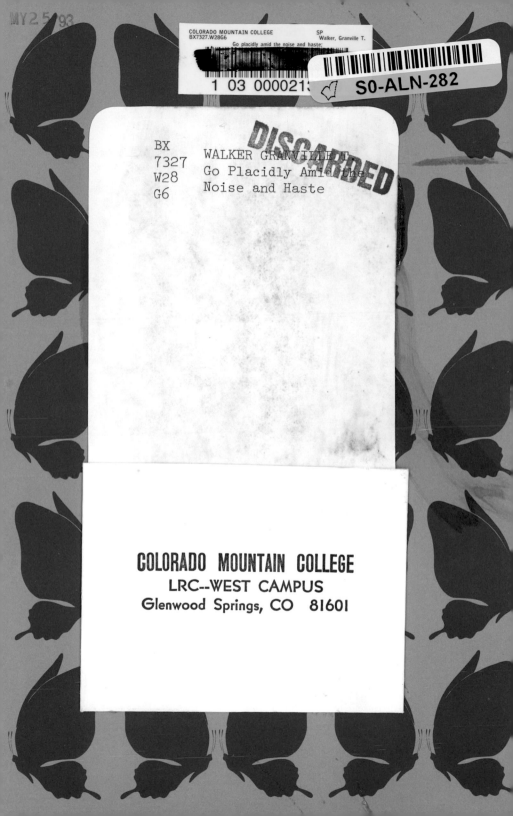

Go placidly amid the noise and haste

MEDITATIONS ON THE "DESIDERATA"

BY GRANVILLE T. WALKER

NO. 2, 1973
TCU PRESS

THE TEXAS CHRISTIAN UNIVERSITY PRESS, FORT WORTH, TEXAS

THE MONDY MONOGRAPHS

The Texas Christian University Press in 1968 received a gift from the family of the late Vinal B. Mondy in his memory. In accordance with the wishes of Mrs. Mondy and her son, Lewis, and daughter, Mary Martha, TCU is devoting the funds to a series of monographs in religion of which this is the second.

Mr. Mondy, who lived his latter years in Dallas, Texas, was a churchman, teacher, businessman, and spent much of his free time reading biblical literature and philosophy. He was long regarded as an expert teacher of the Bible in his classes in Christian Churches of Oklahoma and Texas.

The publications committee of the Department of Religion of the University consists of William L. Reed, Chairman, George P. Fowler, and Noel L. Keith, with the latter serving as General Editor for the series.

FOREWORD

The ministry of Dr. Granville T. Walker has been marked by many notable achievements—as scholar and teacher, as pastor and counselor, as administrator and international leader of the Christian Church (Disciples of Christ). Preeminently, though, he is a preacher of extraordinary skill.

These meditations on the "Desiderata," first presented by Dr. Walker from the pulpit of University Christian Church in Fort Worth, Texas, exemplify his exciting, highly intelligent and spiritually powerful preaching. If the essential nature of a sermon is such to make it impossible for printing to reproduce preaching, as Fosdick once suggested, it is true in Dr. Walker's case only to the extent that the reader is deprived of the forceful impact of his intimate and compelling speaking style.

Always an exponent of intelligent Biblical preaching, Dr. Walker in this unique series uses the obviously restated Biblical ideas from the popular "Desiderata" to proclaim the "essentials" (the meaning of "Desiderata") for human conduct. Ranging from "the passive virtues of humility and peaceable relationships" to "Christian action in meeting the vast and immeasurable needs in our world," there is help here for the reader in making day by day moral and ethical decisions and in finding Christian answers to some of the baffling problems that plague our culture. If the essential purpose of preaching is to enable persons to come to such an insight into their own condition and the condition of their world, that they may be free to live their lives as authentically as Jesus Christ lived His, this is preaching at its best!

Go Placidly amid the Noise and Haste is an excellent companion piece to Dr. Walker's earlier work, **The Greatest of These,** meditations on the thirteenth chapter of First Corinthians published on the occasion of the twentieth anniversary of his service as minister of University Christian Church. The publication of this present volume coincides with the remarkable confluence of four significant events: the centennial celebration of Texas Christian University, the one-hundredth anniversary of University Christian Church, the completion of thirty years by Dr. Walker as pastor of that great congregation, and the announcement of his plan to retire at the end of 1973.

This Foreword provides some opportunity to acknowledge the profound respect and affection held for Dr. Walker by members of the congregation and a grateful brotherhood. Complete objectivity may be too much to have expected in the writing of this Foreword from one so much affected by his preaching, pastoral care and friendship.

Kenneth L. Teegarden
Executive Minister,
Christian Church
(Disciples of Christ) in Texas

TABLE OF CONTENTS

With all becoming grandfatherly pride,
this book is lovingly dedicated to
Mary Beth Chowning
Anne Chowning
and Christopher Walker Wilson
assured that the message of the Desiderata
will be as needed in their maturer years
as it has been in ours.

PREFACE

The publication of this volume coincides with several important anniversaries. One is the centennial of University Christian Church; another is the centennial of Texas Christian University. (The two institutions came into being simultaneously at Thorp Spring in the fall of 1873.) Still another is my thirtieth anniversary as minister of this church; and the fourth is my sixty-fifth birthday. All of these dates fall within a month of each other—a confluence of events which crystallized my long pondered thoughts on retirement.

These years of relationship to Texas Christian University and to University Christian Church I look back upon with deep gratitude and joy. All but a very few years of my adult life have been spent either as a student or as a faculty member of the University, or as minister of the University Christian Church.

The publication of this book is being made possible by the University Press of which Dr. James Newcomer is Director. To him I acknowledge a great debt for his helpful suggestions about form. Words written to be spoken and words written to be read represent different disciplines and my writing for the most part has been for speaking purposes. My appreciation also is extended to Miss Judy Oelfke who has designed the book and done the art work, as she has done for many of the works of art in University Christian Church; and to my secretary, Mrs. Joyce Valentine, who with painstaking care has typed and retyped, and proofread the manuscript several times. And for the friendship and love of the fine people who comprise the membership of University Christian Church which Erline and I have served for thirty years and more our gratitude is inexpressible.

Granville T. Walker

July 1973

go placidly amid
THE NOISE AND HASTE

After Adlai Stevenson's death in 1965 it was discovered that he had intended to send out as his Christmas card a reprint of the "Desiderata," which is a list of suggestions for human conduct, easily converted into commitments for a new way of life.

The authorship of the "Desiderata" was for a time obscured by the fact that the work appeared in print bearing the legend that it had been discovered on a plaque installed in St. Paul's Church in Baltimore when built in 1692—a claim which caused a bit of controversy and investigation and which was never confirmed. Indeed, there seems to be little question now but that the author of the "Desiderata" was Max Ehrmann, for the work appeared in a book of poems authored by him and published in 1948.

In any event, the "Desiderata" (or "essentials" as the word may be loosely translated) is now a part of American literary lore. Among its virtues is the fact that it restates in fresh and vivid manner ideas that are thoroughly Biblical, but our very familiarity with them dulls the way they strike us. Indeed, there is a remarkable likeness in the "Desiderata" to the sayings and proverbs in the Wisdom Literature of the Old Testament, and to the practical, ethical admonitions which are to be found scattered throughout the writings of Paul.

1

I

Hear then the wisdom of the wise:

"Go placidly amid the noise and the haste, and remember what peace there may be in silence.

"As far as possible, without surrender, be on good terms with all persons. Speak your truth quietly and clearly; and listen to others, even to the dull and the ignorant; they too have their story.

"Avoid loud and aggressive persons; they are vexations to the spirit.

"If you compare yourself with others, you may become vain or bitter, for always there will be greater and lesser persons than yourself.

"Enjoy your achievements as well as your plans.

"Keep interested in your own career, however humble; it is a real possession in the changing fortunes of time.

"Exercise caution in your business affairs, for the world is full of trickery. But let this not blind you to what virtue there is; many persons strive for high ideals, and everywhere life is full of heroism.

"Be yourself. Especially do not feign affection. Neither be cynical about love; for in the face of all aridity and disenchantment, it is as perennial as the grass.

"Take kindly the counsel of the years, gracefully surrendering the things of youth.

"Nurture strength of spirit to shield you in sudden misfortune. But do not distress yourself with dark imaginings. Many fears are born of fatigue and loneliness.

"Beyond a wholesome discipline, be gentle with yourself. You are a child of the universe no less than the trees and the stars; you have a right to be here. And whether or not it is clear to you, no doubt the universe is unfolding as it should.

"Therefore be at peace with God, whatever you conceive Him to be. And whatever your labors and aspirations, in the noisy confusion of life, keep peace in your soul.

"With all its sham, drudgery and broken dreams, it is still a beautiful world. Be cheerful. Strive to be happy."[1]

II

Now out of all these consider only the first:

"Go placidly amid the noise and the haste, and remember what peace there may be in silence," a difficult exhortation to follow, and probably the more important because it is difficult! It would be easier to help make the noise and join in the haste. But if we take this option we are the losers.

One need not be a rebel against the technological achievements of our age to perceive that the noisiness of it, and the speed which has conquered space, have together robbed mankind of something dearly needed and which if possible must be regained. The result is that it is a rare person who knows what silence really is or who, being alone, can manage his solitude! Rarer still are those who have retained in private experience what speed and rush have taken from most others.

A very thoughtful and popular theologian of our time, C.S. Lewis, recalled in his autobiography that it was one of the blessings of his childhood and youth that his family had no modern means of transportation. Most of their friends did. Sometimes these friends would take him for a drive.

"This meant," he said, "that all those distant objects could be visited just enough to clothe them with memories and not impossible desires, while yet they remained ordinarily as inaccessible as the moon. The deadly power of rushing about wherever I pleased had not been given me.

"I measured distances by the standard of man, man walking on his two feet, not by the standard of the internal combustion engine. I had not been allowed to deflower the very idea of distance; in return I possessed 'infinite riches' in what would have been to motorists 'a little room.'

"The truest and most horrible claim made for modern transport is that it annihilates space. It does. It annihilates one of the most glorious gifts we have been given. It is a vile inflation which lowers the value of distance so that a modern boy travels a hundred miles with less sense of liberation and pilgrimage and adventure than his grandfather got from traveling ten."[2]

Fortunately or not, we live in an age in which space is being conquered, not just for astronauts who experience the adventure and the thrill, but for ordinary folk who speed through the park and never see the flowers, who fly from one metropolis to another and never see the mountains. We have lost our ability to measure distances by the standard of a man on his feet. One wonders whether the gain is worth the loss! It might be—if we develop a commensurate competence to move placidly amid the noise and haste and remember the peace there may be in silence.

III

Can we slow the hurried pace? Can we learn now and again to be still and know that God is God?

One has a fellow feeling for J. B. Priestley, who once wrote an essay in his book, **Delight,** on "not going." Said he, "One of the delights known to age and beyond the grasp of youth is that of **Not Going.** When we are young it is almost agony not to go. We feel that we are being left out of life, that the whole wonderful procession is sweeping by, probably forever, while we are weeping or sulking behind bars.

"Not to have an invitation—for the dance, the party, the game, the picnic, the excursion, the gang on holiday—is to be diminished, perhaps kept at midget's height for years. To have an invitation and then not to be able to go — oh, the cursed spite!

"Thus we torment ourselves in the April of our time.

"Now, in my early November not only do I not care the rottenest fig whether I receive an invitation or not, but after I have received it, I can find delight in knowing that I am Not Going.

5

"I have arrived at this by two stages. At the first, after years of illusion, I finally decided I was missing nothing by not going. Now, at the second, and I hope, final stage, I stay away and no longer care whether I am missing anything or not!"[3]

Of course we cannot live as Priestley suggests, turning away from our fellows with unmeasured gracelessness. But we know what, in essence, he meant. He did mean that whatever the circumstances of a man's life he ought not to allow himself to be pushed around and beleaguered by meaningless demands of one sort or another, that a wise man will slow the hurried pace if it falls within his power to do it. In our rush we miss too much. We are like the woman whose maid, observing her daily mad rush, quietly suggested to her that she was running past more than she was catching up with!

"Go placidly amid the noise and the haste, and remember what peace there may be in silence."

IV

The peace there may be in silence! Peace? But there is much more than peace. For silence is the moment of listening, and no man learns anything while he is talking! But in the silence he learns. He may then hear the call of his fellowman for help. He may then hear God's voice, offering him new courage, new direction, new spirit. But some never give God a chance. They do not go placidly amid the noise and haste.

6

They are never silent. They rush through life, never stopping to think. They move from one thing to another. Every hour is filled; they are afraid to be alone. The silences of God are never given a chance. So, never relaxed, or quiet or silent, they are never in a mood to receive. It is a way of life which cannot for long be sustained, for they cannot move as fast as everything is moving and they cannot keep the pace. Consequently something takes place which they did not foresee or anticipate.

And then in a moment life itself makes a silence for them. Illness comes. Or grief. Or unexpected failure in what was meant to be a rich enterprise. And the silence is so strange to them. They had never made of it either a friend or a resource, or the occasion of accepting the healing friendship of God! Had they done so, everything might have been different on the side of their own well being. It is a poor way to live in our hurried and noise cluttered world.

V

There is a better way. It is to move placidly amid the noise and haste, and remember the peace there may be in silence. The way is to make room in your life for silence before life makes room for it for you.

This should be for you the hour in which you pray and think, and worship God, and remember in love your fellowman. It should be the hour in which you face your own soul and ask God for the exaltation of His presence within you!

7

For this cause we gather on the Lord's Day in the Lord's house to be silent, to remember and to pray. It is good to be reminded that the Old Hebrew word for Sabbath comes from a root which means "Stop doing what your are doing!"

But the moratorium on rush and noise thus invoked is for a purpose. The purpose is the soul's renewal. The purpose is to get perspective. The purpose is to get away from the meaningless babble and the destinationless rush.

The purpose is to make it possible to live in the midst of the noise and haste with some degree of serenity. The purpose is to make it possible to hear the still small voice of God and discern the difference between life and death.

In a moment of great depression, the prophet Elijah felt that all was lost. He fled to a place of hiding and waited. A noisy blustering wind disturbed the mountainside but God was not in the wind. An earthquake shook the foundations of his world but God was not in the earthquake. Fire burned in all directions about him but God was not in the fire. Then listening when all had become quiet again, he heard a "still small voice," or as one translation puts it "the sound of gentle stillness," and God was in the silence. He listened and found fresh courage for the venture of life!

Let this, then, be one aim of your life: to go placidly amid the noise and haste, and remember the peace there may be in silence.

NOTES

[1] Max Ehrmann, "Desiderata" (Boston: Crescendo Publishing Co., n.d.). © 1927 by Max Ehrmann. All rights reserved. Copyright renewed 1954 by Bertha K. Ehrmann. Reprinted (or quoted) by permission of Crescendo Publishing Co., Boston, Mass.

[2] C. S. Lewis, **Surprised by Joy** (New York: Harcourt, Brace & Co., 1955), pp. 156-57.

[3] J. B. Priestley, **Delight** (London: Readers Union, Wm. Heinemann, 1951), pp. 136-37.

bE ON Good TERMS
witHOUT SURRENdER

"Go placidly amid the noise and the haste, and remember what peace there may be in silence." That was first in the list of admonitions. The second in the list sounds very much like a statement from Paul's letter to the Romans, "As far as possible, without surrender, be on good terms with all persons."

I

Paul's statement is so similar one wonders if the writer of the "Desiderata" had not just read the twelfth chapter of Romans before composing his word of advice: "If possible, so far as it depends upon you," says Paul, "live peaceably with all."

There can be little doubt that the duty to "live peaceably" with all, as far as it is possible to do so, is a duty of such an exacting sort that the person does not live who does not at one time or another need help in fulfilling it. And for that reason Paul goes beyond the simple admonition in the "Desiderata" and lays out certain attitudes and ways of conduct which are calculated not to make it easy to live on good terms with others but (excepting only when the situation is completely out of one's hands) to make it possible to do so.

Read through this twelfth chapter of Romans and you can easily discern that all of these aids to peace and harmony are manifestations of the quality of Christian love. Love is, itself, the guiding principle of the Christian community, and one of its distinguishing features is normally a strong impulse toward harmony among all men.

It is the very nature of Christian love to prevent misunderstandings, or at least hold them to a minimum, or, failing that, to rectify them when they do occur, so that they are not permanently hurtful.

The kind of "being on good terms" or the "living in harmony with one another," which the Christian way suggests, is certainly no mere accident. Rather, it is the result of resolutely avoiding the things that endanger it, on the one hand, and, on the other, of positively doing good to those with whom we are brought in contact.

Both aspects of that quality of life which issues in harmony are under consideration in Paul's Roman letter.

II

On the negative side, Paul urgently pleads that the Christian avoid being haughty and arrogant. For however arrogance may manifest itself, whether in "selfish ambition or in the haughty superiority to which it leads," as Dr. Gerald Cragg has put it, "pride destroys the harmony of the community. It also fatally circumscribes the sympathies of anyone who becomes obsessed with his own importance. It cuts him off from association with those who need him, and who might be able to help him in their turn. . . .

"A man of proud spirit . . . will renounce all dealings with those whom he regards as undeserving of his attention, and he will consequently deprive himself both of the joy which comes from helping those who stand in need of his assistance and the unexpected delight that comes from gaining new insights in places where he did not think to acquire them. Wisdom is not confined to those who think they possess it, and often humble folk have much clearer discernment and sharper insight than many who account themselves far better qualified to make pronouncements about the truth."[1]

And this is a point of great importance in the "Desiderata." "As far as possible, without surrender, be on good terms with all persons. Speak your truth quietly and clearly; and listen to others, even to the dull and the ignorant; they too have their story."

They do, indeed, but it is of the very nature of conceit or arrogance to make one unwilling to test his opinions by those of others and certainly never to subordinate his judgment to theirs.

But the man who would, without surrender, be on good terms with others must be always ready to learn. He must avoid that attitude of mind which is the very nemesis of a person of earnest purpose. By his arrogance he may be led to assume that he has nothing to learn and everything to teach. He will find it easy to criticize and to discredit rather than to praise, an attitude which, to say the least, is quite unattractive to the outside observer, especially to one who is trying to estimate the gospel by the performance of its advocates.

13

III

But, if in seeking to live at peace with others, a man must avoid arrogance and the haughty spirit and condescend to what is lowly, he must also avoid repaying evil with evil. This is a most difficult requirement because when the initiative for a relationship passes out of one's hands, he finds it all too easy to justify a spirit of resentment.

Paul would say, with the backing of what Jesus said about love, that at all costs this attitude must be avoided if possible. In any case, it must not become a settled condition of our human relationships.

There are some sub-Christian levels to which our relationships with other people may descend. One such level is reached when we refuse to do good to those who do no good to us; another is when we are helpful only to those who are helpful to us. Jesus would have regarded either position as the mark of an irreligious man. From His disciples he asked for greater concern for others than either posture would require. If love was, indeed, to be the governing standard of their relationship to others, then to do good only to those who did good to them and to refuse to be helpful to those who were not helpful to them, was to miss the mark of true discipleship. He expected better of his disciples. "What do ye more than others?" was a question which caused them to look deeply within themselves and to their own motives. If the ordinary coin of human discourse is the coin of incivility and unconcern, it is less than Christian, and this was His point.

But the lowest level is the level of vengeance. Aside from the fact that, as Paul says, vengeance

14

belongs to God, when we resort to it we ourselves are conquered by it. Evil can never be conquered by evil. When hatred meets hatred, the dread thing is increased. But when hatred is confronted with love, its only antidote is found. Booker T. Washington once said, "I will not allow any man to make me lower myself by hating him," or, as Abraham Lincoln put it, "The only way to destroy an enemy is to make of him a friend."[2]

IV

"As far as possible, without surrender, be on good terms with all persons," says the "Desiderata." "If possible, so far as it depends upon you, live peaceably with all," says Paul.

Both statements recognize that there may be times when living at peace with others is beyond our control and when the claims of courtesy must give way to the claims of principle. Our Christian faith does not require that we shut our eyes and submit with an easy-going tolerance to everything that happens. On the contrary, there may come times when we cannot escape a genuine battle between right and wrong, and no true Christian will shirk his responsibility in such situations. We can live at peace with others only insofar as we can control the situation. We must resist or surrender.

Paul knew, as we surely do, that there are persons for whom living peaceably with their fellows is more difficult than it is for others, that some have controlled more temper than others may even possess! In like manner, it is easier for some, by

15

nature, to be "good" than it is for others. Knowing this, it should be easier for those who are fortunate in this regard to avoid criticizing and judging those who were not endowed by nature so well. And, with such knowledge, the less fortunate may also find their discouragement softened.

But when things have not passed out of our hands and we have avoided arrogance on the one hand and vengeance on the other, we are still under orders to do positive good even to those who would do us harm.

It is of the essence of Christian conduct that the Christian will bless those who curse him. In the very process he will seek their good, pray for their well-being and do his utmost to answer his own prayer!

The Christian does not return evil for evil; rather, he overcomes evil with good. He prays for those who persecute him. It was Plato who said that a good man will prefer to suffer evil rather than to do evil. And it is always evil to hate.

The great example of this positive response to evil is in both the teaching and in the life of Christ. When reviled, He reviled not again. When nailed to the cross, He prayed for those who were executing Him. And He set the example followed by His disciples. Stephen prayed for his persecutors as they stoned him to death. In all of history there has been no greater spiritual force than this serene forgiveness characterized by Christians who, when in the worst of situations, were the best followers of their Lord.

Consenting to the act and holding the coats of those who were killing Stephen was Saul of Tarsus. No scholar doubts that this episode was an important factor in turning Saul of Tarsus into Paul the obedient servant of the Lord Jesus Christ. St. Augustine wrote,

"The Church owes Paul to the prayer of Stephen."[3]

It was this remarkable spirit in the disciples in the early church which gave them such influence that they were accused of turning the world upside down. That was precisely what they were doing. They were behaving according to standards which were a complete reversal of the standards of the world about them.

When their enemies hungered, they fed them. When they were thirsty, they gave them to drink. When they blessed, whether friends or enemies, their blessing was not mere words. It included deeds performed, acts of helpfulness in return for acts of hurt. They had no illusions about what it means to bless and curse not. You do not bless a hungry man, whether he is good or not, whether he deserves it or not, until you feed him. You bless a thirsty man by giving him a cup of cold water. The disciples never forgot the practical truth that "spiritual fare is poor sustenance for an empty stomach." This is why the program of help in the Great Hour of Sharing is so vastly important. If through it we are able to help the helpless help themselves, then genuine blessing will have occurred and with it the kind of reconciliation of man with man and man with God which reflects the true mission of Christ's church.

V

"As far as possible, without surrender, be on good terms with all persons." You do not surrender your highest principles to do this. In dealing with those who do no good to you, you do good to them. And, in dealing with those you love, you do the same,

17

with the added joy of being able to rejoice when they rejoice and weep with those who weep.

Thus, you are not overcome by evil, but you overcome evil with good.

NOTES

[1] Interpreter's Bible, IX, p. 593.

[2] William Barclay, The Letter to the Romans (Philadelphia: The Westminster Press, 1954), p. 184.

[3] Ibid., p. 182.

speak your truth quietly, and listen

The "Desiderata" is a wise man's list of suggestions for human conduct—a list which must unquestionably have been inspired by the author's knowledge of truths that are common to much Biblical literature, especially the ethical and practical admonitions to be found in the letters of Paul and in the Wisdom Literature of the Old Testament.

"Go placidly amid the noise and the haste, and remember what peace there may be in silence. As far as possible, without surrender, be on good terms with all persons."

This admonition is certainly of such an exacting sort that any person needs help in fulfilling it. In the last chapter we were discussing how Paul, in an almost identical statement, laid down certain suggestions about how this might be done. To live at peace with others without surrender certainly requires, as Paul saw so clearly, that one avoid being arrogant and vengeful, but that rather, in dealing even with one's enemies, he should return good for evil, which is the only way evil ultimately can be conquered.

The "Desiderata" also has some suggestions for being able to live a peaceful life in the midst of the noise and haste and for living on good terms with others without surrender.

I

One such admonition is that we deal gently with others and learn to listen when they speak. To do so does not mean that the Christian man is a man without convictions of his own, but it does mean that you are to "Speak your truth quietly and clearly; and listen to others, even to the dull and the ignorant; they too have their story."

To speak one's truth quietly and clearly calls for considerable restraint on the part of a man of deep convictions, but not to do this is to be vexing to others.

It is not easy to like an opinionated person, even when his opinions are right. So, as the "Desiderata" states it, one is to "Avoid loud and aggressive persons; they are vexations to the spirit." But, more than avoiding them, we must make sure we are not the very kind of person we are trying to avoid!

If we proclaim a positive opinion without being sure of our facts, we may have to modify it with much embarrassment.

Some people with strong convictions can voice them without annoyance, but others let their convictions build walls of alienation and disgust by the haughty confidence with which they express them. Some are always the "devil's advocate" in espousing the opposite side on almost any issue, and, frequently, those who hold strong opinions find it difficult to believe that they can ever be wrong. These are the people in any "town meeting" who draw fire from an opposition that takes great delight in ex-

20

posing their errors. Because we all make mistakes, none of us can afford the luxury of the over-confidence and self-assurance which rules out the possibility of being wrong. If we maintain an attitude of openness, our positions may be accepted with less resistance when we are right, and we can retreat with less embarrassment when we are wrong.

Therefore it is a wise course to speak your truth as you see it, quietly and clearly, and listen to others. Even the best informed people must be prepared to modify their opinions when they are in disagreement with a demonstrated fact. To do this is to experience a wholesome kind of repentance.

And yet it is possible to be too agreeable, so much so that one really has no convictions. A man who does not have convictions and is not prepared to defend them is not worth listening to. There is error in both directions. The too-agreeable are not heard; the overly-opinionated invite resistance and resentment. Says the Book of Proverbs: "Do you see a man who is wise in his own eyes? There is more hope for a fool than for him."[1]

So the truly wise man will speak his truth quietly and clearly and listen to others, even the dull and ignorant; and he will experience the unexpected delight that comes from gaining new insights in places where he did not think to acquire them. Wisdom is not confined to those who think they possess it. Often the humble folk have it too, but they possess it without offense. Speak your truth quietly and clearly, and listen!

21

II

The "Desiderata" gives still another suggestion for the inner life of peace, and that has to do with the measure we use when we begin to estimate ourselves.

"If you compare yourself with others, you may become vain or bitter, for always there will be greater and lesser persons than yourself." We must listen to others, but it is poor business to be always comparing ourselves with them. For if we do, we may find envy and bitterness overtaking us as we see others better circumstanced than ourselves; or we may become vain and entertain feelings of superiority when we compare ourselves with those less fortunate than we.

If a man sincerely desires to escape both bitterness and vanity, his best way is not to compare himself with others but so learn to identify himself with them that he will be able to rejoice when they rejoice and weep when they weep.

This is not easy to do, but such identification is almost essential to the avoidance of vanity and bitterness and the achievement, in their stead, of a genuine quality of humility.

Many a person has envied his neighbor, thinking that he has an easy time of it, when the truth may well be that the envious person never really has seen the inside problems of the other person's life. It is not easy to know the difficulties of another man's job unless we have actually worked at his kind of work. If we have not employed other people, it is difficult to appreciate the pressure of meeting a payroll.

On the other side, if we never have worked for less than a living wage, if we have never been unemployed or faced the grim fact of actual need, we would not find it easy to sympathize with those placed in such situations. Those who have never been ill, or hurt, or hungry, who have never experienced sorrow or great disappointment, must have real depth of compassion to appreciate fully the feelings of people who have gone through these adversities.

In any event, if we really knew, from the inside, the other fellow's true situation, it is doubtful we would want to trade places with him.

There is a story of the man who came to the place where all men bring their burdens, in the hope of exchanging his load for that of someone else. But after looking at the trouble of others, he was willing to take up his own again! As the years go along we come to learn that all men have their full share of troubles, and that, by comparison, some of our own seem much less heavy. When all the facts are known, it is highly probable that folk we may once have envied or thought were troublefree are carrying around in their lives and in their hearts many things that we wouldn't wish to take on, not even if in doing so we could lay down our own load. We do learn, somehow, to live with our own troubles, but it probably would be very difficult to learn to live with someone else's load.

No, we escape vanity on the one hand and bitterness on the other, not by comparing ourselves with others who may be more or less fortunate than ourselves, but by identifying with them in the profoundest possible sense.

III

It may not be easy to see, but bitterness and vanity (or envy) are conquered ultimately by the love which is the undiscourageable goodwill and compassion which we extend to others, and by genuine humility which is a quality of spirit existing when we have made a true estimate of ourselves. The true estimate does not come from comparing ourselves with others, but by comparing ourselves with the perfect standard of Christ, who stands ever ready to help us bridge the gap between what we are and what we ought to be.

William Sullivan once wrote that genuine humility does not arise from the sense of our pitiable kinship with the dust that is unworthy of us, but from the realization of our awful nearness to a magnificence of which we are not worthy!

James Barrie put it in another way: "The life of every man is a diary," he said, "in which he means to write one story and writes another; and his humblest hour is when he compares the volume as it is with what he vowed to make it."

There, indeed, is the only true comparison: the standard up to which we committed ourselves to live, as against the degree to which we have fulfilled it!

This comparison is what leads to the recommitment of a man's life to all that is good and true and holy.

Far from making him envious of another who is more fortunate than he, or vain because he is himself better than others, it makes him humble. For he now knows what he ought to be and what his resources are in Christ for achieving his goal. That could be one of the truly important moments in a man's life. It could be the place where he acknowledges his need and where, by the grace of God, the need is met.

"Go placidly amid the noise and the haste, and remember what peace there may be in silence. As far as possible, without surrender, be on good terms with all persons. Speak your truth quietly and clearly; and listen to others, even to the dull and the ignorant; they too have their story. Avoid loud and aggressive persons; they are vexations to the spirit. If you compare yourself with others, you may become vain or bitter, for always there will be greater and lesser persons than yourself."

NOTE

[1]Proverbs 26:12.

ENJOY
YOUR ACHIEVEMENTS

"Enjoy your achievements as well as your plans. Keep interested in your own career, however humble; it is a real possession in the changing fortunes of time. Exercise caution in your business affairs, for the world is full of trickery. But let this not blind you to what virtue there is; many persons strive for high ideals, and everywhere life is full of heroism."

The "Desiderata" is concerned with a way of life which if followed will enable a person to go placidly amid the noise and the haste and to remember the peace there may be in silence.

One step of that way is to be on good terms with all persons, if this can be done without surrender. Another step is to speak your own truth quietly and clearly, but listen to others, even the dull and ignorant for they too have their story. In the process, you will avoid loud and arrogant persons who are a vexation to the spirit, but you will also avoid being the very kind of person you are trying to avoid.

Still another step is always to keep an honest estimate of yourself and avoid bitterness and vanity by not comparing yourself with others whose real situation you cannot fully understand because you cannot fully know what it is.

Then the wise author of the "Desiderata" comes to deal with that portion of a man's life which consumes most of his time from birth to death—his work, his career, and his relationship to other people in the world where his vocation is fulfilled, whether in business, or a profession, or a craft.

Says he, "Enjoy your achievements as well as your plans. Keep interested in your own career, however humble; it is a real possession in the changing fortunes of time."

I

Enjoy your achievements as well as your plans!

One would suppose it to be a rather common practice to focus most of our pleasure on setting goals and making the trip, rather than the joy of actually arriving. Robert Browning must have had such a thought in mind when he wrote:

"Ah, but a man's reach should exceed his grasp,

Or what's a heaven for?"("Andrea del Sarto")

It is an unsatisfied hunger to achieve which spurs us on, but once having arrived we have no peace until we have chosen a new destination and have begun to move again.

Take almost any area of human endeavor which has succeeded in this century and you will see without much argument that this is so. In 1903 the Wright Brothers flew the first airplane. Fourteen years later aircraft factories were in operation and the first planes flew in World War I. Unsatisfied with such meager beginnings, in 1927 Charles A. Lindbergh flew the Atlantic, as much a pioneer in aviation as the astronauts have been in space. He was the first man to cross the ocean, non-stop, in a plane.

Now 20,000 people cross it daily in jets. Unsatisfied even with that tremendous accomplishment we have put men on the moon, and it is not unthinkable that within the lifetime of some people now living interplanetary travel will be common, that even hospitals will be aloft in space.

Free of the pull of gravity it is possible, says Edward Lindaman, that "A rest home in space could be a permanent haven for the crippled and infirm, since they would no longer need crutches or wheelchairs. They could dive, float, sail and roll languorously at will, and move from place to place with a finger tip push. Their lives could be far more self-reliant and useful than on Earth . . . .

"An orbital hotel, with variable gravity suites and possibilities for exhilarating new kinds of recreation was seriously discussed at a 1967 symposium on 'Commercial Uses of Space.' "[1]

At this moment there are several hundred satellites orbiting the earth sending back reports which reasonably could change the whole life of mankind on this planet: discerning the location of additional resources we have not yet discovered, reading the weather for long periods in advance, warning of coming floods sufficiently early to save hundreds of lives and countless millions of dollars in houses and buildings, serving as relay stations for worldwide television and radio broadcasts so that we can see and hear in a matter of seconds what is happening on the other side of this planet.

This has been, despite the terrible social problems of racism, of overpopulation threats, and the pollution of our natural resources, a great time in which to live.

II

One of the virtues of this period is that those who have had the remarkable privilege of being involved in these accomplishments have enjoyed moment by moment what was going on. It really is the only way to live. Following the ancient admonition, "Whatsoever thy hand findeth to do, do it with thy might," scientists and workmen have felt themselves a part of something vastly greater than themselves, in itself a deeply religious mood.

For to be religious, in the profoundest sense, is to have the feeling that what you are doing has meaning and significance, not only to yourself, but to others; and, in the area just cited, that significance may be for all mankind for all time to come. It is then that your personal religion is relevant. It is then that you can give yourself completely to the task at hand.

On Arturo Toscanini's 80th birthday someone asked his son, Walter, what his father ranked as his most important achievement. The son replied, "For him there can be no such thing. Whatever he happens to be doing at the moment is the biggest thing in his life—whether it is conducting a symphony or peeling an orange!" Well, no religion is irrelevant if it helps people to see the hidden glory of the common things they do as well as the uncommon things which may represent their greatest achievements as the world measures their work.

III

Here, too, is a clue to at least one major secret of happiness; for, as Aristotle long ago taught, happiness comes chiefly by some productive act, a working in the way of excellence. "Our happiest moments," says Elton Trueblood, "are not those in which we ask how to be happy, but rather those in which we so lose ourselves in some creative task, which seems to us important, that we forget to take our own emotional pulse. When we plant trees, write books, build houses, or make roads, we often find that we have been having a wonderfully good time and that we are not immediately driven to do something to have fun. We have had, all along, something better than anything which commercialized and self-conscious entertainment can ever provide."[2]

IV

Behind the massive youth drop-out in our culture one of the factors may be that work as they have witnessed it in the life of the older generations has become meaningless. They have observed that for many the only real satisfactions in life have come not

31

from their work by which they have made their money, but from the empty gratification they have received only from the spending of money!

The really fortunate people in our culture are those whose work has become their pleasure. James Barrie once said that nothing is really work unless you would rather be doing something else! Work which offers no pleasure is work indeed. But work which it is a joy to do, work which is regarded as sacred to the worker because he believes this is God's world and anything he does to improve man's life is within the limits of God's plan, that is the work for which the pain of drudgery has been made endurable and to which the joy of relevance has been added. If this is truly God's world, then, as Trueblood has said, any true work for the improvement of man's life is a sacred task and should be undertaken with that fact in mind.[3]

Henry David Thoreau once asked an Irishman how many potatoes he could dig in a day and was well pleased with the reply: "Well, I don't keep any account. I scratch away, and let the day's work praise itself."

That surely is a Christian view of a menial task, for the day's work cannot finally praise itself unless it has been rendered in service to mankind. Some do not reach that pinnacle. They work to eat and eat to live and live to eat, and so on. They wind up like Sam whose boss recently discharged him. "Where's Sam?" asked an acquaintance. "Sam doesn't work here any more," came the reply. "Do you have someone in mind for his vacancy?" To which the answer came, "Pshaw, when Sam left he didn't leave no vacancy." Poor Sam, he could enjoy neither his achievements nor his plans!

V

You can enjoy your achievements as well as your plans if you are able, when the day is done, or the task accomplished, to affirm that because it served mankind there is dignity in what you have done. You will have a sense of glory in it because you have regarded your work as having a sacramental significance. Without that, no good work will continue. If on a wide scale a negative view of work were felt, our civilization would cease to advance. As Alfred North Whitehead observed, "A civilization which ceases to advance is already in full decay, because advance and decay are the only choices open to mankind."

With the "sense of glory" and the "feeling of dignity" in a finished task you can enjoy it and have a right to enjoy it. Helen Keller's biography of Anne Sullivan Macy, her teacher whom you saw portrayed in "The Miracle Worker,"recounts the fact that it was without regret that Anne Sullivan left the world on October 20, 1936. A few weeks before the end one who meant to comfort said, "Teacher, you must get well. Without you Helen would be nothing." "That would mean," Anne Sullivan replied sadly, "that I had failed." For her basic aim had always been to make Helen free—even of her. But there was no sadness,

33

only the joy of accomplishment, for the teacher had not failed.[4] Though she had given her entire adult life for only one person, Helen Keller, she could look back with pride that her pupil, blind and deaf and dumb when she began her work, was now as complete a person as one who lived with sight and hearing and voice.

VI

The line between one's plans and one's accomplishments can be drawn only when the job is done, but, even then, for the man who continues his labors in some creative form, planning and achieving really become one.

This is why the author of the "Desiderata" added one more word: "Keep interested in your own career, however humble; it is a real possession in the changing fortunes of time."

It was Jesus who said, "My father worketh hitherto and I work. We must work the works of him who has sent me while it is day for the night cometh when no man can work."

And Thomas Carlyle had a word for it: "Blessed is he who has found his work; let him ask no other blessedness."[5]

"Keep interested in your own career however humble; it is a real possession in the changing fortunes of time." It is, indeed. But that does not mean that a man must do the same old thing in the same old way in the same old place. To keep interested

34

may require movement—new situations, new faces, new people to deal with, new problems to tackle. This is only so one can have the real joy of both his plans and his achievements.

On the tombstone of the novelist, Winifred Holtby, are inscribed these words:

God give me work
Till my life shall end
And life
Till my work is done.[6]

Cardinal Newman, in a prayer with which he ended a sermon in the mid-1800's, summed it all up in an ardent supplication:

"O Lord, support us all the day long of our troublous life, until the shadows lengthen and the evening comes, and the busy world is hushed and the fever of life is over and our work is done. Then in thy great mercy grant us a safe lodging and a holy rest and peace at last. Amen."

NOTES

[1] Edward Lindaman, Space, A New Direction for Mankind (New York: Harper and Brothers, 1969), p. 125.

[2] Elton Trueblood, The Common Ventures of Life (New York: Harper and Brothers, 1949), p. 93.

[3] Ibid., p. 85.

[4] Recounted in Gerald Kennedy, A Second Reader's Notebook (New York: Harper and Brothers, 1959), p. 1.

[5] Ibid., p. 346.

[6] Ibid., p. 322.

be not blind
TO WHAT VIRTUE THERE IS

"Exercise caution in your business affairs, for the world is full of trickery. But let this not blind you to what virtue there is; many persons strive for high ideals, and everywhere life is full of heroism."

While most of the "Desiderata" deals with the passive virtues of humility and peaceable relationships, a portion of the wise man's sayings is devoted to those disciplines of selfhood which have to do with daily work: "Enjoy your achievements as well as your plans. Keep interested in your own career, however humble; it is a real possession in the changing fortunes of time. Exercise caution in your business affairs, for the world is full of trickery. But let this not blind you to what virtue there is; many persons strive for high ideals, and everywhere life is full of heroism."

That admonition can be summed up in the simple statement: Be careful but not cynical!

The two approaches balance each other, and each needs the other for completion.

One does need to be cautious in dealing with others, for the world is indeed full of trickery. But one may become so careful of getting hurt, or cautious of being "taken," as to go through life suspicious of nearly everyone he meets.

Somehow a man must learn to exercise

37

reasonable caution on the one hand and reasonable trust in his fellow man on the other if he is to "remember what peace" comes from wholesome human relationships. Few qualities are more calculated to rob a person of genuine happiness than the quality of being suspicious of others, of feeling that everybody has "an angle." It is better to trust and be deceived than never to trust at all.

I

The world is full of trickery, but let this not blind you to what virtue there is.

Many are blinded to what virtue there is, that many persons strive for high ideals and that everywhere life is full of heroism.

Their blindness results in distrust, in suspicion, and, indeed, in cynicism.

Could it be that Raymond Massey was right when he said that most of our suspicions of others are aroused by our knowledge of ourselves? Is it our knowledge of ourselves, unconscious but nevertheless real and definitive of our attitudes toward others, which causes us to live with a sense of distrust?

We do not believe in the heroism of others because we have serious questions about our own. We do not fully trust the idealistic commitment of others because our own commitment is weak and flabby. So, we project our weaknesses, the things about ourselves which we most despise in others. We project these weaknesses on to other people and then hold them in suspicion!

II

It is a fact that we tend to wear masks to hide our real selves from others so that they will think more highly of us than we deserve, and to keep ourselves from acknowledging the truth about ourselves. This causes us to discount the fact that many strive for high ideals and that everywhere life is full of heroism.

Let us explore this fact about ourselves for a moment. By reason of our animal nature we enter life with organic hungers and biological urges, with capacities for lust and fear, rage and hate. Often we find it difficult to hold these native drives in check. Frequently we are ashamed of them; sometimes we are embarrassed by them. But on the other side of our native equipment are hopes and dreams, godlike powers, aspirations after goodness and brotherliness, and fellowship with God which often we find it difficult to achieve.

These contending forces are at work in each of us, but we want to present ourselves to the world at our best and not our worst. Indeed, we want to be our best, and we want to have a high opinion of ourselves. The self-image as well as the image we wish to project toward the world is important to our sense of identity. So we wear masks to make sure that others think more highly of us than we deserve and to disguise our baser impulses from ourselves. Our true destiny, of course, is not found in wearing these masks but in achieving the real spiritual potential which is ours as children of God.

Yet we wear the masks. And we wear them not because we are all bad, but because above all we want to be good. Nevertheless with the masks we tend to deceive ourselves more than the world outside. In turn, because unconsciously we know we wear them, we assume that all others do so, too, and this blinds us to what virtue there is, the high ideals and the inspiring heroism with which life is full.

III

It is important that we should come to know our real selves, that we should really and honestly understand ourselves with all the masks removed if we are going to learn the first principles of trusting others and of running the risk of that trust!

There are several ways by which such self-understanding can be brought about. Some people are so self-deceived that only in-depth study by a trained scientist of the human mind can unearth their disguises. Although most people are not abnormal, all of us, to some extent, go through life self-deceived. In any event let me propose a review of some questions advanced by Richard L. Evans under the title "Self-searching," which was his effort to get the common run of us to look honestly at ourselves.[1]

Perhaps as we probe these questions we may for the moment trade our masks for mirrors and see ourselves as we actually are, an exercise which may start us on the way of becoming what we ought to be. Here are the questions as they appeared in a little book by Richard Evans:

"If you were choosing someone you had to trust, could you trust yourself?

"Would you like to meet yourself when you are in trouble?

"Would you like to be at your own mercy?

"If other men did not put locks on their homes, on their barns, and on their banks, would you ever walk in where you knew you had no right to walk?

"If there were no accounts, no bonding companies, no courts, no jails, no disgrace—none of the usual fears except your own soul inside of you—would you ever take what you knew you had no right to take?

"Would you serve a man without influence as fairly as you would a man with influence?

"Would you honor an unwritten agreement as honestly as if it were written?

"If you found a lost article that no one else could possibly know you found, would you try to return it or would you put it in your own pocket?

"Would you stay with your principles no matter what price you were proffered for forsaking them?

"Would you compromise on a question of right or wrong?

"Do you talk as well of your friends when they aren't around as when they are?

"If you make a mistake, would you admit it or would you pretend to be right even when you knew you were wrong?

"Could you be trusted as well away from home as you could where you are known?

"Do you think the world owes you a living or do you honestly know that you should work for what you want?

"Do you make an earnest effort to improve your performance or have you been hoping for an undeserved improvement in your pay or your position?

"Do you try to get the job done or have you been loafing along for fear you were doing too much?

"Would you hire yourself? Would you like to work for yourself?

"If you were your own partner, could you trust yourself?

"If your partner were to die, would you treat his family as fairly as if he were alive?

"If he lost his health, would you still deal with him not only justly but generously?"

Well, that's a tough list! But there are times when in order to become what we ought to be, we need to know and understand ourselves as we are. Indeed, if we are convinced that the world is mostly filled with trickery so that we discount the heroism and idealism and the virtue that are everywhere, could it not be that our suspicions are rooted in an unadmitted awareness of our own moral turpitudes and weaknesses?

IV

Of course that is not the whole story. But it might just give us an insight into how we appear at least at times to other people. Dr. Leiper tells the true story of an American gentleman who was taking the channel steamer from Fusan in Korea to Nagasaki. This happened quite a while ago, before World War II. The American found himself sharing a stateroom with an Oriental gentleman. After the steamer had left port the American went to the purser and said, "I don't like the looks of that Jap in my stateroom. I want you to put my valuables in your safe." "All right, sir," said the purser, "he brought his down about half an hour ago!" It could be that they were both wrong in their misgivings about each other, but if both learned what had gone on both might have discovered how they appeared in each other's eyes.

Such self-knowledge is the beginning of wisdom. But of course the negative side is not all of it.

For the other side of it is that we are possessed of godlike powers, hopes and dreams, aspirations after goodness and brotherliness and fellowship with God, and we deeply want to be our best. Moreover, most other people are like that, too, a fact about both them and ourselves which we do not often enough allow for.

Perhaps our problem is that we do not care to see these qualities in others because to do so is to admit that there are those who are better than ourselves. If we do not look for these virtues in them, they will in all likelihood not look for them in us.

V

We do not need to pretend to be other than we are when we trade our masks for mirrors and see there not only our evil inclinations but our good as well.

The truth is that Jeremiah was right when he said that the heart is deceitful above all things and dreadfully wicked. But Jesus also was right when He said that the good man out of the good treasure of his heart brings forth that which is good.

For love and goodness and hope are there as well, and every man's foremost problem is to see himself as he actually is—faults and virtues together—and then determine what he shall do with his life.

When we remove the masks and look in clear mirrors, we are on the way to becoming what we ought to be. Within us all there are possibilities for strength and potentialities for good which we never have developed fully, and which some of us never have recognized as being there at all.

When we see them and determine to live up to our full stature, we shall learn to trust ourselves first of all. Beginning there, we will not let the trickery which we know to be in the world blind us to what virtue there is.

Many persons put the weight of their lives on the side of the good and strive for high ideals. Everywhere there are those who face life's misfortunes with unconquerable courage, inspiring the rest of us when we are tempted to be cowards and run away, and everywhere life is full of heroism.

NOTE

[1] Richard L. Evans, **Tonic for Our Times** (New York: Harper and Brothers, 1952), pp. 19-20.

bE yourself

"Exercise caution in your business affairs, for the world is full of trickery. But let this not blind you to what virtue there is; many persons strive for high ideals, and everywhere life is full of heroism.

"Be yourself. Especially do not feign affection. Neither be cynical about love; for in the face of all aridity and disenchantment, it is as perennial as the grass."

It would not be a difficult undertaking to prove that one of the major preoccupations of large segments of our culture is with such questions as "Who am I?" If we start with the admonition from the "Desiderata" to "Be yourself," then the question is "What self?"

The emergence in the past few years of sensitivity training, whereby persons examine their own deep emotional responses to life in an effort to come to understand themselves and their own drives and urges more fully, is certainly one indication of this preoccupation with one's selfhood.

There are phrases which have come into the current vernacular which also signal this concern: such as, that a person ought to "do his own thing," that one ought to "tell it like it is," or that this or that type of involvement either is or is not "my bag."

Many of the youthful drop-outs in our culture

justify their way of life on the ground that they are searching for their own true selves, and even those who indulge in the use of hallucinogenic or other types of drugs do so claiming that they are, by this experience, achieving a deeper awareness of themselves. Rarely has so important an issue had to bear the burden of so many questionable forms of the human search or been used as a means of rationalizing behavior which in previous generations has been regarded as open to highly adverse moral judgment.

I

When we come to deal with the simple admonition "Be yourself," it turns out not to be so simple. For in order to "be" ourselves, we need first of all to know who we are. What is the true nature of our humanity; what is the meaning of our selfhood?

In the last chapter we were saying that perhaps one reason we are reluctant to trust other people is that we cannot trust ourselves. We wear masks to keep our true feelings from being known by others, and, by the same token, we hide these feelings from ourselves. Also, if we are not to be blind to what virtue there is, the time must come when we trade our masks for mirrors in which we take an honest look at the reflection and remember what we see. This is part of what we see: by the very nature of our animal ancestry we enter life with organic hungers and biological urges—lust, fear, rage and hate—

which we often find difficult to hold in check and by which we are often embarrassed and ashamed; on the other side of our natures are hopes and dreams, godlike powers and aspirations after goodness and brotherliness and fellowship with God which we find difficult to achieve.

While this inner civil war is going on within us, we want the world to see us at our best and indeed we want to be our best and have a high opinion of ourselves. While we want others to think the best of us, we want to think the best of ourselves as well.

This is why we wear masks, but it is also why we must trade our masks for mirrors until we accept ourselves as we actually are.

II

The principle of self-acceptance comes first if we are to be ourselves. At this point, the trouble with many people is that they know their own faults and hate themselves for them, a circumstance which makes it impossible for them truly to love anyone else.

When they trade their masks for mirrors, they despise what they see. Instead of making peace with what they see, instead of accepting themselves for the good within them which should be encouraged and the evil which must be overcome, they despise themselves. Consequently, they find it impossible to trade their mirrors for windows that look out lovingly toward other people.

One erroneous assumption frequently made about the requirements of Christian faith in action is that while we feel we must describe in detail how one man ought to treat another, the same man can be expected to be spontaneously wise in dealing with himself. But anyone involved in counseling people who face all manner of problems soon discovers that underlying many of these problems is a tragic quality of self-hate. People need to be taught that it is quite as immoral to hate themselves as it is to be cruel and callous toward others. One's attitude toward himself can be psychologically just as complicated as his attitude toward others, and it is certain that until he loves himself properly he will find it impossible to love his neighbor as he ought.

We do not often give enough attention to this precondition of loving our neighbors. Jesus did, and the Hebrew tradition out of which He spoke did also. The command was simply "Thou shalt love thy neighbor **as thyself!**" A proper self image and self respect are essential to obedience to that commandment.

III

Self-acceptance is achieved and properly loving ourselves becomes reality when we look at our weaknesses and admit them; when we eliminate the picture of perfection, which we cannot achieve but which keeps us living with a sense of failure and inferiority to others; when, in short, we cease trying to be someone else and start being ourselves.

For nothing is more likely to create within us a sense of inferiority, along with the remorse and guilt which go with it, than an unswerving insistence on a perfection within ourselves which we cannot attain. The perfectionist is never satisfied with himself. As a businessman, he must be first in his field. As a professional he must be highly thought of. Socially he must have the biggest home, the largest salary, the most expensive car. The good qualities in other persons, other races, and other cultures usually escape his notice and his appreciation, despite the fact that, more than most people, he is governed by what others think of him. At whatever cost he must maintain the fiction of his perfection and superiority over those about him. He is never satisfied with himself and therefore he hates himself, a fact which spoils even the good he is able to do.

IV

But once he admits to himself and to his God that he is what he is and nothing more, then he makes important discoveries not only about himself but about God as well. To his amazement he discovers that God loves him with a love that will never let him go, that God loves him not because he is good and makes no mistakes but because God is truly God.

It is then that a man is released from the terrible burden of being perfect and is able to put aside all pretense and insecurity and false pride and give himself to making the most of what he is. A divine trust has been imposed upon us and we know it,but we also know that because we are finite and He is infinite, because He is loving and understanding and we are weak, our mistakes do not speak the last word, and our failures are not final. Therefore though we may be truly penitent concerning them, we are not overwhelmed by them. We do the best we can with what we have and are relieved of the awful necessity of making "a good impression" either on God or on our fellows.

In short we have been set free to accept ourselves for what we are, and in this freedom we find release to be ourselves. No longer must we act a part. No longer must we leave the right impression on others. We simply resolve to do the best we can with what we have, to accept the fact of our humanity and the consequences of it without fear. When we fail we know it is our fault; when we succeed we know that life has been good to us. In failure we make no alibis but look to ourselves to see why.

When the Dean Martin Golf Tournament at Tucson was shown on television Bobby Nichols was in the lead until the last few holes. On the 18th he still stood a chance. As he addressed the ball at the tee, a baby in the gallery began to cry. Nichols stepped away from the tee momentarily, then returned to hook his ball into a parallel water hazard on the left side of the fairway. His chance of winning had fallen into the water with that ball. Later when reporters tried to get him to blame that shot on the crying baby, he refused to do it. He simply said he should have had better control of himself—the baby and no one else in the gallery was to blame, only himself. That was the essence not only of good sportsmanship but of honest self-acceptance. When something goes wrong a healthy minded man will find out what it is and do what he can to correct it. He will assume personal responsibility for his bad shots which cost him the tournament as well as the good ones which permit him to win.

This is precisely what should take place in the larger game of life. We have to admit ourselves to be what we are, accepting our weaknesses as well as our strengths and determining to make the most of what we have.

We simply accept ourselves for what we are. We simply "be" ourselves and no one else. As Samuel Johnson once put it, "No man was ever great by imitation." He may be taught by others, but he cannot be what they are because he is himself and himself only.

This means a creative form of resignation to the limitations life has imposed upon us. When a man reaches that point he is able in utter honesty to say concerning himself, "Now I know what I have to work with. I wish it were more, but it is not, and with it I will do the best I can." And there is no way of reckoning where such resolution will come out.

The late Dr. M. E. Sadler had a personal motto by which he lived his very impressive and creative life. It was a motto allegedly written by Edward Everett Hale. It went like this:

I am only one, but I am one.
I cannot do everything,
    but I can do something.
I will not let what I cannot do
    interfere with what I can do.
Well, some remember what a remarkable life was built upon that. It was a life of complete self-acceptance and self-reliance.

Ralph Waldo Emerson wrote: "There is a time in every man's education when he arrives at the conviction that envy is ignorance; that imitation is suicide; that he must take himself for better, for worse, as his portion; that though the wide universe is full of good, no kernel of nourishing corn can come to him but through his toil bestowed on that plot of ground which is given to him to till."[1]

Surely that is what it means to accept yourself and be yourself and to love yourself properly so that you may then be prepared to love your neighbor as you ought.

NOTE

[1] Quoted in Harry Emerson Fosdick, **On Being a Real Person** (New York: Harper and Brothers, 1943), pp. 60-61.

do NOT feiqn affection

"Be yourself. Especially do not feign affection. Neither be cynical about love; for in the face of all aridity and disenchantment, it is as perennial as the grass."

When we come to this statement in the "Desiderata" we are brought once again to ideas made familiar to the Christian community by the Apostle Paul in the twelfth chapter of the Book of Romans.

"Do not feign affection. Neither be cynical about love," says the "Desiderata." "Let love be genuine," says Paul. "Hate what is evil; hold fast to what is good; love one another with brotherly affection."

The Phillips translation gives freshness to these verses from Romans: "Let us have no imitation Christian love. Let us have a genuine break with evil and a real devotion to good. Let us have real warm affection for one another as between brothers, and a willingness to let the other man have the credit."

"Do not feign affection!" In the Christian community **agape**—or Christian love—is a feeling of undiscourageable goodwill toward others which can exist even when you may not like the person who is the object of that goodwill. But in the Christian fellowship, Christian love is almost bound to result in some degree of affection, of filial love, of love of the sort which has in it genuine feelings of identity with the person loved.

When Paul speaks of this "love" in the twelfth chapter of Romans he is talking about the kind of love within the Christian community which at its best does result in some degree of affection. Paul is saying in essence that this is a level of relationship between human beings which you do not play with or play at. It is either genuine or it does not exist. It does not have the quality of play-acting in it. It must be completely sincere. If it is an imitation Christian love, it is not love at all.

I

With all of this the "Desiderata" is in agreement: "Be yourself. Especially do not feign affection. Neither be cynical about love."

The reason these admonitions put such weight upon the necessity of genuineness with respect to love and affection is that love lies at the very heart of life's meaning; it is the focal point of the Christian Gospel both in its revelation of the nature of God and in its hope for the ultimate possibilities in human nature.

Because love is the central commitment of the Christian Gospel, it has the power to transform every type of human relationship. Gerald Cragg has observed that Christian love "takes up and enriches natural affection, so that the warm emotion

56

characteristic of the family relationship at its best is brought into the family of God."

Says he, "It expands and enlarges that narrow circle to which we usually restrict the action of our love and brings an ever wider area of human life within the scope of its power.

"But it also achieves the transmutation of a force which often works to destroy our peace and to poison human relationships. One of the marked features of our lives," says Dr. Cragg, "is the drive provided by the natural desire to excel. We crave superiority. In seeking to achieve pre-eminence we often embitter our own lives and those of others. . . . But in the Christian fellowship . . . the redirection of our craving to excel is manifested. We outdo one another in showing honor; each is quicker to recognize worth in and give recognition to others than he is to make claims on his own behalf." Love has the power completely to transform every type of human relationship.

This is so because, as Paul insisted, love is **the** quality which underlies the whole of God's redemptive activity. It is, as Dr. Cragg has observed, "the secret of all that God has done for us."[1]

Love, then, is the one quality which, more than any other, must characterize the Christian community. For this very reason it must be absolutely without hypocrisy. Pretense is so antithetical to the nature of Christian love that the two cannot live together. Love is either genuine, without pretense, without hypocrisy, without imitation, or it does not exist.

II

This ought to be said: we live in a synthetic world where almost any good product can be imitated. We can buy across the counter a reproduction of almost anything we want, a fact which permits a working girl to wear jewels that look for the world like those which Queen Elizabeth wore in her coronation.

Some years ago when it was still thought that "cultured pearls were worn only by uncultured people" the Tecla Pearl firm ran the following ad in a national magazine. It was entitled "A $10,000.00 mistake":

"A client for whom we had copied a necklace of Oriental Pearls, seeing both necklaces before her said, 'Well, the resemblance is remarkable, but this is mine!' **Then she picked up ours!**"

You may be sure that ad sold a lot of pearls.

This art has not by any means been confined to the area of personal adornment. During World War II when we were cut off from the sources of supply of genuine rubber, the Allies rolled huge caravans of war material from one battlefield to another on synthetic rubber. To meet a critical need, scientists developed a process for making imitation rubber which might have spelled the difference between defeat and victory.

Indeed when you canvass the field of synthetic products, it will amaze you to discover to what extent the clothes we wear, the furniture with which we outfit our homes, the drugs and vitamins that help keep us alive are made of synthetic imitations of something else. They are, in some instances, better in the synthetic form than in the original, and far less costly.

III

This is not true, of course, of all imitations. Most of man's first efforts in this direction were for purposes of forgery, to get something for nothing, or at least for little.

It is when an imitation parades as something that it isn't that folk rebel against it. The danger of a counterfeit is that it brings the genuine under suspicion. Counterfeit money can wreck an economy if it is not detected. That is why during the War high American authorities voted against the proposal to drop counterfeit money all over Germany with the thought that the resultant inflation and confusion would wreck what was left of German economy before it could be detected. The proposal was turned down, according to one account, because it would have violated the ethics of war!

For purposes of forgery it is only the valuable and the costly that is reproduced, for these can be passed on to the unsuspecting as genuine. Against all such, wise and intelligent people must be on guard.

IV

While this is true of material goods, it is even

more important to be alert to counterfeit values, spurious ideas, imitation virtues.

This is supremely true of the principal virtue— Christian love. Says Paul, don't ever be a hypocrite with that. Says the "Desiderata," don't ever feign it, or fake it, or be cynical about it, for it is the one value we must not eliminate or dilute. Genuine love has some indispensable qualities and characteristics of its own which, if our life is to be good and meaningful, we cannot live without.

For one, it has the power to discriminate between that which is good and that which is evil. It is morally sensitive to the values of life, cleaving tenaciously to the good and making a genuine break with evil.

Genuine love can discriminate not only between what is good and what is evil, but also it has a remarkable capacity to discern the good possibilities in people and to bring into actuality "the things which it detects while they are merely possibilities."[2] Imitation love, a love that is faked, simply cannot do that.

Yet this fact about love is one of the major themes of the New Testament, continuously exemplified in the Gospels, particularly in the life of Jesus.

It would be unrealistic to assume that Jesus really did not know what the true condition of some of the people He dealt with actually was. Mary Magdalene was a woman of the streets almost wholly in the grip of evil forces. He knew that. But He also detected in her what almost everybody else failed to see, namely, the making of a saint! Zaccheus was a rascal who had sold out to the Roman Government as a tax collector among his own people, but Jesus recognized him as one to whom salvation might yet come. Probably few people even suspected such possibilities. In any event, a faked love would never have seen it.

Says Dr. Cragg: "Love alone possesses the power of discerning what is good and what is evil because love alone has the secret of the necessary insight. So far from being naïve and gullible, only love is free from the deceptions which mislead us in our judgments about men and movement."[3]

V

The "Desiderata" adds another word about it: "Neither be cynical about love; for in the face of all aridity and disenchantment, it is as perennial as the grass."

Of course! Those who are cynical about love never give it a chance to determine either what they do or how they judge other people. They look upon it as sheer sentimentalism when, in very truth, it is the essence of realism. So the "Desiderata" insists that we neither play the hypocrite about love on the one hand, nor be cynical about it when we view it in others. For in the face of everything that can go wrong, love lives on, it is the one perennial in life's garden of values.

You can neither be hypocritical about love when it is yourself you are thinking of, nor cynical about it when you discern it in others, cynical because you think they too are acting a part and are not genuine. You can do neither of these things and come óut with the kind of love which holds life's profoundest secrets; because, only genuine love underlies the whole of God's redemptive activity in our behalf.

This is, indeed, the quality which must mark the Christian community if it is to be Christian.

You will find no better description of what genuine love really is than in Paul's letters to the Corinthians and to the Romans.

Genuine love, Paul insists, is love that is morally sensitive, cleaving tenaciously to the good and making a genuine break with evil, discerning the potentialities in others and doing what it can to bring them to the fore.

It is love which in humble self-effacement seeks to outdo one another in showing honor.

It is love which in unquenchable enthusiasm boils over, glowing in spirit.

It is love which is irrepressibly optimistic, full of joy, hope and patience, even "in tribulation."

It is love that draws upon the divine resources, being "constant in prayer."

It is love which causes men to sympathize with one another in brotherly affection, in every circumstance, rejoicing with those that rejoice and weeping with those that weep.

It is love which is never haughty or conceited, willingly giving itself to humble tasks. It is love that never avenges itself, but overcomes evil with good.

This is genuine Christian love as Paul describes it. And then he adds, as the "Desiderata" centuries later did, do not feign love. Let us have no weak imitations of it. For only the real article, the genuine thing, can count. And the genuine thing which Paul describes is a set of fundamental principles delineating love in moral action. Love is not something about the Christian faith which you sit in a corner and contemplate. It is something to do. It is a set of attitudes that determine your relationship to yourself, to your God, and to your fellowman. It is the Way, the Truth, the Life.

What it does no imitation Christian love—no love that is faked—can possibly do. What it does no one who is cynical about it can possibly do.

For love is the very moral and spiritual grain of the universe. It hopes all things, believes all things, endures all things, and in the face of all aridity and disenchantment, it is as perennial as the grass.

NOTES

[1] Interpreter's Bible, IX, pp. 586-87.
[2] Ibid., p. 587.
[3] Ibid.

TAKE kindly THE COUNSEL of THE YEARS

In all the "Desiderata" there is probably no admonition more difficult to follow than this: "Take kindly the counsel of the years, gracefully surrendering the things of youth."

It is an admonition to grow old gracefully, to move from one period in one's chronological life to another, recognizing both the joys and inspirations of the new time and the things from the old which ought to be relinquished.

The Bible recognizes this necessity:

"Lord, thou hast been our dwelling place in all generations. Before the mountains were brought forth, or ever thou hadst formed the earth and the world, even from everlasting to everlasting thou art God. . . .A thousand years in thy sight are but as yesterday when it is past, or as a watch in the night.

. . . .The years of our life are threescore and ten, or even by reason of strength, fourscore; yet their span is but toil and trouble; they are soon gone and we fly away. . . . So teach us to number our days that we may get a heart of wisdom."

Paul is even more emphatic: "When I was a child, I spoke like a child, I thought like a child, I reasoned like a child; when I became a man, I gave up childish ways."

"Take kindly the counsel of the years, gracefully surrendering the things of youth."

I

If we take kindly the counsel of the years, we will realize that it is the spiritual and emotional and not the chronological index in a man's life which is most important, so that if we advance chronologically and do not advance spiritually, gracefully relinquishing the things of youth, we are in for trouble. We rob our lives of both power and beauty when we do not see this.

Hardly anything is more pitiful to witness than a person growing into maturity but refusing gracefully to surrender the things of youth. And yet there are those who do just that. They grow old but they do not grow up. They refuse to release at least some of the things that properly belong to their younger years, forgetting that each stage in the advance of life has its own compensations. When the Psalmist wrote, "Teach us to number our days that we may apply our hearts unto wisdom," he was surely talking about the wisdom which recognizes the completeness of life at each of its levels and which requires a graceful surrender to the demands of time and a constant renewal of the values of the spirit which are the only abiding values.

Without such discipline a man or a woman presents the pathetic spectacle of refusing to be his age. One way or another, he will change, whether he wishes to do so or not, and the change may be to his peril.

For as Charles Crowe has said, "The confidence of youth easily becomes the stubbornness of age. Ambitions unrealized can turn idealism into cynicism. The unreasonable accidents and tragedies of the years can harden into stone the gentlest hearts. Love loses its luster when it is undernourished. The once generous and unselfish soul can become petty and cantankerous. And faith in God and in life, when it is not renewed from day to day, dissolves into doubt and skepticism!"[1] For this cause the Psalmist cried, "Create in me a clean heart, O God, and renew a right spirit within me." Take kindly the counsel of the years, indeed.

II

The great need of our time is for people who do just that, who take kindly the counsel of the years; who become emotionally and mentally mature as they grow older; who are truly adult in their reactions to the emergent situations of everyday living, and who can, therefore, be entrusted with responsibility.

Some manage to do just this. If you become discouraged because of advancing years, remember that Immanuel Kant wrote his **Anthropology, Metaphysics of Ethics** and **Strife of the Faculties** at 74; that Tintoretto painted his "Paradise" and Giuseppe Verdi produced his masterpiece "Othello" in their mid-seventies; that at 80 Verdi produced

67

"Falstaff," and at 85 his "Ave Maria," "Stabat Mater," and "Te Deum." Lamarck at 78 completed his great zoological work, **The Natural History of the Invertebrates**. Oliver Wendell Holmes at 79 wrote **Over the Teacups**. Cato at 80 began the study of Greek, and Goethe completed his **Faust**. Alfred Lord Tennyson wrote "Crossing the Bar" at 83, and Titian at 98 painted his historic picture of the "Battle of Lepanto."[2]

All these were people who took kindly the counsel of the years. Instead of growing old, they gracefully surrendered the things of youth and grew up! They did not forget that true life is of the spirit and not of the flesh! They kept their minds and hearts growing with the years. They knew that, as Jesus said, life is more than meat and the body than raiment.

III

Now these remarkable people could not have done what they did had they not gracefully surrendered the things of youth and adjusted the pace of their lives to suit their changing needs.

Relinquishing the things of youth is no easy matter. Dr. Harry Emerson Fosdick once confessed that he was almost 50 years old before he quit using the phrase, "We of the younger generation." Of course he was no longer "of the younger generation," but few important lives lived in this century have reflected a greater capacity for taking kindly the counsel of the years than did his. On becoming a man, like Paul, he gave up childish things.

It is not easy to do. We enter this world wholly dependent upon the care of others, and without that care we would most certainly die. But, as we grow into adolescence, one of our major objectives is that of becoming independent. How many problems have unwise parents permitted to fret them because they did not accept the fact that the time must come when their children will be on their own and that if that time does not come, the child himself will not be taking kindly the counsel of the years.

Then the adolescent becomes a man and makes or would better make a new discovery about his relationship to his fellowmen. He can no longer be wholly dependent. He must stand on his own feet. Nor can he be wholly independent, for mutuality is at the heart of things.

Somehow the mature person who has taken kindly the counsel of the years and has gracefully surrendered the things of youth has found a synthesis. His dependence, as in infancy, was good but not good enough. His independence, as in adolescence he strove for, was good but was of itself not enough. Ultimately the synthesis of these two must be achieved: interdependence which gathers up the truth in dependence and the truth in independence into a living blend.

It is then that the mature person emerges. Paul recognized this truth. Every man shall bear his own burden, he says. This is independence. But one sentence farther on he says, "Bear ye one another's burdens and so fulfill the law of Christ!"

Law of Christ? Yes, His law—a cosmic law that

dependence is good but not enough, that independence is also good but not enough, that the
conscious blending of the two into a man who, insofar
as he can, bears his own burden, but recognizes, too,
that others are bearing a part of it, and who con-
sciously and willingly beyond his own dependence
goes out to bear the burdens of others!

IV

So do we surrender gracefully the things of youth,
and in the process we adjust the pace of life to suit our
changing needs. There can be no doubt that this is
what Paul meant when he said, "When I was a child, I
spoke like a child, I thought like a child, I reasoned
like a child; when I became a man I gave up childish
ways."

That was Paul's way of saying that one should
accept the mandate of his years, that we are to grow
up in our thinking, in our faith, in our actions, that the
effort to hang on to one's youth is to deny that
maturity brings its own opportunities and its own
responsibilities and satisfactions. It is these opportunities and satisfactions which we should
welcome with the advancing years, and adjust to
what they demand and require.

V

If we accept the mandate then we will remain

eager and enthusiastic participants in the wider sphere of life all about us.

There are areas of service which cry out for our help, and we remain vital persons by giving ourselves to them. There are opportunities of fellowship, in the church and beyond the church: literary organizations, musical groups, groups that meet just to play and enjoy life, groups that gather for creative work, other groups that meet for study and worship. Such activities are mushrooming over the nation and more and more people, as they grow older, are taking advantage of them.

What could be more important, if we are to take kindly the counsel of the years, than that we keep alert and sensitive to the larger currents and events of our time.

To live vitally and significantly in our day; to feel the winds of God in the sails of your life, however humble; to look out and see some of the great hopes of mankind being fulfilled in the world; above all, to see history as a sphere for the operation of God's will— that is what is required if we are to take kindly the counsel of the years.

It is to live on a new frontier. It is to realize that we live in an age of a thousand miracles, where space, time, and distance are no longer obstacles to our mobility, but where the great conquest yet to be made is the conquest of the inner man, and where the true meaning of life is achieved only by those who know that life itself is of the spirit and not of the flesh.

VI

In First Kings the story is recorded of the Lord's appearing to Solomon in a dream and telling him to ask for whatever he wanted. The event took place at Gibeon, where Solomon had gone to offer a sacrifice at the altar. Solomon responded to the offer with singular wisdom. Said he:

"Thou hast shown great and steadfast love to thy servant David my father . . . and now O Lord my God, thou hast made thy servant King in place of David my father, although I am but a little child: I do not know how to go out or come in. And thy servant is in the midst of thy people whom thou hast chosen, a great people, that cannot be numbered or counted for multitude. Give thy servant therefore an understanding mind to govern thy people, that I may discern between good and evil; for who is able to govern this thy great people?"

The prayer was pleasing to the Lord and God said to Solomon: "Because you have asked this, and have not asked for yourself long life or riches or the life of your enemies, but have asked for yourself understanding to discern what is right, behold, I now do according to your word. Behold I give you a wise and discerning mind . . . I give you also what you have not asked, both riches and honor . . . . And if you will walk in my ways, keeping my statutes and my commandments, as your father David walked, then I will lengthen your days." (I Kings 3: 5-15)

It was a wise and humble prayer and one that might well rise from every man's lips. The results sound very much like Jesus' promise, "Seek first the Kingdom of God and his righteousness and all these things will be added to you." For when we seek first of all from God and from life those values which ought to be first, our prayers are often answered more abundantly than we ask or think, as the years of our lives go by.

Take kindly the counsel of the years, gracefully surrendering the things of youth. Create in me a clean heart, O God, and renew a right spirit within me. So teach us to number our days that we may get us a heart of wisdom.

> Grow old along with me!
> The best is yet to be,
> The last of life, for which the first was made:
> Our times are in His hand
> Who saith, "A whole I planned,
> Youth shows but half; trust God; see all,
>   nor be afraid!"
>
> Browning: "Rabbi Ben Ezra"

NOTES

[1] Charles M. Crowe, Getting Help from the Bible (New York: Harper and Brothers, 1957), pp. 50-51.

[2] Aaron N. Meckel, Living Can Be Exciting (New York: E. P. Dutton and Company, Inc., 1956), p. 158.

seek spiritual strength for the unexpected

"Be yourself. Especially, do not feign affection. Neither be cynical about love; for in the face of all aridity and disenchantment, it is as perennial as the grass.

"Take kindly the counsel of the years, gracefully surrendering the things of youth. Nurture strength of spirit to shield you in sudden misfortune. But do not distress yourself with dark imaginings. Many fears are born of fatigue and loneliness. Beyond a wholesome discipline, be gentle with yourself."

"Nurture strength of spirit to shield you in sudden misfortune." That admonition, like most of the others in the "Desiderata," has the feeling and aura of a Biblical injunction. Where, more than in the Bible, is it made clear that spiritual strength for times of unpredictable misfortune is a cumulative thing, that the crisis does not create the character which can endure it, but only reveals what a man has been doing with his life in order to be ready for such an hour!

I

Once, a decade or so ago, a congregation heard a sermon inspired by the discovery that the Spanish

75

word for "battery" is **acumuladora**—a word derived from the Latin meaning to accumulate, or to store up power and energy to be called into service on demand. This is what a battery is, a reservoir of electricity, an energy bank, representing that margin of power, beyond what is in use, that will carry you through when heavier demands are made upon you. **Acumuladora!** A man's spiritual life should be equipped with precisely that ability. In how many ways can a man accumulate power for future use, laying it by in "storage" so that some day when having forgotten that he had it at all, he is able to draw upon it in a time of need.

II

This is what is always so amazing and so "miracle-seeming" about character at its best, the fact that people from whom you least expect greatness and who indeed least expect it from themselves, are always in a pinch demonstrating far greater capacities than they knew they had, great depths of being from which they are able to live and upon which, like exhaustless wells, they are able to draw!

Indeed, surely that is what character finally is. Character is not something you are born with. What you are born with may help or hinder, but at the last character roots itself in the reserves of spiritual quality which over the years you have been able to accumulate and which at any given moment you may be forced to levy some demand upon.

Great character, therefore, often seems unlikely in the forecast, simply because you don't know what, for any person, has been laid by in store. Don't ever be surprised then when you run into someone who demonstrates greater reserves than you knew he had. What a marvelous thing to see someone facing a bereavement that requires the complete re-organization of life, and doing it in such fashion that his own response leaves a benediction on everyone whose life he touches!

Or here is a person accepting a verdict about his own personal health—a verdict with which he will have to live out his life, accepting it with amazing serenity. Well, somewhere in that life, you may be sure, reserves were being laid away, character assets were being stored up, and now, when the load is laid upon him he has the power with which to stand beneath it.

There are folk, therefore, who remind us of the burning bush which Moses saw and wondered why it was not consumed. It was afire, according to the story, and it should have been burned to ashes, but it was not. Seeing a character like some of these we have been describing, like Moses we want to turn aside and see why the bush is not consumed.

III

Often when we find the answer to that question,

at the center will be the fact that repeated experiences of the worship of God have left a deposit of spiritual power in their lives.

There is a story to the effect that when George Matheson began going blind the girl he was engaged to broke the engagement because she did not want to marry a blind man. Matheson had every justification for becoming utterly despondent and embittered. Instead he wrote a hymn which we sing until this day, "O Love that will not let me go."[1]Nurture strength of spirit to shield you in misfortune, indeed!

A man facing such a turn into the future alone and in the dark who still holds high his head and instead of weeping at his loss, sings for joy at what he has that still remains, and will remain forever, such a man has rooted his faith in acts of worship until he knows God face to face.

Sometimes we fail to reckon what happens to us in worship. We go to church Sunday after Sunday. We repeat the Lord's Prayer. We hear the sacred Scriptures read again and again. We go through the formalities of the Lord's Supper. And we listen with varying degrees of attentiveness to a sermon. How routine it may all seem in our less inspired moments.

Looked at from that standpoint, how formal and meaningless may it all become. There is danger there, to be sure, and no intelligent worshiper will discount it. But even so, what we cannot measure at all is the spiritual power that is being accumulated over the periods of time in these acts of worship when we commit ourselves week after week to those values apart from which life loses its sanctity. Even when

78

we think we do not, we go away stronger than we came in. This is what the Psalmist meant when he said, "Wait on the Lord and He will strengthen thy soul!"

Nurture strength of spirit, indeed. Thank God for the spiritual reservoirs, filled over the years in the worship of God which provide us with the power we need when we need it.

This is the power which will enable Christian people in our community and throughout the land to find Christian answers to some of the problems that plague our culture. One reason why we should have no fear of the ultimate outcome of the crucial issues confronting us in these days in America is that by and large Americans are a worshiping people, and though here and there in the name of religion violent things may happen, in the long run as a nation we have spiritual reserves, and the spiritual commitments which will guide us into right courses. We will find the answers which will show respect and honor the dignity of all people and which will enable us without fear or shame to bow before the altar of Christ.

IV

Surely another contributing factor to our spiritual reserves is to be found in an experience which you would least suspect of being a source of power: the discipline of suffering. Leslie Weatherhead once said that many people ultimately find suffering to be a "frozen asset" which "later events unfreeze to their great enrichment and the confounding of their doubts." Weatherhead is right about that. For multitudes of people the discipline of suffering has turned out to be a source of spiritual wealth.

That was surely the case with Charles Dickens, who, as a boy, lived in a succession of shabby houses in an "atmosphere of sordid makeshift and continual debt." Ernest Tittle describes Dickens' father as done to the life as Mr. Micawber in **David Copperfield**. He was in and out of luck, in and out of debtor's prison, waiting for something to turn up.

"Prisoners for debt were permitted to see their families as often as they wished or the families wished. In fact, the wife and children of an imprisoned debtor sometimes moved in with him, having no other place to go. Mrs. Dickens once, when nothing was left, moved with the younger children into Marshalsea Prison, where her husband was confined. Charles, who had attained the ripe age of ten, was given a garret room outside, loaned to the family by some relative or friend, but he got his breakfast each morning in the prison. Yet even in this case such adversaries as lonely nights in a garret room and humiliating breakfasts in a debtors' prison were made to contribute to personal growth and achievement."

The experience did become a frozen spiritual asset which thawed out in Dickens' later life and became liquid in Nicholas Nickelby, Tiny Tim, Little Nell, Little Paul, Little Oliver, and "no little support for humanitarian movements that abolished England's debtor prisons and cleansed her schools of unspeakable barbarity."[2]

It is one of the most incredible things, when you ponder it, that suffering which all of us would like to avoid, but each of us must now and again endure, can itself be a source of spiritual power. I suppose that it is so because in the midst of suffering many a person has for the first time really found God because he has been driven to God.

Marty Mann, for example, was once a hopeless alcoholic. She is now a national worker in the field of alcoholism and a tremendous power for good. But years ago she was literally living in Hell as an alcoholic. But she says, "In the midst of my suffering I came to believe that there was a power greater than myself that could help me, to believe that because of that power, God, there was hope and help for me."[3] So in the midst of suffering she found God, and in Him Power, power to rise above her own weakness into His strength, power to become a force for good instead of evil in the world.

This is the testimony which most truly great spiritual giants can bear: that what they have had to suffer, far from being a source of weakness, has time and again turned into a source of strength. One would suppose that this past generation never produced a greater spiritual giant than Harry Emerson Fosdick. Well, consider this autobiographical word which he wrote a few years ago:

"In my young manhood I had a critical nervous breakdown. It was the most terrifying wilderness I

81

ever traveled through. I dreadfully wanted to commit suicide, but instead I made some of the most vital discoveries of my life. My little book, **The Meaning of Prayer,** would never have been written without that breakdown. I found God in a desert. Why is it that some of life's most revealing insights come to us not from life's loveliness but from life's difficulties. As a small boy said, 'Why are all the vitamins in spinach and not in ice cream where they ought to be?' I don't know. You will have to ask God that, but vitamins are in spinach, and God is in every wilderness.'' [4]

V

Another source of spiritual reserves is to be found in the personal disciplines which we place upon ourselves and which build up the reservoir of power.

It was the great psychologist and man of religion, William James, who once observed that if a young person will give himself to the disciplines of the career he has chosen for himself, staying with its requirements day in and day out, never giving up, then one bright morning he will wake up to the discovery that he is no longer a novice but an expert in his field! The only way one becomes an expert in any field is by yielding to the disciplines of it until he is able to do unconsciously, and with the artist's touch, what formerly he did by crude and studied effort.

All of this and more goes into the reserves of power which give to life the margin of depth which makes it worth the candle. Nurture strength of spirit, indeed. What an admonition to send us in a search of soul to see how we fare with our spiritual reserves! Here they are, disciplines which none of us can live well or greatly without: the discipline of work, the discipline of suffering, the discipline of worship, the discipline of self.

"Nurture strength of spirit to shield you in sudden misfortune. But do not distress yourself with dark imaginings. Many fears are born of fatigue and loneliness. Beyond a wholesome discipline, be gentle with yourself."

NOTES

[1] Harry Emerson Fosdick, **What Is Vital in Religion** (New York: Harper and Brothers, 1955), p. 53.

[2] Ernest Fremont Tittle, **A Mighty Fortress** (New York: Harper and Brothers, 1950), pp. 14-15.

[3] Fosdick, **op. cit.**, p. 9.

[4] Ibid.

you ARE A child of tHE uNiVERSE

"You are a child of the universe no less than the trees and the stars; you have a right to be here. And whether or not it is clear to you, no doubt the universe is unfolding as it should."

When Max Ehrmann wrote this sentence in the "Desiderata" in the first quarter of this century, the word "ecology" meant little if anything at all to the vast majority of people in the world. Within the past year or two you have probably heard more, read more, and witnessed more about "ecology," especially as it relates to the problem of pollution, than almost any subject other than the Vietnam War and the generation gap.

Ecology is defined as the science that deals with the mutual relationship between organisms, living things, and their environment. And the ecologist is concerned with that balance of nature in the environment best calculated to result in the well being of all living things.

I

What makes the issue current is that within the past decade or so we have become suddenly conscious of how mankind is polluting the soil on which he grows his provender, the air which he breathes and the water he drinks; how he is denuding the

85

forests, placing great scars upon the face of the earth without attempting to heal them, and turning the living streams of water into streams of sludge and refuse. And this in turn confronts us not only with the scientific problem of sheer survival, but also with a problem which somehow must be faced prior to the scientific, namely, what is the role of man in his universe?

Is he, as the "Desiderata" says, a child of the universe no less than the trees and stars, or is he in some sense independent of it, in control of it, but not responsible for it? Is man nearer to the truth when he stands in awe of the universe or when he thinks of himself in terms of domination over it?

Both of these moods are sounded in the Eighth Psalm: "O Lord, our Lord, how excellent is thy name in all the earth. . . . When I consider thy heavens, the work of thy fingers, the moon and the stars which thou hast ordained, what is man that thou art mindful of him and the son of man that thou visitest him?"

There is the expression of awe and wonder and an admission that man is a child of the universe, no less than the trees and the stars.

But the Psalm ends with an affirmation which **can** mean the opposite of that, though it was probably not intended to do so. Listen: "Thou hast made him but little lower than God and hast crowned him with glory and honor. Thou has given him dominion over the works of thy hands, thou hast put all things under his feet—all sheep and oxen, and also the beasts of the field, the birds of the air and the fish of the sea and whatever passes along the paths of the sea. O Lord, our Lord, how excellent is thy name in all the earth!"

II

Which is he then? A child of the universe, interdependent with all its forms of life, or some near-angelic being who can do with nature what he wills to do, his dominion over the natural order meaning domination? Later we shall attempt to see the relationship between man as a child of the universe and man made in God's image and given dominion over the earth. But, for this moment, let us observe that in nature all living things appear to be interdependent with one another for sheer survival, and that whenever genuine imbalance occurs, all of nature seems to be affected by it.

Take, for example, this illustration from a lecture by Joseph Sittler.

"On the bank of a river that flows between high hills is a village. It has been there for centuries. The village has made an arrangement with the vernal and autumnal moods of the river: the houses and shops know how much the river rises with the spring runoff of the snow water and with the fullness of the autumn rains. Well up the bank they keep their distance.

"High in the forest-covered hills, too, a right relationship exists between trees and earth and forest animals and insects. By virtue of a marvelous ecological balance the life of each is regulated by the function of the others.

"Under the bark of the trees, for instance, there are millions of beetles which, undisturbed, would destroy the trees. But they do not destroy the trees because beetles are food for woodpeckers and the birds devour the beetles in such numbers as to keep the margin safe. On any summer's day . . . one can hear the birds about their happy ecological business! But one day a great beetle-infested tree so falls upon the soft-mounded earth that its underside is inaccessible to the birds. Thus protected, the beetles proliferate in the rotting timber. They spread from tree to tree now in such numbers that the bird-beetle balance is destroyed.

"Tree after tree is attacked, invaded, killed. The first ravaged acre increases to a dozen denuded hillsides. The billions of miles of earth-gripping hair roots die. When the rains come and the melting snow water gathers to a flood, the earth sponge, loosened now, nonfibrous and helpless, pours the water down the slope and with it the accumulated rich earth of unnumbered forest seasons. The old rhythm of the river is broken by a process that began with a strangely falling tree. The shops and houses at the river bank are flooded in the spring because the beetles on the far hills had an uninterrupted cycle of life."[1]

III

This story illustrates an inescapable fact of life: namely, its interdependence. As Rachel Carson once phrased it, "The history of life on earth has been a history of interaction between living things and their surroundings." And while the story illustrates what happens in the natural order without man's manipulation or interference, the fact remains that man is the only creature who has acquired significant power to alter the nature of his world.

And he is rapidly altering it. Says Rachel Carson, "During the past quarter century this power has not only increased to one of disturbing magnitude but it has changed in character. The most alarming of all man's assaults upon the environment is the contamination of air, earth, rivers and sea with dangerous and even lethal materials. This pollution is for the most part irrecoverable; the chain of evil it initiates not only in the world that must support life but in living tissues is for the most part irreversible."[2] And Miss Carson speaks of the pollution as a universal contamination of the environment. And this, not by the falling of a tree in a forest but as the result of the tremendous scientific and technological developments within the past few decades. But enough of this. You are surely aware of the results in smog in our industrial centers; the turning of our streams and rivers into sewage currents and the devastation of our forests. These are the results of the action of man. And man himself is part of the problem, for the population of the world is increasing faster than man's ability to increase agricultural production to match it.

IV

All of this means that the issue is not merely one of the scientific and technological knowledge, but of man's own understanding of nature and his own relation to it. That is first and foremost a theological matter. It is highly doubtful whether ecological

89

catastrophe can be avoided simply by applying to our problems more science and more technology. Real catastrophe can be avoided only by changing our understanding of the true nature of man in relation to his environment.

Some insist that man's abuse of nature has grown out of his religious conviction that nature is here primarily to serve man and for no other purpose; and that man's dominance which the Genesis account records is really not dominance in the sense of stewardship, but dominance in the sense of domination.

Which view is right we must leave to the experts. But this we know without a doubt: that man's current attitude toward the natural order and his relationship to it must undergo a significant change if man himself is not to die out of the universe as a result of his abuses.

For man has acted as though he were superior to nature, as if he were contemptuous of it and has been willing to use it for his slightest whim. In defense of the devastating commercial harvesting of the sequoia forests on the West Coast, a prominent politician is alleged to have remarked, "When you've seen one redwood tree you've seen them all." Is it possible that to a Christian man a tree is only a physical fact? Or is there some sense in which all living things are sacred because God has made them; and even though they are subject to man's use for his own survival, they are not to be abused or exploited as though they had no value except in terms of dollars and cents?

Whatever theologians have had to say about it, it does not follow, simply because the Genesis account urges man to be fruitful and multiply and to have dominion over all creation, that man was to abuse either of these privileges—either that of over-populating the earth or of exploiting wastefully the natural resources which sustain life upon this planet.

V

There is some evidence that there have been saints in the past who saw dominion as stewardship and all of life as something to be revered and not merely to be exploited.

St. Francis of Assisi is probably the greatest example from the Middle Ages. He was, at this point, a radical of the first magnitude. Lynn White has said that "The key to an understanding of St. Francis is his belief in the virtue of humility—not merely for the individual but for man as a species. Francis tried to depose man from his monarchy over creation and set up a democracy of all God's creatures. With him the ant is no longer simply a homily for the lazy, flames a sign of the thrust of the soul toward union with God: now they are Brother Ant and Sister Fire, praising the Creator in their own ways as Brother Man does in his." [3]

St. Francis preached to the birds because he believed there was something sacred in all the life God has created. In his own unique way he was rebelling against what man even in his time was

91

doing to nature and with it. He is regarded by some as the greatest spiritual revolutionary in Western history because he proposed an alternative view to the prevailing one regarding nature and man's relation to it: "He tried to substitute the idea of the equality of all creatures, including man, for man's limitless rule of creation. He failed."[4]

Whether man's having dominion over nature was meant to be unrestrained domination or reverent stewardship is no longer on logical grounds debatable. Unrestrained domination has brought us to the brink of disaster, and the roots of our trouble are essentially religious roots. Until we come to see and act upon the belief that St. Francis was in some profound sense correct, we are under threat. Someone has suggested that St. Francis be named the patron saint of the ecologists.

In modern times he had a counterpart in Albert Schweitzer, the great medical missionary, theologian and musician, whose philosophy of reverence for all of life would be a welcome message to the ecologists who are now so concerned with man's environment. According to the story, Schweitzer would not permit the killing of any animal except for food or unless the animal endangered human life, and even the life of insects he guarded against unwarranted destruction. As a medical man, but mostly as a devoted Christian, he took his position in full knowledge of the delicate balance which must be maintained in nature if living things are to continue living.

Frederick Elder in his meaningful book, **Crisis in Eden**, suggests that somehow we must in our time come to a new asceticism, not the old asceticism which denied the flesh as evil, but a new one which recognizes the value of human good in its relation to all the universe. Three words describe the new asceticism which he advocates: restraint, quality existence, and reverence for life.[5] The discipline of restraint would suggest restraint in the demand and acquisition of "things" which cause so much waste and pollution and restraint in the matter of human reproduction which would be a direct attack upon over-population.

An emphasis upon quality existence, instead of quantities of things, would bear upon this problem of pollution and destruction of natural resources. We have moved from a Puritan ideal of thrift into a state of conspicuous consumption, a course which somehow must be reversed. The new asceticism, as Elder contends, would not be world-denying, but life affirming, with a concern not only with what we acquire but with what we preserve as well. If what we really wanted were a better life rather than more goods and if we were willing to accept the discipline of it, it would make a significant difference in the manner in which multitudes of people in our affluent society live.

The third element in Elder's proposed asceticism is the Schweitzer principle of "reverence for all of life," which would put ethical considerations foremost in all of our decisions. [6]

We will have to come back to the simple admonition of the "Desiderata" to achieve this new asceticism: "You are a child of the universe no less than the trees and the stars; you have a right to be here." Accepting that simple principle you may go on to affirm as the "Desiderata" does, "And whether or not it is clear to you, no doubt the universe is unfolding as it should. Therefore be at peace with God."

NOTES

[1]Joseph Sittler, The Ecology of Faith (Philadelphia: Muhlenberg Press, 1961), pp. 3-4.
[2]Rachel Carson, Silent Spring (Boston: Houghton Mifflin Company, 1962), pp. 5-6.
[3]Garret DeBell, ed., The Environmental Handbook (New York: Ballantine Books, 1970), p. 24.
[4] Ibid., p. 26.
[5]Frederick Elder, Crisis in Eden (New York: Abingdon Press, 1970), p. 145ff.
[6]Ibid., p. 150.

bE AT pEACE

"You are a child of the universe no less than the trees and the stars; you have a right to be here. And whether or not it is clear to you, no doubt the universe is unfolding as it should. Therefore be at peace with God, whatever you conceive Him to be. And whatever your labors and aspirations, in the noisy confusion of life, keep peace in your soul. With all its sham, drudgery and broken dreams, it is still a beautiful world. Be cheerful. Strive to be happy."

The "Desiderata" begins with the admonition to go placidly amid the noise and haste and remember the peace there may be in silence. This is one kind of peace, the peace of tranquility and the contemplative heart. But the "Desiderata" goes a step farther and urges peace with one's fellows: "As far as possible, without surrender, be on good terms with all persons." This is the peace of good human relationships. Without it all other forms of peace are threatened.

But toward the end of the "Desiderata" are two other admonitions concerning peace. ". . . whether or not it is clear to you, no doubt the universe is unfolding as it should. Therefore be at peace with God . . . . whatever your labors and aspirations, in the noisy confusion of life, keep peace in your soul."

These are forms of peace denied those who have

not yet learned that they are not ultimately responsible for how the universe turns out.

In the last chapter we were speaking of man's "dominion over nature" as dominion which had more to do with stewardship than with exploitation. However good a case one may make that man is responsible for the uses which he makes of the material universe, the fact remains that the universe is God's; and while we have it within our power to deface, pollute and even destroy this world and the atmosphere about it, in the long run God reigns over all creation and over all history. The Christian man will do the best he can with what he has and encourage his fellows to do the same and leave the results in the hands of God.

On these two inseparable aspects of peace, so prominent in the "Desiderata" and in the Bible, let us think for a few moments.

I

". . . no doubt the universe is unfolding as it should. Therefore be at peace with God . . . . in the noisy confusion of life, keep peace in your soul."

How does one come by this, the profoundest need of the individual life?

Well let us begin by observing that the two are inseparable. Peace with God and peace within are two sides of one experience. If we gain the first, the second is its by-product.

As one searches the Scriptures and delves into

96

the deepest experiences of the saints who have stood in the Christian tradition, he may discern that there are several basic steps to attaining peace with God and peace within.

The first is obvious: to give yourself to God so completely that His rule in your life is not in competition with any other force in the world or with any god less than God.

We find peace with God when we accept God as the basic fact and factor in human life and history. In the "Desiderata" there is a qualifying phrase, and a good one. "Therefore be at peace with God, whatever you conceive Him to be ." And that "whatever" is an open door to continued growth in your understanding and knowledge of God. Every man has a right to pose his questions about God, but for the believing man the questions will have to do with God's meaning, His will and His purpose, and all such questions fall within the circumference of confident faith in God's reality. Really to find peace with God is to accept the fact that in His will is our peace and to learn to say, "Not my will but thine be done."

It was Thomas a Kempis who said, "For immediately you have given yourself unto God with all your heart, and have sought neither this nor that according to your own will and pleasure, but have together settled yourself in Him, you shall find yourself united and at peace, for nothing shall give you so gratifying delight as the good pleasure of the will of God."[1]

Let there be no question, to keep peace with your own soul you must be at peace with God, and to be at peace with God is to find it in doing His will. William Law, a towering religious figure of the early 18th century, wrote in his **Serious Call to a Devout and Holy Life** that "If there is any peace and joy in doing any action according to the will of God, he that brings the most of his actions to this rule, does most of all increase the peace and joy of his life."

II

Of course this is true. The experience of multitudes of people through the ages bears witness to it. For the will of God has to do with day to day ethical and moral decisions, and there is no such thing as peace with God or peace within your own soul apart from fulfilling the ethical conditions of it.

To put it simply, a man cannot feel right unless he does right.

Somewhere along the line, if we are going to achieve for ourselves some center within that is serene and undisturbed, we will be obliged to quit fighting the claims of our higher selves. No man can feel right unless he does right!

This is a prescription for inward peace which for multitudes of people is not easy to take. We have been in recent years bludgeoned by the pseudo-psychologists who preach a gospel of relaxation as though Jesus had said, "Take up my cross and relax . . . Go into all the world and relax." But that is not what He said. A man with a guilty conscience cannot relax and for that very reason. His conscience ties him in knots.

An issue of **Time** magazine recorded the fact that the Liberian translation of the Lord's Prayer, by a misplaced inflection, has long had the Liberian Christians praying, instead of "Lead us not into temptation," "Do not catch us when we sin."

Well that would be a convenient escape, if we could arrange it. But it cannot be done. When we make evil choices, when we do wrong, it may be that no one else will know about it. You might even convince yourself that it has escaped the notice of God. But it will not escape your own conscience. For however poor our consciences are, they are nevertheless witnesses to the fact that we allow for a difference between right and wrong.

Our consciences testify to the existence of a moral universe where we cannot get by with what is essentially evil. The mercy of God may be infinite, indeed it is, but His demands are nevertheless inescapable. Do not catch us when we sin, my word! We never escape! Certainly one condition of peace with God and peace within ourselves is in Dante's famous phrase, "In His will is our peace," by which he meant at least this: that there are ethical considerations which must be met before any kind of peace at all is possible.

III

Consider two other conditions which must be taken into account if such peace is to be achieved.

One is certainly that we set our minds on what is

highest and best and, in the words of the "Desiderata," remember that with all its sham, drudgery, and broken dreams, it is still a beautiful world.

There is of course a lot of sham and drudgery and broken dreams. There is a lot of war and poverty and hatred in this world. We cannot escape it. We should do what we can about it. There is a lot of injustice in the world and we should do what we can to rectify it.

But any person who dwells constantly on what is wrong, what is evil and what is indecent and unfair in our world, even having done what he can about it, is calculated to have his emotional balance disturbed and even his mental equilibrium threatened.

It is not to be unrealistic occasionally to put the emphasis on the good, the true and beautiful in our world and affirm that with all its sham, drudgery and broken dreams there is much in which we can rejoice.

Paul did not consider it unrealistic or irrelevant to do this. He wrote his letter to the Philippians from a jail cell, and prison conditions in those days were horrible. Yet he says to his readers, "Rejoice in the Lord always; again I will say, Rejoice . . . Have no anxiety about anything, but in everything by prayer and supplication with thanksgiving let your requests be made known to God, and the peace of God which passes all understanding, will keep your hearts and your minds in Christ Jesus . . . . "

"Finally, brethren, whatever is true, whatever is honorable, whatever is just, whatever is pure, whatever is lovely, whatever is gracious, if there is

100

any excellence, if there is anything worthy of praise, think about these things . . . and the God of peace will be with you!''

The only people who can meet this standard are those who, having done all they can about what is wrong with our world, quietly surrender their efforts to God in the conviction that the God who made this universe, and the God who needs our help in seeing that our portion of it is done right, nevertheless is the God who **runs** the universe and we can trust Him with ourselves and our loved ones in both life and death!

IV

If our peace is in His will, then it is His will that we become as St. Francis prayed, instruments of His peace. We do not leave everything to God. We leave only the results to Him, having done what we could, having done the best of things in the worst of times and hoped them in the most calamitious.

The prayer of St. Francis has become a part of classical Christian literature, for it expresses the kind of concern for goodwill and justice which the Christian must manifest toward all of God's creatures if he, himself, is to have any peace at all.

The prayer was St. Francis' way of saying not only that we must be identified with the other man's needs in order to find peace, but that we must get our own selves off our hands. Our preoccupation with our own selfish concerns must be taken out of the center of our interests before we can have a peaceful world, before we can have peace with God or peace with ourselves.

This is a day in which there is available unlimited opportunity for Christian action in meeting the vast and immeasurable needs in our world. We cannot wash our hands of those needs, however much at times we would like to do so. We must do what we can to bring a just peace to a war torn world; to bring economic justice to the underprivileged minorities in our own nation and in the world; and to help bear the burdens of suffering mankind, if we shall ever have peace with God or peace with ourselves. We must get ourselves and our selfish interests out of the center, and forgetting ourselves, take on "the burden of the world's divine regret."

Having done this, we can rejoice that with all its sham, drudgery and broken dreams, it is still a beautiful world. "Be cheerful. Strive to be happy." Here endeth the reading. Let us pray:

"O Lord, our Christ, may we have Thy mind and Thy spirit; make us instruments of Thy peace; where there is hatred, let us sow love; where there is injury, pardon; where there is discord, union; where there is doubt, faith; where there is despair, hope; where there is darkness, light, and where there is sadness, joy. O divine Master, grant that we may not so much seek to be consoled as to console; to be understood as to understand; to be loved, as to love; for it is in giving that we receive; it is in pardoning that we are pardoned, and it is in dying that we are born to eternal life." In Thy will is our peace. Amen.

NOTE

[1]Quoted in **The Christian Reader**, ed. by Stanley I. Stuber (New York: Association Press, 1952), p. 190.

THIS BOOK WAS DESIGNED BY
JUDITH M. OELFKE
PRINTED IN TEN-POINT NEWS 4
ON WARREN'S OLDE STYLE EGGSHELL BOOK
BY MOTHERAL PRINTING COMPANY
AND BOUND BY
JOHN D. ELLIS BINDERY

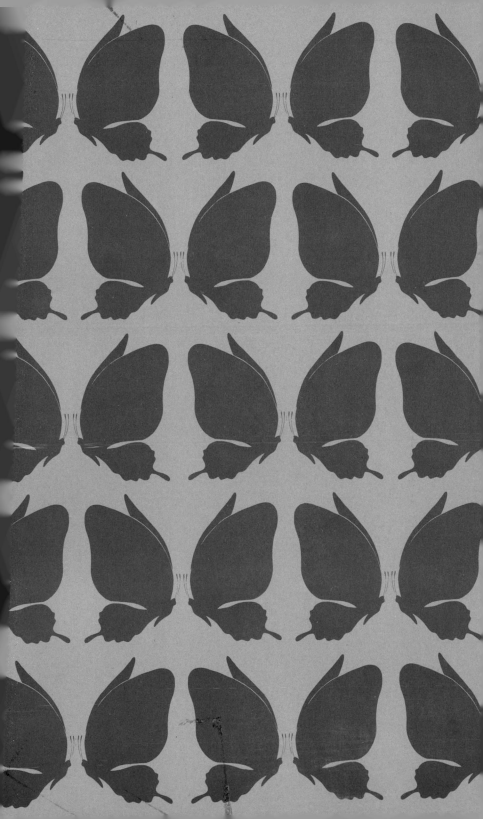

CALVIN
A Life

CALVIN
A Life

by Emanuel Stickelberger

TRANSLATED BY

David Georg Gelzer

John Knox Press

RICHMOND, VIRGINIA

Library of Congress Catalog Card Number: 54-8505

DEDICATED
to
The honored theological Faculty
of the University of Basel
a token of gratitude
for having granted the author the
degree
Doctor of Theology, *honoris causa*

Concerning Emanuel Stickelberger

The stormy experiences of the First World War awakened a new vision in Emanuel Stickelberger, then a young business man of thirty. His first book, a novel, *Hans Waldmanns Letzte Tage (Hans Waldmann's Last Days)*, 1916, created a real stir. It is the story of a man living in Basel, the ancient city of commerce and of the arts which is also the ancestral home of Stickelberger. Among Stickelberger's ancestors are Humanists and Reformers, tradesmen and statesmen. Hans Holbein the Younger's coat of arms can also be found among Stickelberger's armorial bearings.

After several successful works, Stickelberger turned to the writing of historical novels. In the 1920's, the Reformed Church of Switzerland celebrated the beginning of the Reformation. Here the poet Stickelberger found ample material to give expression to his skill and faith. He published *Zwingli* and *Reformation*, books that were eagerly read in Switzerland and Germany and soon translated into Dutch and Hungarian. The University of Basel granted him the honorary degree of Doctor of Theology for his Anniversary Play commemorating the Reformation at Basel. In gratitude, Stickelberger dedicated to the University of Basel his next book, *Calvin*. This scholarly work, not a novel, is a painstaking interpretation of the life and work of John Calvin, drawn from the original sources. *Calvin* has already been translated into French, Hungarian, and Dutch, and has enjoyed as wide circulation in those countries as in Germany and Switzerland. Stickelberger's most recent achievement is his Holbein Trilogy.

"Emanuel Stickelberger," writes Dr. Schwarber, Head Librarian of the University of Basel, "in his works is a citizen of Basel, a Swiss, a world citizen, and an evangelical Christian. His poetic gifts are nourished by these four streams. He possesses, as hardly another poet of his kind, the spirited, pointed dialogue, finding for every situation, for sorrow, fear, or the saving laughter, the fitting form of expression. The scene of his imagination is the past. He leaves the events as history has told them. His personalities live in the environment and with the problems of their day. He does not clothe them with the sorrows and joys of the twentieth century. This timid and wise reticence lends to his works inward truth and the stamp of perfection. Although Stickelberger's works vary in their subject matter, there is nevertheless one steady course and conviction recognizable in all: the firm faith that above the course of history there rules the hand of God. This recognition is not the fruit of objective reasoning. It is deeply anchored in the recognition of the providence of God in all human affairs and thus illumines, without coerced insistence, the course of his narrative, now with exaltation, encouragement, now with direction and purpose. . . ."

Hermann Burte says about *Calvin:* "This work, in genuine Swiss tradition, gives evidence of two of Stickelberger's characteristic gifts, first, the ability to do the research to find out what has happened in the past, and second, to present his material in such a way that it lives in the present, and is to everyone understandable. He does not invent history, he animates and illumines it.

"In gratitude for the high honor of the degree of Doctor of Theology, *honoris causa,* bestowed upon Stickelberger, a layman, he created *Calvin.* In this work the poet stands behind the scholar but the artist remains sovereign and knows how to describe the spirited and spiritual Calvin in form and figure, so that the life of this man, freed from mysteries and prejudices that surround it, becomes a compelling figure for the present. What distinguishes Stickelberger both as a scholar and a poet is his ability to see through intricate, mysterious, and dark facts; to comprehend the central issues, and to present them in such a way that everyone with the right will, understands them. What scholarship has discovered in and about Calvin becomes through Stickelberger the common good of all."

And Gottfried Bohnenblust says: "The judgment of the greatest student of Calvin, Prof. Doumergue, 'Vous animez l'histoire, vous ne l'inventez pas' (You animate history, you do not invent it), concerning Stickelberger, the most ardent poet of Calvin, shows that he does not develop history from imagination, but from the given facts. But the heartbeat is higher so that Stickelberger's zeal is unmistaken, expressing the past life and history of Calvin as eternally present."

* * * * *

Citations are from:

Dr. Karl Schwarber, *Der Dichter Emanuel Stickelberger*, Verlag Huber & Co., Aktiengesellschaft, Frauenfeld.

Hermann Burte, *Der Dichter Emanuel Stickelberger*, Verlag von J. F. Steinkopf in Stuttgart.

Gottfried Bohnenblust, *Emanuel Stickelberger*, printed by Rudolf Schwabe.

DAVID GEORG GELZER
Translator

Yale University
New Haven, Connecticut

Contents

CALVIN
A Life

I.

Preparation and Achievement

(1528-1534)

EARLY IN 1528, as the Picarde, Jean Cauvin, whose nineteen-year-old head was soon to be decorated with the Doctor's hood, was leaving the College Montaigu in Paris, a limping Basque moved in, clothed in voluntarily chosen beggar rags. His eyes glowed in fanatical ecstasy, for he too desired to equip himself with the tool of Science for the fulfillment of the task which he had chosen: He was Iñigo Loyola.

"There is no chance. . . . Our sluggish mind which is unable to ascend the heights of God's providence calls chance what lies in His decree."[1] These words originate in Calvin and are typical of him. Thus it may have been inscrutable providence that the man who, preparing himself to cross the lifework of the other, ere this one had begun, and who was to become the strongest support of the tottering Holy Chair, should have attended the same school as the most inflexible enemy of Rome at the time. Inscrutable? Perhaps Calvinism would not have retained the firm inner strength which proceeds from it to this day had it not been for the rationalized hatred, the spiritually proud defense, and the well-planned, cruel persecutions of the disciples of Loyola.

Obedient to the command of his father, Calvin had early exchanged the study of theology for that of the law, wherein he made astonishing progress under Pierre de L'Estoile, the keenest lawyer in France at the time. It was no friend but a bitter enemy who testified, "He surpassed all in the perceptive faculty and strength of memory . . . his themes were of marvelous clearness

15

and rare beauty of language." And in another place, "A peine eut Calvin son pareil" ("Calvin scarcely had his equal").[2] His industry was matchless. He ate little, slept hardly a third of the night. In iron self-discipline he repeated each morning upon awakening all that he had learned the day before, so that his natural memory, enhanced to amazing power, was admired by friend and foe alike.

Yet through the restless mental work which denied the body its rights, he laid the foundation for a stomach disease and a general frailty, perhaps even for his premature death.

The Parisian Doctor continued his studies in Orleans and Bourges. He confined himself no longer to Jurisprudence alone, but threw himself into all fields of Science within his reach. It is perhaps an exaggeration—no less a person than Gui Patin, the witty physician, called the twenty-two-year-old Calvin the most learned man of Europe.

Already the spiritual revolution which was going on across the Rhine made itself felt increasingly in the West. His cousin Olivetan, a German roommate who threw off the Franciscan cowl, and his Greek teacher Volmar from Rottweil had already been seized by it. Once begun, the talk about it never ceased. He resisted, defended with all the harsh tenacity that was in him the only saving Church against the pernicious teachings of Luther. Oh, he was not won that lightly. Yet, pressed by the ardent desire for truth, he too began to search in Holy Scriptures and lost himself more and more in the Gospels and the letters of the Apostles. Then he read the Church Fathers. He made use of his natural ingenuity and the knowledge acquired in law and philosophy in the interpretation of religious questions, finding himself more and more opposed to the teachings of the ruling Church, which he now discovered to be in disaccord with the Divine law, that Divine law which was revealed to him with growing clarity. And behold, from one hour to the next the pale youth changed into a confessor, a warrior unafraid of death, in whose future life each separate day would be a testimony to the spiritual fortitude of his faith.

Is this, then, supposed to be a scholar, buried in books and

He had to obey, obey against his will.

He was led into the homes of wealthy people, into the shops of laborers, into the halls of the University, even into the surrounding villages, and finally into the pulpit, zealously denouncing the abuses of the Church of Rome. It surprised even him that his speech was able to win followers everywhere for the pure doctrine.

Truly his persuasive power was convincing. The vehemence of his arguments overcame the pretexts of the scholars. The deep moral earnestness of his appearance won him those who were pure of heart, his fiery oratory warmed the lukewarm, shook them up, pulled them along.

Unintentionally the young Picarde became the spiritual head of the secret gatherings.

POINTENT, a surgeon from Savoy and one of the most zealous visitors at these gatherings, told his patients, priests and monks who were full of shameful diseases, only too openly the cause of their illnesses: "It's all a punishment for anti-Scriptural celibacy which hardly anyone keeps!" Without mincing matters, the honest man exalted marriage for priests as a remedy for such immorality and its consequences. Finally, all too outspoken, he was arrested and condemned to burn at the stake because, unwilling to recant, he courageously confessed the pure doctrine. Before that, however, the hangman cut out his tongue because he dared to blaspheme the institutions of the Church.

Paler than usual, horror and embitterment in his look, the young preacher stood among the spectators who were watching the execution at Grève Place. His features became preternaturally tense, he could hardly stand the torture of his fellow believer which was being extended upon the command of the judges. Etienne de la Forge who stood beside him realized that this fiery spirit was about to commit an indiscretion and thereby rob the congregation of its spiritual head. He pulled him away by force and against his will.

In the evening when the believers were gathered around Cal-

vin to receive new strength from his sermon—one can easily guess
the text, "Be thou faithful unto death!"—they entreated him not
to risk his life. All felt that this loss would be irreparable for the
Church of Christ.

He promised to be on guard. Yet an opportunity came to
propagate Reformed views from a significant place. It was an
opportunity which his conscience demanded he use.

Cop from Basel, an evangelically inclined medical man, had
been elected Rector. Immediately Calvin saw him, importuned
him with entreaties, "Give the pure Word a chance in your rectorial address. After centuries of silence, let truth be proclaimed
from the pulpit which is respected by the world of scholars in
Europe as no other!"

The physician hesitated, "That would be audacious!" "It
will succeed. Think of the success for our cause." Finally Cop
consented. He was, however, not at home in the field of theology.
Therefore his friend was to write the manuscript. It would be
done.[7] During cool October nights they were together, by candle-
light, carefully choosing word after word. Courage was accompanied by wit, which pointed to the title: "Christian Philosophy."
Who could object to that? Under its pretense the nature of the
Gospel should be demonstrated and a confession to the Reformed
faith should be made before the entire land. The academic position, the high rank of the speaker—his father is the King's personal physician—should protect him from persecution.

On All Saints Day the University convened in its traditional
pomp in the Church of the Mathurins; many monks could be
found among the listeners, in particular Franciscans. The court
was also present. But there were also groups who belonged to
the new faith who were waiting in the background for the address
of their fellow believer, among them an insignificant pale youth,
the unknown author of the words which would shake both the
University and the entire land. He stood there afraid, hoping,
praying for the act which was to be the beginning of the turning
away of France from Rome.

The voice of the young Rector who began to speak trembled
very audibly at first sight of the distinguished congregation. Yet

soon it regained its impressive force. His first words already awakened astonishment, "Let us praise the Sciences." He mentioned them one by one. "Let us praise them for the sake of their usefulness. Yet what do all of them mean next to this honored philosophy which has what all philosophers have sought but none has found: God's grace which alone redeems from sins."

Shaking their heads, the listeners heard it. It was All Saints Day. There was not a word that concerned itself with that day, as the usual custom was. It would probably come later. They listened again: "Let us plead to Christ who has great mercy and who is the only Mediator with God, that His Spirit may enlighten our hearts that all our being and striving might praise Him, feel Him, and bow before Him in awe, so that the Divine Redeemer may fill our hearts and immerse them in His grace. . . ." Dark looks were seen in the pews of the monks. Christ the only advocate—and all this should happen on the day dedicated to the Saints! Now the speaker touched upon the Sermon on the Mount. In a new, unusual manner—in evangelical manner—he exposited the Beatitudes of the poor in spirit, those who mourn, and those who hunger and thirst after righteousness . . .

Never had the University heard anything like it from this place. Here and there the listeners applauded. But it could not compare with the disapproval of the followers of Rome. Two Franciscans were seen leaving the church. They had been disturbing the audience with remarks of disapproval for the last half hour. "Grace, pardon of God, Holy Spirit," they said; "that's all this speech is filled with. Nothing about indulgences, good works—where will it lead to?"

They ran to Parlement as plaintiffs. The University heard about it; the representatives of the faculties came together to hold council over this peculiar case. The philosophers and medical men defended the Rector, the theologians and lawyers were against him. "Here freedom and the Gospel; there Popery, tradition, subjugation!"

They did not agree.

The King's sister, the Queen of Navarre, heard about it, discovered Calvin's part in it, and asked him to come and see her. She congratulated him and assured him her intercession.

In Parlement, where the opponents of the new faith were in majority, no one troubled about the University's own jurisdiction. The Rector was summoned. He decided to obey the call and to defend the special privileges of the University which had been disregarded. Clothed in the impressive garb of his office, preceded by herald and beadles carrying their golden scepters, he entered the palace.

But there was no thought of giving him a chance to speak. The king was outside of Paris and the time was opportune to strike. The heretic's seizure and immediate execution was a foregone conclusion. Their opponents would bow before the inevitable; they would find out, much to their horror, that the guardians of the old faith would not stop even before the dignity of the Rector Magnificus. Thus the initial growth was nipped in the bud and imitators were hereby warned.

One of the evangelically-minded members of Parlement succeeded in warning the threatened man just in time. The messenger met him accompanied by many students and citizens, drew up to him, and whispered in his ear, "Flee, otherwise you'll be in jail today and at the stake tomorrow!"

Some of the students heard the warning and formed a crowd through which the Rector was able to disappear into a side alley. An hour later he was on the road to Basel in disguise.[8] Furious over this mishap, those of the old faith decided to capture the real author of the rectorial address instead of the straw man, for the secret had leaked out. But the students who helped the Rector to escape were clever. Without losing any time they hurried to Calvin, who, trusting in God and in the protection of the Queen of Navarre, quietly sat over his books. He had to flee head over heels. As it is told, friends let him down out of a window on bed sheets as the bailiffs were knocking at the door.

In his exposition of the Acts of the Apostles, Calvin remarked about the flight of Paul from Damascus which was similar to his, "And already the Apostle's time to carry his cross began . . ."

The first powerful attack of the awakened giant against the

Roman bulwark was frustrated. But God had not abandoned him who, "Romae mentis terror ille maximus,"[9] was to become the greatest terror to the crumbling Rome.

THE FUGITIVE was driven hither and yon. The richly endowed scholar who could see ahead of him a splendid future as lawyer or humanist chose the modest and very hazardous activity of an apostle of an outlawed sect.

Directing his way toward the noonday sun, he crossed the plains and valleys of Touraine, the meadows and forests of Poitou, finally to find pleasant shelter in the house of the choir director du Tillet in Angoulême. In the large library of this friend—it contained thousands of volumes—he found the quiet and composure which would harden him for new battles. He took his Paris manuscripts dealing with the Christian faith, elaborated upon the ideas, supplemented and documented them.

"This is the blacksmith shop upon whose anvil this new Vulcan manufactures the lightning which from now on he hurls every direction . . . here the wool for the *Institutes* has been spun, for this Koran of heresy."[10] Thus writes an angry historian, hostile to him, as he mentions the home of the prebendary, du Tillet.

Calvin's Wartburg.

Yet like Luther in his Thuringian refuge, Calvin could stand these four walls no longer. He visited the neighborhood and, overcoming his natural shyness of public appearances, worked for the Gospel. In Nérac he visited his old teachers Roussel and Lefèvre d'Etaples. The first was frightened when the youth told him of his plans to restore the Church to its original purity.

"For heaven's sake, be moderate, so that you won't tear down the house of God which you intend to purge!"

Calvin's answer was firm: "The building is too rotten to be patched up. It must be torn down and in its stead a new one must be built!"

"Take heed that you may not be killed by the cracking walls . . . ," remarked the troubled old man.[11]

But the eyes of Lefèvre filled with tears as he heard what the young, determined fighter said. "You are chosen as the mighty instrument of the Lord. Through you God will erect His kingdom in our land."[12]

Anew the youth went wandering, everywhere preaching the pure Word. He held secret meetings in the caves of Saint-Benoit. From all around they came. Already the uncared-for congregations partook of the Lord's sacrament of the Holy Communion in both kinds.

He was persecuted, and in order not to fall into the hands of the enemy had to assume a different name: Charles d'Espeville. He appeared in cities, in market places, in castles, always working for the cause, preaching. Even more, he sent men who were aroused by the Gospel, meagerly equipped for this task, out into the land as messengers of the Gospel.

HE COULD NOT STAY AWAY from Paris any longer. Mightily he was drawn to the congregation which considered him as its head despite his youth.

But first he returned to his home in Noyon, the little city with all its past and its majestic cathedral whose two towers rise high in the air, and where his parental home was located at the "grain place." His conscience drove him to renounce in every respect the prebend which his deceased father had acquired for his livelihood. He wanted no offices, no privileges, from the Church of Rome.[13]

He discarded all precaution as, following his longing, he returned to the capital. But Etienne de la Forge, who received him cordially, was worried about his safety and made him promise not to speak in public.

Therefore he visited the members of his congregation secretly, among others the lame cobbler, Milon; the book-hungry cloth merchant, Jean du Bourg; the Royal lieutenant, Fosset; the mason, Poille; the famous lawyer, Canaye—nobles, officials of the court, and professors alongside of craftsmen and students. The common folk outnumbered the others. They were most zealous and most willing to sacrifice. Everywhere they received him with gladsome eye; his words of encouragement found ready ears.

There were still other opponents of the old Church who sought his acquaintance—the Libertines, the Freethinkers who misunderstood the Evangelical freedom and gave their own interpretation to the Scriptures. They had heard about this learned, daring young man, and would have liked to get him on their side. Yet their most subtle reasonings did not catch him. All the cleverness that human wisdom knows how to produce was repulsed by the superior knowledge of the power of the Word of God. There he stood before the men who seemed to themselves nine times as wise as he, strong as a rock on which the surf dashes. This insignificant figure seemed to grow giant-like as he said:

"The Word of God is immovable, faith in it towers high above human imagination."

And as they pressed him further, he continued, "Take heed: he who strays away from the Word of God may run as fast as he likes, yet he will not reach the goal because he will wind up in the wrong path. It is better to limp on the right way than to run on the wrong . . ."[14]

His point of view was supported by reason, proofs of such logic as admitted of no argument. He was able to win this one and that of the Libertines to the faith.

Only with one all efforts failed. He was one who could not be taught because he was of the conviction that he alone possessed all knowledge. Michael Servetus, the highly gifted Spaniard who was only two years younger, not only wanted to reform Roman Catholicism but also the Reformation itself. His thoughts were distorted, he appealed to revelations, took himself for Michael of the Apocalypse.[15] At the age of twenty he had an opus on the Trinity printed in the town of Hagenau in Alsace. In vain he pleaded for understanding with the Reformers in German and confederate lands. Oekolampad and Melanchthon, the mildest of them, desired to have nothing to do with his dangerous doctrine. "My God," cried Melanchthon, frightened, "what tragedy can this matter yet bear!"[16] The gentle Bucer from Strasbourg called him a beast, and Zwingli seriously warned against this destructive doctrine.

Disappointed, embittered, he shook the dust of German soil from his feet. "May God destroy all tyrants of the Church! Amen!"[17]

He hoped to find more understanding in France because the French mind is more flexible. He was told that the young Reformer was going farther in his religious reformation than Luther. He could become *his* man. He offered him a religious debate, convinced he would win him for his views.

The undertaking was dangerous. Yet Calvin did not hesitate to accept the challenge. He, too, had confidence in his power to convince the Spaniard of his errors. "I shall do whatever stands in my power to heal Servetus . . . I know: I shall endanger my life through such a public debate . . ."[18]

But he waited in vain for his challenger in the house at Rue Saint Antoine which had been designated for the battle of wits. The Spaniard, who under a false name was studying medicine in Paris and, for safety's sake, attended the Roman Mass regularly, was struck with fear at the last moment. For Rome he would be an even more valuable catch than his opponent—humility was not his strong side.

Thus an opportunity passed unused which, twenty years later, could perhaps have prevented the terrible incident at Geneva, that incident which, even though repeated unnumbered times in the Church of Rome for centuries, occurred in the history of the Reformation just once, yet once too often.

IT HAD BEEN NOISED abroad that the man who knew so well how to spread his heretical thoughts through the mouth of the fugitive Rector was back in the capital. Already people whispered in the alleys behind his back.

Etienne de la Forge entreated him, "Leave, before it is too late!"

The host did not imagine that within a few months he himself would die as a heretic in flames. His wife would languish in prison and his happy home be destroyed . . .

Had the young Reformer stayed in Paris, remarks Merle d'Aubigné in his classic history of the Reformation,[19] within a short time he would have been burned at the stake and the story of his life in Crespin's "Martyrologue" would have filled one paragraph.

Heavy-hearted he heeded the warnings. One prospect eased his decision: would that he could find a quiet spot in the German lands in order to devote his full time to the work which increasingly occupied his heart and mind, the writing down of his articles of faith! Just recently he had published a book against the Anabaptist doctrines on the state of the soul after death which was accepted favorably. The planned writing, however, would be much more valuable, in fact, so important that he needed concentration for it.

Accompanied by his friend du Tillet, he rode eastward. At Metz he took leave of his beloved homeland in which he was not allowed freely to confess his convictions.

Then through Strasbourg, where Bucer, Capito, and Pastor Zell received him heartily. He found there too much activity and not enough resoluteness and turned therefore to Basel. An old fable (is it really a fable? Then the fable makes sense[20]) has it that in Freiburg, unable to deny his reverence, he visited the head of all Humanists, Erasmus, who gave back to Christendom the New Testament. Disappointed, he left him. He who paved the way for the Reformation discovered that out of the egg which he had laid an entirely different bird had been hatched by Luther and Zwingli than he had envisaged. Already he had withdrawn himself from the New Thinkers and offered his services to the Pope in order to restore the unity of the Church. And now an even more blustering fellow than the others appeared!

The aging scholar had nothing left for those who perceived the consequences of his conclusions. The pure zeal for truth which was in the young man from Picardy revealed to him a new variety of folly. Indeed he sang the *Praise of Folly,* but it was the mocker who praised it.

II.

The Immortal "Institutes"

(1535?-1536)

STRIPPED OF MEANS, the travelers arrived in Basel. On their way—already before Strasbourg—du Tillet's servant, that pickpocket, had left with all the cash the travelers carried with them. Calvin chose a humble lodging which probably could still be found among the small Gothic houses in the suburb of St. Alban.[21] He called himself Lucanius in order to hold himself aloof from undesired visitors.

Here he was undisturbed, had few contacts, except with Nikolaus Cop, the former rector of Paris, some scholars, and religious refugees from France, among them Viret, who later became Reformer of Lausanne, and Courault, formerly a monk, then court preacher for the Queen of Navarre. In spite of frailty and partial blindness, he had been able to flee the persecutions just in time, traveling from Paris to Basel on foot. Occasionally Calvin saw Myconius, the successor to Oekolampad. He enjoyed the leisure to which he had been unaccustomed for so long. Then, too, there was the unknown bliss of living among a people of his own faith, in a city where Mass was repudiated, without the processions that offended his eyes. Although they spoke a language different from his own, and their customs varied from those of his country, he felt at home. Indeed, here he could work . . .

ALL HE HAD TO DO was to put his pen to paper, hardly ever glancing at his notes. The manuscript stood clearly in his mind before he even began to write the first line.

In the unrest of the last days he had thought the plan through many times, formed the individual chapters—he could say them from memory.

Thus, aside from Luther's translation of the Bible, there came into being the most powerful work of the Reformation, the classic handbook of the Reformed Church: *Institutio religionis Christianae*—instruction in the Christian religion.

True, this first Basel Edition has only six chapters. To Thomas Plater, the same who started as a poor Wallisian goatherd and became a professor of Greek and a publisher, who once under the guise of a chicken merchant took care of the news service between Zwingli and the Evangelicals participating in the religious debate at Baden, to him belongs the glory of having published the work. In the course of twenty-four years these chapters steadily increased. Not patchwork but free growth like that of a tree whose crown unfolds mightily. Moreover, the author never had to retract one sentence. Vainly one searches among other Reformers and among scholars in general for a second example of such directness of work from the very beginning. Letter upon letter, all came as if cast. Almost incredible is the consistency of this work—and that of the author!

Six chapters at first: concerning the law, faith, prayer, the sacraments and the false sacraments, and Christian liberty.

Out of the original six chapters grew eighty in the edition of 1559, four mighty books. "All wisdom if it is to be called true, full wisdom, consists in the knowledge of God, and in the knowledge of ourselves. Both are interwoven in such a way that it is hard to say which comes first and which follows." [22]

Thus begins the first book. [23] Here not the Christian but the philosopher wants to speak who sees the Divine hand in all things created and who endeavors to enter the human soul.

Nevertheless, he does not postpone leading the reader upon the right track: "Self-knowledge . . . ? In our innate pride we think ourselves just and perfect, unless we are led to believe otherwise through convincing arguments of our unrighteousness and foolishness . . . By nature inclined to hypocrisy, we are satisfied with the vain show of righteousness instead of the reality.

Surrounded by filth, we assume that to be pure which is the least defiled, just as the eye which is accustomed to black paint can take gray for snow white."[24]

With whom are we to measure ourselves in order to recognize our unworthiness? "Man will never arrive at a clear knowledge of himself unless he holds up his weakness against the glory of God."[25]

In the margin are references to Holy Scripture. The author wants every argument documented.[26]

Chapter after chapter in unrelenting consistency the way points to the knowledge of the Creator in order to measure our smallness by Him. God reveals Himself in the world, in the wonders of nature, and in Holy Scripture.

The first book is followed by three that deal with redemption, the appropriation of salvation in Christ, and the external means of salvation. It is a mine of information for the searching Christian, a theology of action, a perfect exposition of Scripture.

Catholic, Protestant, and even Reformed historians have described Calvin's teaching as Old Testament-like. This conception is also found in his biographer Ernst Staehelin.[27] It is not tenable. Calvin sees the will of God, to which one has to submit, in all of Scripture. He knows only *one* Holy Spirit, not one for each Testament. That which is particularly Christian and evangelical does not stand in the background, but he finds free grace with Moses as well as with the Apostle Paul who in the ninth and following chapters of Romans refers frequently to Moses.[28] Moses for the state, Paul for the justification of souls, this is Calvin's stand. One finds in him the same contrasts as in the Prophets and Apostles. They were men of iron consistency yet of tender and affectionate heart, full of zeal for the truth, never against it, really incomprehensible to merely sophistic consideration. Every attempt to press them into stereotyped forms leads to wrong conclusions and causes confusions.

Calvin takes the *whole* Bible absolutely seriously: this the secret of his being reveals.[29]

THE SUPERIOR demonstration of forceful conviction which is aware of its perception attracts the reader tremendously. The conclusions are of a clarity that brings each link of the chain into tangible nearness. There is no trace of the vanity of Humanism. Calvin did not want to glorify himself through his writing. He sought as little personal honor in this as he ever sought during his entire career. There is no trace of the pompousness of quoting, a means with which other learned contemporaries encumbered their books. Rarely is a name cited from ancient Rome, a reminiscence of antiquity; in its place there is an abundance of divine knowledge. Calvin's amazing memory had been fed by Holy Scripture and the Church Fathers. He did not write for the sake of publishing a book—his aim lay far beyond. The book shows the way to his aim.

Like his thinking, so is his style: not ambiguous, but crystal clear, despising unnecessary flowering of language, a mirror of his purity. In fact, the French language, in which he wrote a great deal later on, owes much to his style. No history of literature underestimates his pioneering significance.

Space is too small to linger over the *Institutes*. Only the doctrine of predestination will be discussed since it is the most disputed teaching of the Reformer. Through free choice, God has determined man's salvation from eternity, independent of his works.

With a certain discomfort one begins to read the expositions[30] on this question after having read the marvelous chapters on the freedom of the Christian man and on prayer. Predestination! The word is repugnant to the modern frame of mind.

However, if one reads through these much reviled chapters once, the impression is different from the expectation. What causes resentment is perhaps the cold, dogmatic presentation. Nevertheless, one feels moved. What, after all, does this election by grace show to the attentive reader? What is this doctrine of salvation that cannot be earned through works, this clarification of the unconditional mercy of God? It is the deep humility of the creature before the Creator. Again and again it recurs, "We are nothing, less than nothing, compared to the Being who is all."

And if the dogmatic expression of this feeling does not cause Christians to tremble in terror, then it is because they see in this confession the greatest sacrifice that man can bring unto God, to measure his misery by the infinite grace of the Creator.

This doctrine of election, which Calvin, like Paul an Apostle by grace, derives honestly from Holy Scriptures, was not his discovery. The Church Father, Augustine, already had taught it. With him as with Calvin, and for that matter also with Paul and in the Gospel of St. John, it is not just a special doctrine concerning the question of whether God will save one portion of humanity by predestining them and not another, but it is broadened here to form the basic doctrine of grace.

"Wherein lies the personal assurance of salvation of the Christian?" This is the question which leads Calvin to the doctrine of election. And he answers, "Alone in the grace of God." If this grace is to be real grace, then the acceptance of it cannot depend upon the work of man and his will, not even in the least. The ground and nature of grace is the free will of God. Man has nothing to do with it. Grace is the sole work of God. Whoever possesses it has been called to a new life. He is a new creature. Whoever lacks it remains in death and slides with each passing day deeper and deeper into the depravity of the old nature. Therefore, since grace comes from God alone, and the possession or lack of it—there is no in-between—decides the life or death of the soul, it is evident that through the gift of His grace God saves some to eternal life. In order to clarify this, Calvin developed his doctrine of election. It is the doctrine of grace which comprehends its real meaning as a freely given gift of God in the most logical and deepest sense.[31]

Luther and Zwingli upheld the doctrine of election in its full dimensions.[32] In later Lutheran polemic it is just the interpretation of grace which is, in attempt, set alongside of Calvin's doctrine of election, and out of his doctrine a philosophical system of God's predestining the destiny of man is read in artificially.

One cannot criticize or condemn this doctrine if it is torn out of the context of the entire life work of its most noble proclaimer. It is wrong, however, as is so often done, to make this the "central dogma" of the *Institutes,* else it would not have been put as late as at the end of the third book. Other doctrines could be mentioned, such as the divine law, the Church, or the people of God, the honor or lordship of God, which put the doctrine of election into a questionable first place. Calvin's thinking, indeed, has more than one central point.[33]

God loves the world, Christ sheds His blood for the sins of the world—and yet the world consists in reality and according to the eternal decree of God of the few whom the Son of God receives through the Father from all equally lost and perishing flesh. The question is not: "Is the doctrinal system of Calvin correct?"— it is answered through Scriptures—but: "Did Calvin know the arguments against this system, and how did he deal with them?" To that it can be answered that he never feels himself bound through his doctrine not to offer to everyone who comes the grace of God with the most solemn adjurations. His dogmatic conclusions are not chains that prevent him from being the messenger of the Good News to everyone.[34]

In vain one searches in Calvin's theology, in his practical applications, or in his life for traces of that fatalism which his opponents try to find in this "terrible" dogma.[35] No one admonishes himself and others more strictly to loyalty, sacrifice, devotion, and progress in the Christian life than he. No one more zealously urges work for the Kingdom of God. "Let each one of us seek to make those whom we meet partners of our peace; yet our peace will only rest upon the children of peace. Let us speak to the heart of each one whom we meet, let us offer him the remedy of salvation, so that he and through him others may not perish. But it belongs to God to bless our words in those whom He has chosen."[36]

Actually free will is not lost in the activity of the Calvinist. On the contrary, this will, made free by grace, possesses an abundance of freedom. The most sincere Christians find in it peace and quiet. Rousseau and other advocates of the greatest personal freedom who thereby seemingly place upon man a much greater responsibility are, as their lives prove, driven by their passions.

By their fruits shall ye know them . . .

"The one-sided force of this iron conception is always nobler and more majestic than the one-sided weakness of a one-sided Pelagianism." Thus wrote Lutheran Tholuck fully a hundred years ago.

History proves that the doctrine of election, which is by no means a non-essential part of Calvinism even as his defenders frequently interpret it, kills neither the ambition to work nor pure morals nor hope. Rather it fortifies men in difficult circumstances within and without.

Therefore no further testimonies by theologians—they are too plentifully represented in literature. Instead those of two historians, neither of whom is Calvinist or Protestant.

Henry Martin,[37] the Catholic: "One might suppose that the doctrine of predestination would result in nothing other than care-free existence, or idle hopelessness, that it would destroy all determination to a devout life. But nothing of the sort with disciples of Calvin. The compelling power of the growing Protestantism is so strong that men, conscious of their salvation, do their work as a natural fruitage of their faith, thereby justifying their doctrine. Even after the relapse from the first great enthusiasm one can see how a strong generation, strict with itself, and of unusual moral and physical vitality, continues to exist."

And Jules Michelet,[38] the unbeliever: "Geneva existed because of its moral strength. It had no territory, no army, nothing for space, time and matter. It was the city of the Spirit, built out of Stoicism upon the rock of election by grace. Against the monstrously dark dragnet in which Europe was caught through the laxity of France, this academy of heroes was needed. To each nation in danger, Sparta sent as an army a Spartan. Thus Geneva . . . Let Loyola undermine the ground, let Spanish gold and the sword of the Guise blind and bribe! In this peaceful place, in this dusky garden of God bloomed blood-red roses under the hand of Calvin for the salvation and the freedom of the soul. If there be any need for martyrs in Europe, the need of a man to be burned or broken upon the wheel, this man is in Geneva, ready to go with the singing of psalms."

AMONG THE REFORMED in Paris there were fanatics who, disregarding the warnings of the sensible, had great bills posted upon the walls all over the city during the night. They were theses containing the pure Evangelical faith, but written defiantly, aggressively, against the Church of Rome. They tried to storm the fortress with iron rams. This was the title: "True articles about the terrible abuses of the papal Mass which have been invented outright against the Holy Supper of our Lord and only Saviour, Jesus Christ."

Indignation against ecclesiastical conditions was set forth in strong words. Perhaps they were too strong—less severe, they might have been more effective. The clergy, the University, and Parliament felt offended; even the king, since the unwise named him too!

What the sensible predicted took place, yet even more terribly than was expected by the fearful. The visitors of the secret meetings were suspected, in all likelihood exactly those who had nothing to do with the posting of the bills. The first one seized betrayed his brethren in order to escape the stake. With knocking knees, full of inward pain, the coward, accompanied by his captors, walked through the streets at twilight, shyly pointing with his finger to the houses of his fellow believers.

Individually, so as to terrify the different sections of the city, the confessors were burnt to death *à petit feu* ("in small fires"). Special whipping gallows had been invented which were lowered into and raised out of the flames in order to prolong the pain of the victims.

There was the arthritic Milon, for years bedfast, who certainly did not post any bills. He was the first victim. Then the cloth merchant, du Bourg, the mason, Poille, and others . . . Even women and girls.

And Etienne de la Forge also.

ALMOST AT THE SAME TIME as the bad news, the calumny came to Basel that those who were executed were Libertines, Anabaptists, Revolutionists against the state . . .

This news cut to the quick the busy writer in the suburb

of St. Alban. In addition to the grief over friends so horribly murdered came the perversion of the truth.

What could he do in a strange land to vindicate the honor of these martyrs and to obtain religious liberty for those Evangelicals still threatened?

While with throbbing temples he was standing above the gushing waters of the Rhine, his eyes lost in the gentle rounding of Mount Blauen in the Black Forest, a thought flashed through him: the work which outlines the faith for which the friends died should be preceded by a letter to their hangman, King Francis. This preface would make the *Institutes* a glowing apology.[39]

Yet he had to overcome certain scruples. One can almost see him now: with a quick movement the body turns around; hastily he sits at his desk and dips his quill decisively:[40]

"To his most Christian[41] Majesty of France, Francis, to his prince and lord, John Calvin wishes peace and salvation in Christ.

"When I began this book I thought of nothing less, Sire, than to write things that would come before your Majesty.

"My sole intention was to give some instruction to those who long to be children of God, primarily among my fellow countrymen. For I saw many in France hunger and thirst after Christ, yet few who received true instruction about Him. The simple and unadorned method of this writing testifies to my intention.

"But when I perceived that the fury of godless men in your empire is becoming so fierce that there is no room for the pure doctrine, I determined this writing should at the same time exhibit before you a confession of faith. May you learn from it what is the nature of this doctrine which drives the anger of the madmen to destroy your kingdom with fire and sword . . ."

And he lays to the heart of the ruler the terrible injustice which is inflicted upon his most faithful subjects. His words become increasingly sharp:

"It is an outrage to pronounce blood-sentences against a teaching with which one is unfamiliar; fraud and betrayal to brand it without reason as revolutionary and hostile to the state . . . No one steps up to oppose the madness. Some who are inclined toward the truth speak of doing something about the ignorance of simple-minded folk. For so they speak, calling that imprudence which is sure truth of God, calling those simple whom the Lord favors with the revelation of His heavenly wisdom . . . It is up to you, Sire, not to turn away your heart and ears where such great matters are at stake: to maintain the honor of God on earth, to preserve the honor of truth, and to continue the Kingdom of Christ among us. What a memorable cause, worthy of your attention, of your judgment, of your royal throne! A true king administers his kingdom as a servant of the Lord. Whoever rules otherwise is a robber, no king!"

Emasculating the lies and prejudices, Calvin criticizes unmercifully those who tolerate the disparagement or even disdain for the faith offered in Scripture so long as the moving spirits stay within the confines of the Church. Point by point the accusations of Rome are refuted. The lawyer in him leads the pen of the theologian. If he were to defend his matter before an unbiased court, his opponent would have a tough time. All arguments, however, are illumined by the spirit of the Gospel. The assurance of his final triumph is victoriously dominated by his conclusions:

"Our God is not a God of anger but of peace . . . Should it please your Majesty to read this confession, without ill will or wrath, then I hope we would regain your favor. Should this not happen because you leave the power in the hands of those who rage against us with dungeon, whip, torture, fire and sword, so that we shall continue like sheep to be led to the slaughter, then we shall possess our souls in patience, waiting for the mighty hand of God, which, when the time is fulfilled, will appear armed to deliver us from our tribulation and to punish the proud and spiteful.

"The King of all kings establish your throne in righteousness!"

"Basel, the first of August, 1535."

Would the Roi-Chevalier read this work? It was said that he was considering the plan of Henry of England to separate the Church of his kingdom from Rome. It was rumored that he was thinking of calling Melanchthon to Paris. If these rumors were true, then reasons other than reasons of faith were working in him. The man of the world will not read an epistle of repentance and punishment, twenty pages long, or even an instruction in the Christian religion. Had he perchance read the exposition on true and false religion which had been dedicated to him ten years earlier by Zwingli? Of course, if it had been an intriguing novel!

The letter which was to be called the classic apology of the Reformation did not reach the one for whom it was designed because he was more occupied with his amours than with ecclesiastical disputes.

SCHOLARS OPENED their eyes when the *Institutes* came off Thomas Plater's press. "Joannes Calvinus— quid est?" What, the young, insignificant Frenchman from the suburb of St. Alban of whom it was said he was assisting in Olivetan's translation of the Bible?

The good lady Klein with whom he was boarding shrugged her shoulders every time a visitor knocked at the door. Gone away!

As soon as the last proof sheet was finished, the author of the book which caused so much commotion took his way into the Ennet mountains. His biographers, who cannot agree on the time of his conversion, are equally divided concerning the motive of this journey. He wanted to greet the dream land of all scholars: "Italia salutanda." Nothing less was in his mind than to bring the Gospel to those areas which lie closest to Rome . . . It is quite true that he had received an invitation from the educated young duchess Renate of Ferrara who drew French fugitives to her court. The poet, Marot, the translator of the Psalms, was her secretary. He belonged to those who, after the posting of the bills, had to flee from Paris. It was he who told her ladyship of the head of the congregation in Paris. These seem to be the circumstances.

Renate, who except for the Salic law would have had possession of the throne instead of Francis I and perhaps would have become for France what Elizabeth later on became for England, had already been engaged to Charles V and after him to Henry

VIII of England. Reasons of state caused these connections to be severed. And it was reasons of state which effected her marriage to the son of Lucrezia Borgia, the duke Hercules of Ferrara.

Already in her youth at the court of Navarre, this charming duchess had been won for the Gospel by Lefèvre d'Etaples. Now living abroad she felt a double need of being in contact with fellow believers. "With them she forms at the court of Ferrara a hearth of anti-Catholic machination, breaks fasting and permits meetings of reformers of the faith to be held in the Palazzo San Francesco. . . ." [42] Thus complained a papal historian.

The young Picarde of whom so many extraordinary things had been told her was received with open arms. He presented to Renate the first copy of the *Institutes*, meanly bound together with proof sheets. She introduced her fellow countryman to her husband as Charles d'Espeville. New life streamed into the colorful, checkered society of Ferrara, taking the shape of a well-grounded Reformed congregation. Like the Waldensian valleys it became an island of faith in the wide sea of superstition.

But Rome was too close. The Papal Church did not yet possess the immovable iron bonds into which the Council of Trent would put her. Disputations on matters of faith and the institutions of the Church were not yet prohibited in Italy. To ask for reform was not yet a crime punished by death—because they knew that those who did so were thinking only of change, not the overthrow of the Papacy. Did not even Michelangelo and Vittoria Colonna favor innovations? And Paul III, the Faranese, the Pope of the Renaissance, was not too strict. He did not like agitators, Loyola for example. But about this avowed nest of heretics in Ferrara he could not do anything but remonstrate, first in a friendly manner, then urgently. Charles V, upon whom the duke depended, added his weight. Hercules demanded the expulsion of the French. In vain did their protectress object, "Leave me these poor countrymen of mine. Had God given me a beard to grow, they would be my subjects!"

But what could she do against force? The warnings of the duke changed into threats; he made her life a hell. Marot's lines run like this:

"She suffers pain in this land,
as if the princess had been banned
like me . . ."

The situation became serious. Only with trouble did Renate
save her faithful people from the approaching Inquisition. They
had to flee, head over heels. She herself was unable at length to
escape the wrath of Rome. Since she remained steadfast against
the attempts of conversion by the inquisitor Ory and the
Jesuits, she was put into prison, her children taken from her
and educated by strangers in that despised religion. . . . Only
much later she yielded outwardly to accept the "Catholic" faith.
Very decidedly she refused to say the "Roman Catholic." After
the death of the duke she retired to her castle, Montargis, in
France, in order as a Reformed confessor to be able to offer
fellow believers an Hôtel-Dieu, a hospital, and a safe place for
refuge.[43]

Beza in his brief chronicle style reported, "When the lady
duchess of Ferrara had seen and heard Calvin, she knew of whose
spirit he was, and as long as he lived, she remained for him a
special instrument of God, faithful in love and devotion."[44]

This is a short episode without any visible influence upon the
life of Calvin, so that I was originally prompted to touch upon it
in two sentences only. Still the Jesuit Tiraboschi says, "Calvin's
stay at the court of Ferrara has brought more damage to Italy than
all the emissaries of Luther."[45] And then—this cannot be over-
looked—the Reformer was in lifelong correspondence with the
much tried duchess and gave her confidence and courage in her
most severe trials. To her deep sorrow, the Duke of Guise, the
great enemy of the Huguenots, became her son-in-law. Even on
his deathbed, Calvin dictated a letter of comfort to her—it was
his last writing in his mother tongue. To her fears of falling into
disgrace with the Evangelicals through this relationship he
answered, "No, Madame, for the very reason that it is evident
that not even this deters you from confessing your faith so
staunchly in word and deed, they love and respect you all the
more . . . I, too . . ."

The letters to the duchess still preserved would, were there no other testimonies available, convey an excellent picture of the writer: this man of God who, without regard for persons, judges and consoles, teaches and warns; and of the man who sympathizes, feels, and hopes for others.

For this is the key to his tremendous power over other minds. He did not exalt himself above anyone, was shy by nature,[46] was tender, sensitive. He lacked daring power and possessed a disinclination for everything which looked like tumult.[47] Yet as soon as the honor of God was at stake, his spirit took on victorious power, his speech reminding one of a prophet of the Old Covenant, perhaps a Micah.

FROM ABROAD Calvin corresponded with the Evangelicals in his native land, reminding them earnestly to stand fast. His former host in Orleans, Duchemin, had accepted a position which brought him in constant contact with the Roman cult. Worrying about him, Calvin wrote, "Look out, faithful man, be on the alert! Let your life be so much kindness, mercy, purity, and innocence, that even the superstitious will have to admit, however unwillingly, that you are in truth a servant of God."[48] Far greater was the sorrow which the newspaper brought to Ferrara, reporting that his teacher Roussel, the same who, much afraid, had warned him in Nérac to be more moderate, had been elected Bishop of Oloron by the Pope. He no longer called him dear friend[49] as he had called Duchemin.

Even the introduction was a reproach: "John Calvin to a former friend, now a Prelate . . ." To a "former" friend: the tie was cut. No fellowship with him who has broken his loyalty to God! Nevertheless he spoke very earnestly to the conscience of the deserter, trying to bring him back: "What happens to one who like you deserts his captain, runs over to the enemy and destroys the ground for the defense of which he swore to give his life? . . . O Rome, Rome! How many of the spirits who were born for the good do you lead astray and how many of these misled do you keep in bondage; how many are you casting into eternal perdition! . . .

"Get out of the swamp, Roussel, before you drown in it!

"You reply: 'What then shall become of the wretched? . . . Should we exchange a comfortable life for one of continual wandering and our full grain bins for the bread of misery in foreign lands?'

"Yes—if you think that such a life is preposterous, you are no longer a true Christian. It is hard—how well I know it—to leave one's home in order to become a pilgrim. And yet the Lord transforms this destiny, which in the eyes of men is so harsh, into sheer joy . . ."[50]

Thus wrote the twenty-seven-year-old Calvin to the bishop. Anyone who leafs through a collection of Calvin's letters will invariably meet the unswerving position to which he held and which he expected to be kept by all believers. He knew no compromise.

It is not hard to see the contrast which this young, unbending man, who felt he belonged to God, presented at the court of the Este, where a Titian and great men, fond of the arts, brought aesthetic enjoyment to its highest development. And again one is reminded of the prophet Micah at the court of King Hezekiah, who could say, "But I am full of strength and of the spirit of the Lord, full of right and power, that I may show Jacob his transgression and Israel her sins."[51]

ONCE MORE the longing for his first congregation overtook Calvin. An edict which assured all "heretics and sacramentalists" a return and a six months stay in their home country—it was hoped to force them thereby to recant their faith—offered the hunted the opportunity to return to Paris for a short time.

With broken heart he stood before the house of Etienne de la Forge in which strangers now lived and sadly sought lodging in an inn. He met the faithful who had escaped the stake; he even succeeded by his persuasive word in winning new followers for the pure doctrine. Even a year later he received a message from a man to whom he brought salvation during that visit. The writer implored him to help him to any kind of position, no matter what, just so that he might be able to attend the Scriptural expositions of the honored teacher . . .[52] Testimony follows testimony to the conquering power which dwelt within the untiring proclaimer of the honor of God as he talked with others.

Yet he could not stay here. He was closely watched. As soon as the designated time of grace was over, the arch-heretic would be rendered harmless.

III.

The First Reformation

(1536-1538)

THIS TIME Calvin left France for good. He took along a sister and his brother Anthony who from now until the last became his faithful helper and secretary. They planned to settle in Basel, or in Strasbourg, or somewhere in Germany where one could live in peace according to his own belief. The author of the *Institutes* longed for a quiet place where he might indulge in his research, where he might work in silent retirement for the progress of the renewal of the faith. Yes, some place where it was quiet. Were there not enough preachers who could speak better than write, to whom the open battle for the Gospel is a need? He could sharpen spiritual weapons which would serve them against superstition and heresy. Only not to appear himself . . .

His first goal was Basel. The road, however, was barred by troops; he had to decide to travel through Lyon and Geneva. In Geneva he planned to stay only overnight.

And now the hand of God reached visibly into the destiny of His Church.

The city located on Lake Geneva had already decided for the Reformation. The transition was rough, even more than in other Swiss cities. It was accompanied by iconoclasm, tumult, and battles with the Bishop and the Duke of Savoy. Famine and inflation were added. The leaders of the Reform movement were put into prison several times, expelled, and by miracle escaped being poisoned. Not only had the superstition of the old faith to be overcome, but the reaction which could already be noticed. Unbelief and immorality realized their opportune moment had come. Unbelief prevailed to an extent which at that time was not expected at all. Yet on May twenty-first, 1536, the citizens assembled in the Church of St. Peter under solemn oath elected the Gospel as the only criterion for faith and life. The city coat of arms as stamped on seals and coins received the motto: "Post tenebras lux"—after darkness light.

Among the preachers of the pure doctrine, three men stand out: Froment, Viret, and Farel. Farel is the most important of the three. To him, the fiery spirit from Auvergne, who through his impetuous attacks had already antagonized Erasmus at Basel, to the Reformer of Neuchâtel, Aelen, and Moempelgard, goes the glory of having broken all resistance. Not only the citizens of Basel but even Oekolampad thought him too impetuous; and they would have asked him to leave, even aside from the fact that he called their celebrated guest, the man from Rotterdam, a Balaam. The French, who are of livelier spirit, need men of his nature. When two opponents get into a squabble, the one who is able to express himself more aptly has an easy victory. And Farel was always skillful, crushing anyone in a battle of words. All deficiencies in knowledge and in the gift of reasoning were overcome by his quick-witted rhetoric.

His insignificant figure was poorly clad, the long red beard neglected, his cheekbones standing out from his freckled face— but the eyes flashed glowing sparks and the voice commanded gatherings in the open, and if heard from the pulpit, rolled like thunder through the sanctuary. Always stirred by the sacredness of his task, filled with hate against the prince of hell whose snortings and roarings he could hear, he was animated with fervent sympathy for the unfortunate who were drifting toward eternal damnation; and like a whirlwind that no dam is able to stop, his speech flowed into the souls of his listeners: wailing, admonitions, threats, entreaties, and terrible anathemas . . .

Not one of the addresses of this man, who is called one of the mightiest of orators of his country, is preserved in his own words. He preached extemporaneously, only for the hour, putting a finger upon every sore point, often in coarse, exceedingly rude, yet always popular language. An evangelist of our own day would be horrified at such popularity; yet it was this with which the never-tiring Farel conquered the unpolished people.

THE PRIESTS were expelled and Farel was master of Geneva. But for how long? Opposition was already felt and the indications were at hand that the enemy would strike a counterblow. He felt he could storm a fortress easier than keep it. Felt it and saw no way out. Being a passionate man of prayer, he wrestled for the city.

There, three months after the memorable meeting at St. Peter's, he met the prebendary du Tillet from Angoulême. He stopped Farel, "Have you heard the latest news? My friend Calvin is here." The preacher almost lost his speech for joy. "Wha-what, John Calvin, the one who wrote the *Institutes*?"

"He is leaving early tomorrow morning." Farel's facial muscles became tense as he said, "He is *not* going to leave! Where is he lodging?" Passers-by were turning around, so loud was the conversation.

And leaving the gasping prebendary behind, he hastened to the inn which was pointed out to him.

Perhaps he was disappointed as he looked at the sickly young man whose black hair gave an even paler appearance to his countenance. Perhaps he expected a stature which outwardly, too, would reveal the creator of this tremendous work which he had read—literally devoured, and already cherished more than any other book written by human hands.

The stranger received him with reluctant gladness. The overjoyed Farel, however, blustered, "You are not leaving, that's all off! There is much for you to do."

"What do you mean? I am sorry, but I cannot remain any longer than one night."

Farel paid no attention. With great eloquence he began to demonstrate to him who was more than twenty years his junior in what miraculous way the city had been won for the Reformation. His words bubbled over as he described this great happening. It was not long before the stranger learned of the tenacious struggle for the victory of the pure Word.

"Look around you: the followers of Rome have been overcome, the abuses checked. Now, however, we need you, just you, in order to teach the Scriptures to the ignorant people who hunger after salvation."

Calvin shook his head, "To teach? I still want to learn. I intend to write several things for which I would not find the time here. I want to talk about these things with Bucer and Capito, also with those in Wittenberg. I want to deepen my knowledge . . ."

Farel heard only half of it. He interrupted him, impatiently shaking and turning his raised right hand with outspread fingers, "Leisure, learning—when it is a matter of acting! Do you want to desert the Reformation of this city? I am at the point of breaking down under the load and you will deny me your assistance!"

"Don't take it as ill-will. My health is not the best; I need a rest."

The Auvergnese went on, "What, rest! Nothing except death brings rest to the servants of Christ!"

"It will never work, here the least of all places. Everywhere they speak of the violence and the constant uproar of the Genevans. To defend myself before council meetings, to withstand riotous crowds, is not my nature; I do not have a fighting constitution, and these Genevans . . ."

With a motion of his hand, Farel cut his word, "These Genevans, these Genevans: tearing wolves they are! But is this a reason for you to leave me alone in the fight against this mob?"

"Why should *I* be the one to help you? Can't you see—" he took the right hand of the other—"I am timid, weak, and fainthearted by nature, and feel myself not equal to such opposition."[53]

Flinging away the other's offered hand, Farel responded, "Do you really believe a Christian may give in to his timid heart so much that he can stay aloof from the battle for the Kingdom of God?"

Calvin quivered. The reproach of putting his personal comfort ahead of the service for the Saviour caused him severe qualms of conscience. Couldn't this determined man see that he was not equipped for the task which he required of him? Once more he pleaded with wringing hands, disconcerted before the strong, demanding look, "In the name of God, have mercy on me! Let me serve Him in a way that is different from your understanding of it. . . . I *can* not . . . !"

"You cannot? Jonah, too, thought he could not when the Lord called him!"

The storm began in the soul of the afflicted Calvin. More and more he resisted, opposing the coercive will of his visitor with his own equally strong one. For a long time both men wrestled with all their might, the one for the completion of the work which he had begun, the other against the threatening turning-point in his destiny.

Farel was determined only to break all resistance, nothing else. He entered the battle with the certainty of reaching his goal. The obstinacy of his opponent drove the blood to his head. His eyebrows lifted in a threat; he forgot with whom he spoke and was no longer concerned with any formality.

"For the last time, do you want to follow the call of God, or don't you?"

The other gnashed his teeth. Uncontrolled, his fingers twisted his black pointed beard, "No! No! No!"

A hostile glance struck Calvin. Now the preacher's stature became erect, it seemed to grow; his eyes hurled lightning.

"You are concerned about your rest and your personal interests . . . Therefore I proclaim to you in the name of Almighty God whose command you defy: Upon your work there shall rest no blessing . . . !"

His facial expression tensed; by force he gripped the hesitant Calvin, his countenance so close that he could feel his steaming breath: "Therefore let God damn your rest, let God damn your work!"

Wide-eyed, Calvin stared at the small lips which had thrown this horrible curse at him. His whole body trembled. A terrible clearness illumined him. It was not the man who stood before him that spoke, but the Lord Himself through his mouth. He felt the presence of the Invisible, seemed to perceive the hand of God which, coming from heaven, descended upon his head[54] and rooted him irrevocably to the place which he desired so much to leave.

A feeling overtook him as bitter as death. He saw himself suddenly torn out of the path which had opened up before him, and found himself stationed in battle and unrest—in the front line. Gone was the hope of work in a quiet, hidden place. Now that he contemplated leaving all this behind, it seemed even more enchanting than he had dreamed. The picture of Abraham came to his mind, of whom the Lord demanded the greatest sacrifice only to reject it at the last hour. God would accept his . . .

The visitor was quiet, his big eyes staring straight at him. Calvin felt the weight of the heavy, invisible hand on his forehead; he wanted to grasp it, so as to free himself of this burden, but was unable to move his right hand.

As if under searing fire, his defiance melted. And as he offered his hand to the preacher, a tear rolled over his caved-in cheek,

"I obey God!"

CALVIN HAD LONG IMAGINED himself an instrument of the Most High, but only now did he realize that always before his own will had ruled, this unbending will which only this day had been broken.

Henceforth the extension of the truth was his only passion.

Almost twenty-eight years later there was found in his exposition on the prophet Ezekiel, the last which he gave, a moving prayer:

"Almighty God, grant us the grace humbly to resign ourselves to Thee, not to falsify our service for Thee by our own imaginations, and in obedience to Thy will to persevere, as it has been revealed to us through Thine only-begotten Son . . ."[55]

IN THE MINUTES of the Geneva Council of September 5, 1536, the following notation is recorded: "Master William Farel explained how important the lectures on the Holy Scriptures are which this man from Gaule (*ille Gallus*) had begun at St. Peter's; wherefore he asked that he be retained (*alimentare*)." The petition was granted.

The arrival of the stranger was given so little attention that his name is not even recorded. "Ille Gallus!" Nor did the Council seem to be much hurried in regard to his salary, for five months later only do the Minutes report: "Calvin is discussed since he has as yet received nothing and it was agreed to pay him five Sonnentaler."

In the daily lectures the young scholar expounded the Pauline epistles. Besides that, he translated his *Institutes* into the vernacular, so that the common man, too, could read them. He was little noticed and modestly stood in Farel's shadow.

News of this excellent expositor was, however, quickly spread among the citizens. The number of his listeners increased constantly. Among them were many refugees from France. The seed which was sown here was to bear fruit in far-distant fields.

As a humble servant of the Word did Calvin begin his work in the Cathedral. Soon his clear, penetrating voice could be heard from the pulpit. And thus began the activity which in a few years Christendom would either blindly admire or furiously hate.

IN LAUSANNE was held a religious debate at the instigation of Berne in order to end the confusion that existed in the Vaud lands. Through such a debate the city on the Aare had itself been won almost overnight to the cause of the Reformation eight years before. In like manner the subjects of the Vaud lands were to be confronted by the pure doctrine, through the power of conviction of the Word.

Viret was already in Lausanne. Farel brought from Geneva the young rector from St. Peter's, "ille Gallus." At seven o'clock in the morning while the church bells were solemnly ringing, the mighty Cathedral was filling up. This Cathedral had been consecrated three centuries before by Pope Gregory X in the presence of Rudolf of Hapsburg, citizens and visitors. In the center of the nave were the seats of the two party leaders, the lawyers, the Bernese delegates clad in official red and black and the participants among whom were one hundred seventy-four Roman priests. The Bishop declined the invitation; His Excellency did not want to get himself into trouble.

The Emperor Charles V caught wind of the meeting at the last moment and swiftly forbade the debate. "Illico annuletis, aboleatis." The Bernese shrugged their shoulders.

Farel addressed the opposition, "Speak straight from the shoulder! We do not dispute with galleys, fire and sword, prison and torture behind us. We have no hangmen for preconceived opinions. Let Holy Scriptures alone be the judge. If the truth is on your side, step forward!"

Different from the debates in which Rome and the Inquisition controlled the meeting . . .

For three days Calvin was silent. As often as Farel nodded to him he shook his head. And in the evening he answered the reproaches by saying, "You and Viret know well how to answer all questions. Why should I interfere?"

Farel wrung his hands, "It is a shame that you have so much insight and knowledge and at the same time so much shyness."

On the fourth day, however, the Lord's Supper was the topic of discussion. Mimard, one of the Romanists, read a carefully prepared speech. He accused the Reformers of holding the teachings of Augustine and other divinely inspired Church Fathers in low esteem.

Farel looked at Viret, Viret back at Farel, who was about to retort, "Human words! Our only basis is the Holy Scriptures."

But it did not come to that. The young lector had risen and in silent scorn he fastened his eye upon the accuser who was looking about himself assured of triumph. Full of amazement everyone stared at the young man. Now he began to speak. "Honor to the Holy Church Fathers: he among us who does not know them better than you, let him beware lest he mention their names. Too bad that you are not more thoroughly read in them, otherwise certain references could be of benefit to you."

Freely, without any manuscript before him, Calvin began to refute the opinions presented. And how he refuted them! Everyone listened attentively because all his arguments were taken exclusively from the Church Fathers. He quoted and expounded

the opinion of Tertullian, added a homily ascribed to Chrysostom
—"the eleventh, about in the middle." Then a passage from
Augustine—"from the twenty-third chapter toward the end";
another from Augustine's book against Adimantus the Manichean
—"about in the middle"; another, from the ninety-eighth Psalm,
and again another, always quoting from Augustine—"the beginning of a homily on the Gospel of John, it must be the
eighth or ninth . . ." He was not yet finished with the presentation
of proofs from the old Christian commentaries, the titles of which
were not even familiar to most of the people present. He had still
another witness for the evangelical interpretation of the debated
question: "In the book *De Fide ad Petrum Diaconum*, we read
this, and in the Epistle *ad Dardanum* the following . . ."

All by heart! Followers of the old faith and the new held
their breath as they listened to the unmatched scholarly presentation supported by a miraculous memory. The opponent who
earlier proclaimed his accusations with a voice of conviction felt
himself shrinking as the small, pale speaker, directing his eye
upon him, continued with victorious expression: "Judge for yourself whether your assertion is not audacious, that we are hostile
to the Church Fathers. Admit that you hardly ever saw the covers
of their works. If you and those who spoke before you had ever
leafed through them, you would have wisely remained silent!"

These scholarly blows are enough. Yet suddenly the surprising
speaker switched over to a different type of attack. He was not in
vain a pupil of de L'Estoile's, the prince of lawyers. Disturbed, the
followers of Rome found themselves defeated by their own arguments. Move by move their opponent, assured of his victory,
placed his chessmen until the enemy was checkmate. Terribly
beaten—with his own weapons!

Clearly the final words could be heard: "A spiritual communion which binds us in truth and reality through everything
which we are able to receive by grace from His body and blood,
which binds us to our Saviour . . . , a spiritual communion binds
through a spiritual bond, the bond of the Holy Spirit: that is the
Lord's Supper." [56]

Calvin sat down and wiped his pale forehead. Absolute silence filled the sanctuary. Even the countless common folk who understood only the smallest part of it felt that decisive words had been spoken.

The startled looks of the priests met each other. No one had a word of rebuttal, no one wanted to expose himself, not even Mimard or Blancherose, their spokesmen.

Then, a Franciscan friar stood up. It was Jean Tandy, well known, a good preacher who zealously spoke against the Reformers from the pulpits of the city and its neighborhood. The speech of the otherwise so eloquent orator was almost tongue-tied today as, pale from emotion, he began to say:

"It seems to me that the sin against the Spirit which the Scriptures speak of is the stubbornness which rebels against manifest truth. In accordance with that which I have heard, I confess to be guilty, because of ignorance I have lived in error and I have spread the wrong teaching. I ask God's pardon for everything I have said and done against His honor; and ask the pardon of all of you people for the offense which I gave with my preaching up until now. I defrock myself henceforth to follow Christ and His pure doctrine alone . . ."

The people were deeply moved. Everywhere there was whispering, even among the preachers. It was obvious that the Franciscan friar was not the only one whose mind had been changed during this hour.

Farel, however, rose triumphantly, crying, "The Lord's name is wonderful, counsellor, mighty God. He makes wounds and heals them, he permits man to fall into the depths of hell and helps him out of it again. Behold and rejoice: The sheep erring among wolves and beasts in the wilderness—He has led it to His pasture!"

The morning after the end of the debate all houses of prostitution were closed in Lausanne, all whores expelled. The religious debate began to bear fruit.

Day after day, clergy of Vaud land declared themselves for the Reformation, within a few months eighty regular and one hundred and twenty secular priests. Among them were some of the most confirmed defenders of the teaching of Rome—even

Mimard who wanted to introduce the Church Fathers into the debate . . .

SOON THE LECTOR of Holy Scriptures received a pastoral office. He became the assistant, the right hand of Farel. In reality, however, it was Calvin who led the fiery spirit. It was not enough to condemn papal abuses and to issue disconnected decrees. Farel had felt that for a long time already. He was only too glad to leave the guidance to the author of the *Institutes*. And Calvin undertook the work to give form to spiritual chaos, and shape to the new church.

Calvin drew up a confession of faith containing twenty-one clauses. It is brief, clearly outlined, and, like the excellent catechism of the Reformed Church, the Heidelberg, based upon it, is worthy of being placed in the hands of all young Christians for instruction. The very first sentence stands out like chiseled stone:

"We confess our faith based alone on Holy Scriptures, without any additions from human wisdom; to desire as the only doctrine for our spiritual welfare the Word of God, without diminution or addition, according to the command of our Lord."

This confession of faith, supplemented by additional theses concerning the Lord's Supper, the church ban, the singing of Psalms, the instruction of youth, and marriage, was submitted to the Council of the Two Hundred—the legislative body—and accepted by it. According to these theses the Little Council[57] had the right to punish any trespass against the law of God; the ministers were to assist the Council therein. The people, through its representation, divests itself of all rights in the matters of faith and places them into the hands of the government and of the clergy.

Thereby the foundation stone for the theocratic state was laid, a state which Calvin strove to attain, in view of the particular conditions at Geneva. It was a theocratic state whose constitution was based on the Reformed faith and which felt itself responsible before God for the behavior of its citizens.[58]

Our century, which is predominantly individualistic, has a

sympathetic smile for such a concept of the state. What is left of that precious gift, freedom of conscience?

Admittedly, to the age of the Reformation the word "tolerance" was unknown. Who does not keep this in mind lacks understanding of the history of this epoch, be he historian or even biographer of Calvin. He who sees the events of the past through the spectacles of his own age and views them in its "knowledge," sees them distorted. Calvin was a child of his century. If he wanted to build up what was torn down, he could not have proceeded any differently. Faith was to him the highest wisdom, it was the content of life. He did not go halfway, but drew all consequences from this assumption, for the Church and for the state, as well as for every citizen. And his theocratic state, even though one may be critical or hostile towards it, was something magnificent, impressive, and moving.

Only recent research has designated Calvin as the definite author of the confession of faith of 1536. It was Farel who put it into the minds of the Council. Calvin, who against his will entered the service of the Genevan Church, still stood in the shadow of Farel, who showed an affectionate respect for his colleague twenty years younger. Constantly he wanted to bring him to the fore, to give him the honor, but his efforts failed every time because of the other's reluctance and humility. Calvin would much rather remain "ille Gallus" and sit at his desk than to appear before the public.

His next work was a catechism. He prefaced it with verses from the First Epistle of Peter, "Long for the spiritual milk as new born babes, being ready always to give answer to every man that asketh you a reason concerning the hope that is in you." [59]

The booklet is a condensation of the principal parts of the *Institutes*. It not only was to anchor the Reformation spirit in this city for which it was primarily written, but carry it out into the world and form a bond of the reborn churches. Thus it stands written in the Preface, and for that reason the first edition of the Catechism was published in Latin.

One realizes what could already be noticed in the *Institutes*: the twenty-seven-year-old Calvin had more in mind than an

Evangelical local congregation. He worked for the holy catholic Church.

The following words can be read in this Catechism: "We believe that all the elect are united in one Church, one communion, one people of God, whose prince and leader is our Lord, Christ . . ."[60] This communion is catholic, that is, ecumenical, for there are not two or three. All the elect of God are to be united and bound to Christ as their head, that as members of one body they grow with Him and have the same faith, the same hope, the same love, and therefore also the same spirit of God, and have been called to the same inheritance of eternal life."

This is the compelling essence of a holy conviction. Whoever wants to understand Calvin, let him grasp this thought not only in its Biblically grounded inner greatness, but also in its effects as soon as the personal conviction becomes the basis of the state.

Now THAT CALVIN and Farel had the sanction of the law, they proceeded against vice, transgressors, and the unworthy. All sores on the body of the theocratic state must be removed so that it may be sanctified. Courault, who was now totally blind, had joined them. With his gripping enthusiasm for the pure doctrine and the daring punch of his preaching he supplemented what he perhaps lacked in spiritual penetration. All of them, the seeing and the blind, superintended the moral mandates and the congregation's respect for God. It would seem that he who lacked eyesight had a special sense in detecting sins and censuring them.

The Little Council seemed to be filled with a new spirit which went hand in hand with the spirituality of the devout, convinced Reformed mayor, Ami Porral. It punished without respect of persons what morality reprimanded. One of the first to feel the strict consequences of the Church law was a councilman, Ami Curtet. Right after him Matthieu Manlich, who was held in high esteem, was chastened. The instigator of an indecent jocular masquerade had to do public penance, kneeling in the Cathedral; another who owned a gaming house was put in the pillory for an hour, adorned with a necklace of cards. A perjurer whose lying right hand was tied above him, was put on display on a ladder; an adulterous couple was led in disgrace through the alleys of the city, and parents who refused to send their children to school were fined. Even Bonivard, the darling of the town, who had been freed from Savoyan captivity in Chillon, could not get away with his debauchery. He, like the first transgressor, received a reprimand from the Council.

Strangely, the people themselves seemed to approve this strict regimentation. It gave them satisfaction to see that it called a halt not even before the most noble. This type of justice appeals to the common man. Gloating, he rubs his hands when one who heretofore has been safe because of his position falls victim to a defamatory penalty.

A contagious power seemed to proceed from the labors of the preachers. From everywhere they received assistance. During the worship services the churches were overcrowded. And there were many worship services, five every Sunday, two on each weekday and never at the same time, so that eager churchgoers might attend the services in sequence. Saunier, a religious refugee, opened an Evangelical school which became famous almost overnight and received pupils even from England.

Everywhere in the old city springlike spiritual life began to sprout. Secret opponents who might still be present were hiding before the powerful attack of the Gospel. They waited in their lurking places for an opportune time to strike again.

And the opportunity was not far off. The preachers were not satisfied that the Council had accepted the Confession. The citizens themselves should swear to the Confession as well. This will give forceful expression to the conception of the congregation as it is contained in the above-mentioned outline of the Catechism. The solemn oath was being taken, but many were missing, all too many. The Council threatened, decreed banishment. Now the fists clenched in pockets appeared in the open. The residents of the Rue des Allemands, so called after the German-Swiss, united in order to refuse the oath. All of them were commanded to leave.

The enemies of the Reformation rejoiced, for when a government sets up such rules as these which are impossible to be carried out, it weakens its authority.

And now the opposition dared step into the light: Libertines; those whom traveling preachers had won to Anabaptism; those who in their hearts were still followers of Rome; old Genevans to whom the regimentation of foreign clergymen did not appeal; and all those people who are always present to oppose any existing government. In a town meeting strong words were expressed concerning foreign domination and this unbearable yoke. Anyone who had something on his heart spoke up freely. Ami Porral was accused of bringing the city under the ferule of Farel. The preachers were reprimanded for their concern with other than spiritual matters.

The citizens' meeting was encouraging to those Councilmen who themselves were against this strict order. Already the Council was afraid to carry out blindly all suggestions that came from the preachers.

The fine unity which marked the history of Geneva up until late in the fall of 1537, was seriously endangered.

THE PLEASURE of the citizenry was as changeable as April weather. Beating the bushes against the Reformers was instigated. He who agitated against them found followers. "Do you also belong to the brothers in Christ, eh?" were the words of mockery in craftguilds and inns. "The deuce, you will soon regret it!" Loathsome songs were sung under the windows of the preachers, and the Lord's Supper itself was mocked and mimicked.

And in February of 1538, the majority of newly elected Council members belonged to the dissatisfied. The four new mayors were definitely opposed to Farel and Calvin.

And once again, to the astonishment of the voters, that which has repeated itself in history so many times occurred once more. As soon as the heads of the minority party became the rulers, they began to compromise. The new mayors suddenly felt the responsibility that rested upon them and they realized that the city was near a state of anarchy. And when the preachers pointed to the increasing brutalization, the bailiff's horn was soon heard sounding through the streets. A mandate of the Council was proclaimed:

"Since it has been reported that disgraceful disorder and nightly disturbance of the peace are rapidly taking over . . . we order that no mocking songs are to be sung in which mention is made of the names of citizens who live in Geneva; furthermore no one shall be found on the streets after nine o'clock without a light, and let everyone beware of uproar and noisy arguments. All these things are punishable with imprisonment in the tower, the ration of food being bread and water for three days in the first and six days in the second and nine days in the third case."

The Libertines were surprised to hear such a mandate. What, those who owed their political offices to them were now trying to tell them what to sing during their drinking parties!

The opposition increased since messengers of the King of France made a proposal to annex the city to the empire, and since Berne, hearing of this action, began to intervene. The officials of Berne saw a dangerous symptom in the peculiarities of the church of Geneva which deviated in certain points from the practice of the German-Swiss. They demanded the retention of the four holidays which Farel had done away with—he had retained Sunday only—and the use of unleavened bread, or wafers, at the Lord's Supper. The Council agreed to that, in order to please Berne. The Reformers refused even when a synod in the Bernese Lausanne decided to do it that way. No worldly power shall decide over ecclesiastical matters, but a general confederate synod, which was to meet in Zurich that summer.

Immediately the opposition aligned itself with the cause of Berne. The Libertines expressed a passionate desire for unleavened bread at the Lord's Supper. Whatever they could do to vex the hated Reformers was done. Pamphlets filled with ridicule of the preachers were printed; indecent songs were sung again and the Reformers were threatened with force. An infidel, mocking the Lord's Supper, went up and down the main street. Instead of "La parole de Dieu," they cried, "La parole d'André."

André was probably a well-known fool. And there were still meaner, more despicable things which I will not mention.

The Council did little, if anything, any more to check the increasing disorder. The officials understood the hints of their voters.

The servants of the Word continued unflinchingly to preach against the mockers, against the ever-increasing unbelief, and finally against the Council members themselves. Courault, the old blind man, who expressed his anger too freely, was put behind lock and key.

SINCE EASTER was approaching, the Lord's Supper was to be observed for the first time in the Bernese custom. Thus had the Council decreed it. The Reformers refused especially to distribute the sacrament at that very time. The peace-meal of the Lord at this moment? Who among the participants in the Lord's Supper could answer the question, "And has no man aught against his brother?"

Nevertheless, on the evening before, the master sergeant came to Calvin and Farel to ask them to yield. In vain.

Then the Council arrived at a serious decision: to forbid the obstreperous the pulpit.

Soon the rumor raced through the city: the preachers gave no heed to the prohibition!

A restless night descended. The tumult on the streets permitted Calvin no peace. Angry fists hammered against the door of his house; rocks beat on the shutters; he heard curses and the cry, "Into the Rhone with the traitor!" Musket shots frightened him incessantly: he counted more than sixty.

And behold! at the appointed morning hour he mounted the pulpit of St. Peter's Church. To him who was the enemy of all kinds of excitement, meek in nature, who had spent a sleepless night, the short walk was bitter as death. Yet cost what it would, he obeyed God more than man. At Easter the city must not remain without the Gospel.

His sermon, as always, was clear, plain, convincing. Freely he touched on the controversial points: "Before all of you we testify that it is not a question of leavened or unleavened bread which prevents us from celebrating with you the Lord's Supper. Think of the strife, the revolt against the Gospel, the blasphemy which prevails among you. Think of the manifold defiance against the Word of God and the Lord's Supper . . ."[61]

Many of the listeners came armed, but no disturbance took place. The language of the preacher was too moderate, his reasons too sound, to give rise to an uproar. Unmolested he returned to his dwelling.

It was otherwise in the Church of Saint-Gervais where Farel, as was to be expected, gave free rein to his gloom. It was necessary for his friends to intervene in order to protect him from the molestations of his enemies who threateningly crowded around the pulpit.

For the afternoon sermon which Calvin delivered in the Franciscan Church, his enemies had assembled. They listened quietly to the beginning of his exposition, but it was the quiet before the storm. The first word which touched upon existing conditions would release the tumult. And truly the worship service from one moment to the next changed into an ugly fist fight, arms resounded, drawn swords flashed in the broken light of stained-glass windows. As in the morning for Farel, the faithful ones grouped themselves around the preacher to protect him with their bodies from the mob. A contemporary reported as a miracle, "une espèce miracle," that in the heated battle no blood was shed.[62]

Still on the same day the Little Council assembled and on Easter Monday the Council of the Two Hundred. The accusers were careful to avoid the preacher's words which were directed against the government and existing conditions. A discussion of these words might have taken an embarrassing direction. They confined themselves to criticizing the disobedience of the Reformers: they had preached despite the prohibition. After hours of deliberation (among other things the imprisonment of the obstinate was suggested) the resolution was drawn up: Farel, Calvin, and Courault were to be exiled. They were to leave the city within three times twenty-four hours.

Calvin received the sergeant of the Council with moving magnanimity.[63] "If we had served men, we would have been poorly rewarded; but the Lord whom we serve thinks of His servants beyond measure!"[64] Even Farel from whom one would have expected an outburst of vivacious spirit quietly accepted the message, saying, *"A la bonne heur!* It comes from God, therefore it is good."

ON APRIL 25 Courault tottered out of jail and on the same day the three Reformers, leading the old blind man in their midst, left the city to which belonged their life and work.

In one of Calvin's letters to the ministers of Zurich[65] one reads concerning that time: "Since I with my faithful colleague, Farel, assumed the direction of this church, I have faithfully endeavored to find all the means to preserve it; although the burden which I assumed rested heavily upon me, I have never thought about how to get rid of it. I saw myself placed in this position by God and I did not dare move from it. Were I to tell you only the littlest things of the misfortune—what am I saying?—of the adversity which virtually crushed us during the course of one year, you would hardly believe me. I am convinced that not a day passed in which I did not long for death ten times . . ."

Is it a wonder that the man who saw himself suddenly relieved from the activity which he had carried on with inward opposition and solely out of obedience to God, breathes deeply relieved?

"When I was chased away, I was not magnanimous enough not to enjoy my new-won freedom—to enjoy it more than I could answer for. Freed from my calling, I was now permitted to live in peace without a public office," he wrote later.[66]

Nevertheless the exiles did not feel that they had been relieved of their responsibility. After Courault had been lodged with the minister of Thonon, Calvin and Farel went to Berne and Zurich in order to report to their fellow believers. Bullinger and the delegates of a synod which was just meeting at Zurich urgently advised their return. They sent a conciliatory message to Geneva and encouraged Berne to throw its weight in the scales on behalf of the exiles. However, in the city by the Aare bitter humiliation awaited them on their way back from Zurich. A malicious message had arrived from those in power in Geneva. And it was believed. The bear showed his claws. The Bernese treated the two Romanic gentlemen roughly in Bernese-German-French. Finally, however, the resolution was made to send with them a delegation to Geneva to effect their reinstatement. It was in vain. In the city by the Rhone they were politely given to understand that, fundamentally, all this was being done for the sake of the Bernese. Moreover, "alea jacta est," the die is cast. The exiles were curtly refused entrance into the city. The Council of the Two Hundred was summoned for a special session in order to consider the request. The few who had the courage to raise their hands in favor of the preachers were rebuked outright and swords were drawn against them: Kill them! Flight was their only hope. No one wanted anything to do with the Reformers.

Geneva seemed lost to the pure doctrine, a plaything of the Libertines, perhaps a ripening fruit for Rome, one which might fall into the hands of the archenemy waiting across the border.

THE SCHOLARLY PRINTER Oporin of Basel gave shelter to the friends.[67] They were in need of care. The struggles and trials of an especially arduous journey pressed hard upon them and weariness almost overcame them.[68] One of them barely escaped the waters of the swollen Aare.[69]

Calvin was definite in his decision not to enter any more commitments which would bring him into contact with church affairs. During a visit in Strasbourg he wrote, "Above all I fear to return to the yoke from which I have been freed . . . At that time God's call held me bound . . . Now I fear I would tempt God were I to assume again such a burden which, as I have discovered, is unbearable for me."[70]

However, he was without means. What he had left was money given to him by his former friend and fellow traveler, du Tillet, who left Geneva without saying good-bye and returned to the

Roman Catholic fold. It was hard to have to live on funds supplied by a deserter who warned him that his expulsion from Geneva was God's sign of disapproval of his work.[71] Myconius, Oekolampad's successor as head of the church in Basel, the noble Grynäus and other friends helped all they could, but they did not have much to spare. Calvin sold books and worked hard on a greatly enlarged revision of the *Institutes* which promised him some honorarium.

Farel had been called back to his old congregation in Neuchâtel. He would have liked to have Calvin close by, but if that did not work out, then in Bonneville. The latter was also wanted in Lausanne. Even in Basel there was talk of creating a French pastorate for him.[72] He declined all these offers, even refused the honored call of Bucer to come to Strasbourg.

Nevertheless, the people of Strasbourg did not give up. To have the author of the *Institutes,* that great theologian, within their walls would bring to the city fame and respect even though it possessed no university. They urged him with repeated insistence. As once before, they cited the prophet Jonah as a warning example. The pressing poverty in which he lived reinforced the entreaties of the people of Alsace. The need overcame the inner disinclination.

For ten weeks he resisted the overtures. Then early in September of 1538, a staff in his right hand, he strode through the gate of St. John toward Strasbourg.

IV.

Pastor, Teacher, Writer

(1538-1541)

THE FAITHFUL BEZA reports in the biography of his master: "At Strasbourg he was received like a jewel by such excellent men as Bucer, Capito, Hedio and others who themselves like precious stones adorned the Church of God at the time. Empowered by the Councilmen and the regents of Strasbourg, he established a French congregation in which he introduced the church discipline which could never be accomplished by the Germans in their churches. He also gave theological lectures which were admired by all."

Truly his fears of coming under a new yoke in Strasbourg were unfounded. Yet he was never lacking in work. He preached four times a week, taught Holy Scriptures, conducted debates. But he met no opposition in the church whose head he was. How consoling were the solemn celebrations of the Lord's Supper with brothers who for the sake of their faith had left their country and with one mind approached the table of the Lord, devoutly, humbly! With horror Calvin recalled the hordes of guzzlers, gamblers, and mockers who flocked to the sacrament in Geneva. Now they came from far away to hear the famous teacher. Many of the Anabaptists and Romanists, sure of victory as they arrived to debate with him, were won over and became members of the Reformed Church, faithful until death. Already Strasbourg was called the New Jerusalem, the new-risen Antioch in the book of the Acts.

The Strasbourg theologians were devoted to him with loving

reverence. In the wretched dispute over the Lord's Supper they stood between the Wittenbergers and the Swiss. They would have liked to mediate as they had nine years before in the unfortunate Marburg dispute. One of them, Martin Zell, exclaimed with grief, "Am I really to believe that in the holy Lord's Supper I am receiving the body and blood of the Lord 'substantialiter, essentialiter, realiter, naturaliter, praesensialiter, localiter, corporaliter, quantitative, qualitative, ubiqualiter, carnaliter'? It is the Devil who sent us all these words out of the deepest abyss of Hell! Christ simply said, 'This is my body.' If all these strange descriptions had been necessary, He would have no doubt employed them."

Calvin also condemned the sophistry which misled the layman. While Bucer and Capito were framing comparisons and ambiguous phraseology in order to bring about an agreement, "the Genevan eagle took a higher course: he exhorted Christians to be of one mind in that they look to the one and same sun and hold to the one and same truth."[73]

In a "Brief Treatise on the Holy Lord's Supper"[74] he spiritualized, intensified, and deepened Zwingli's doctrine:

"The meaning of the institutional words 'this is my body, this is my blood' becomes clear as soon as we are convinced that the entire blessing of this holy supper is dissolved into nothingness unless Jesus Christ is offered in it as essence and foundation. If this is true, the holy supper would nevertheless become a void and superfluous act, were we to deny that in it we are offered real communion with Christ . . .

"Bread and wine are visible symbols of Christ's body and blood through which He reveals Himself to us. Our communion with the body of Jesus Christ, in itself hidden from our senses, incomprehensible to our mind, is thereby perceptibly placed before our eyes." At the end of his treatise, the reading of which would be of value to every Christian to this day, he touched briefly upon the sad controversy over the Lord's Supper: "Without a doubt Satan unleashed it in order to hinder the course of the Gospel and, if possible, to foil it; I would that the controversy could be consigned to oblivion . . ."

He took issue with Luther on the one hand, with Zwingli and Oekolampad on the other, and arrived at this conclusion: "The mistake common to both parties lay in this, that they did not show the patience to listen to each other in order to follow the truth without passion, regardless of which side it might lie upon . . ."

With grief he noted that as yet no statement of faith had been found which represented a common agreement among the Evangelicals. He hoped that it might soon be given to them so that all might say:

"We confess with one accord that when, according to the institution of the Lord, we receive the sacrament in faith, we become partakers in reality of the true body and blood of Christ.

"How this happens some are able to explain better and clearer than others. Above all, however, it is to be emphasized, in order to exclude all material conceptions, that one must lift his heart on high, to heaven. One cannot bring the Lord Jesus down so that He becomes confined in transitory elements."

The treatise concerning the Holy Supper is the most moderate among his polemic writings. Every sentence reflects the will not to pour oil on the fire but to serve concord on this question which is, for the Christian, the most holy.

A contemporary describes vividly how, surrounded by students, Luther returned from a lecture and entered the bookstore of the Wittenberger Moritz Goltsch. The latter had just come back from the Frankfort Fair: "Moritz, what is new in Frankfort—are they ready to burn the arch-heretic Luther?"

The book dealer answered, "I did not hear anything about that, honorable Sir. However, I brought with me a little booklet which John Calvin first wrote in French. Now it has again been published in Latin. They are talking about Calvin; though a young man, he is reported to be pious and scholarly. In this booklet Calvin is supposed to show wherein your honor, but also Zwingli and Oekolampad, went too far in the controversy."

"Please give me the booklet," said Luther. He sat down with the tract and with particular zeal began to read in it. As he returned the tract he spoke in deep contemplation, "Moritz, he is certainly a scholarly and pious man. I might well have relegated the whole matter of this controversy to him from the very beginning. I confess for my part if the opposition had done likewise, we might soon have reached an agreement. Aye, if Zwingli and Oekolampad had so declared themselves from the start, we would never have been involved in so lengthy a controversy."[75]

One would like to write these words into the scrapbook of many an opponent of Calvin from the Lutheran camp. It is important to remember Calvin's heartfelt exposition of the Lord's Supper which bridges the extremes between Zurich and Wittenberg in the knowledge of which even the giant, so stubborn at Marburg, had to bow.

THE TREATISE on the Lord's Supper was not Calvin's first work in Strasbourg. He had already published the new edition of the *Institutes,* begun at Basel. It was now three times the size of the first edition. With marvelous admiration, Luther read it long before the reported discourse with the book dealer in Wittenberg. Writing to Bucer he did not fail to add: "Give my respectful regards to Calvin, whose book I read with especial pleasure."[76] And Melanchthon's letter to the Strasbourger reports, "Calvin stands in high favor with Luther."[77]

An exposition of the Epistle to the Romans was the next fruit of Calvin's untiring labors. With deep emotions he approached his task which, as one feels on every page, he undertook to carry out with all his strength and with the unbounded love he had for the Scriptures: "To praise the blessing of Romans for Christian knowledge would be a vain undertaking. Our words do not reach the height of this Epistle. It must speak for itself. Who enters into it receives the key to all the hidden treasures of Holy Scriptures . . ."

So begins the introduction.

SERMONS, PASTORAL COUNSELING, and a rich literary activity constituted Calvin's ever-increasing work. However, to provide a meager income for the ceaseless laborer did not come to anybody's mind at first. He himself, bashful and modest, did not find the courage to ask for it. Indeed, he was always a welcome guest with Bucer and others, but it went against the grain to fall to the burden of his fellow brethren who themselves had not been blessed with earthly goods. Having spent the rest of his cash possessions, he was forced to sell household utensils and his library in Geneva. "My poverty is so great that at present I do not even have a Sol. Therefore it is not easy for me to guard my health as you recommend to me in your concern," he wrote to Farel during that time.[78] Only after eight months did the famous author of the *Institutes* receive a salary for his lectures. It was wholly insufficient, a Gulden a week![79]

Calvin was forced to accept boarders into the household run by his brother and sister. Obviously they were often even poorer than Calvin himself. He picked them out, future servants of the Word whom he wanted to train. Among them was Sebastian Castellio, who one day would be the leader of all attacks against him and who would bring much sorrow upon him.

About this time death notices arrived which grieved his tender heart deeply. Courault, his blind fellow laborer in Geneva, and his cousin Olivetan, the translator of the Bible, had suddenly passed away. Both, it was said, were poisoned. Calvin's sorrow was so great that he had to apologize because his letters had become shorter and less clear. He knew friendship in its most noble meaning, sacrificed to it his last strength—as his correspondence shows. The loss of a friend each time cut a wound that was slow to heal.

CALVIN'S LIFE was not confined to labors in Strasbourg. As early as 1539 he participated with Bucer in the Frankfort Diet for which a great religious discussion was planned. He wanted to call the situation of fellow believers in France to the attention of the German princes and become acquainted with Melanchthon. And behold, the two men were drawn to each other. A lifelong bond of friendship grew which was clouded only by the occasional lack of firmness in the German. Melanchthon exclaimed once, "Oh, that I might die at his heart!"[80] With a good deal of dislike, Calvin attended the religious discussion itself which was first held in Hagenau, then in Worms, and finally continued at the Diet in Regensburg. In Regensburg, where the presence of the Emperor at the meeting added luster and significance, he represented the city of Strasbourg, which upon the expressed wish of Melanchthon had elected Calvin as its delegate.[81]

Unfortunately, Calvin never met Luther personally. A meeting of the two great spirits of the Reformation might perhaps have yielded unforeseen fruits for a united Protestantism, particularly with the presence of Melanchthon who was a friend of both. Calvin himself had no greater wish than for a united advance of all Evangelical churches. And his admiration for Luther was boundless: "Remember what a great man Luther is. How marvelous are his gifts, how bravely, how firmly, how ably, how scholarly, how effectively he has constantly labored in the destruction of the Anti-Christ and in the spread of the doctrine of salvation. I hold to what I have repeatedly said, 'Even if he would call me a devil, I would yet honor him and call him an excellent servant of God.'" In this fashion he defended the Wittenberger against Zwingli's successor Bullinger.[82]

ONCE WHILE SITTING at table with Calvin and other friends after a strenuous day and noticing the former's silence and absent-mindedness, Melanchthon jokingly lifted a finger and cried, "Well, well, it seems to me our theologue is thinking about a future spouse!"[83]

Indeed, the twenty-nine-year-old longed for a life partner. A quarrelsome shrew who disturbed the peace among the brothers and the sister, friends who had picked out just the right girl for the sickly man steeped in work—all these things add up. Still at one time he expressed himself in this way: "I shall not belong to those who are accused of attacking Rome, like the Greeks fought Troy, only to be able to take a wife . . .!"

Of course, no one was going to force a wife on him. He warded off the excessive good intentions of his friends, he refused the hand of a rich noble lady who was suggested to him, although he might indeed have been able to use her dowry. Likewise he refused another young lady whose characteristics did not seem to justify the praise given her.

"The grace which might capture me for a woman is discipline, gentleness, modesty, good housekeeping, patience . . ." [84] This was written to Farel because he, too, was recommending a charming girl as a wife for his friend.

Was the picture of Idelette de Buren, the friendly widow of Jean Stordeur, the Belgian, perhaps already before the eyes of the writer as he enumerated these qualities? The Stordeurs came to Strasbourg as Anabaptists; against their will they were converted by Calvin's exposition of Scripture. The latter, in the course of instruction which he offered the couple upon their wish, still saw the thoughtful eyes of the woman upon him. He discovered nothing in these eyes but the fervent desire for truth.

Shortly after the couple became new members of the French Reformed congregation, and together partook of the Lord's Supper, Jean Stordeur died of the plague. And Calvin, pronouncing the benediction over the casket of the Wallonian, noticed his widow, Idelette, clothed in black with two little children at her hands. In her expression, sorrow and anxiety concerning an uncertain future outweighed confident trust in the providence of God.

Perhaps the picture of the unassuming woman with those fine, spiritually deepened features was before his eyes when he wrote "chaste, indulgent, patient . . ."

In August, 1540, Calvin married Idelette de Buren. Farel himself came from Neuchâtel in order to solemnize the union of his younger friend. [85] Calvin who had never wasted a superfluous word upon his own circumstances of life—what did he tell us concerning his youth?—rarely expressed himself about his spouse. The few testimonies reveal a tender and sincere love. Unfortunately, their life together lasted only nine years. The delicate, fine woman, like himself, was sickly. Three children which she bore him died shortly after birth. But she shared his strong faith. In her death struggle one could hear her, already on the brink of eternity, exclaim, "O glorious resurrection! God of Abraham and of all Patriarchs . . . I trust!"[86]

Letters are preserved in which Calvin gave voice to his deep grief over the loss of his wife. Instead of citing them here, there follows an excerpt of a message of consolation by Viret, the Reformer of Lausanne, to Calvin, because the writing is characteristic of the recipient as well:

"As with one voice I hear from all the friends in Geneva what marvelous composure you show in your deep grief. These testimonies impress me so much that I would like to write you rather a letter of congratulation than one of condolence. I know, friend, your innate tenderness. They call you soft—your composure in this grief is certainly not that of a weak soul! With admiration and adoration I experience the power of God's Spirit who works in you and shows Himself in you as comforter. How well do I know how deeply this has wounded you, for nothing more difficult could have happened to you. How you must feel, you whom the grief of others moves so deeply . . . And yet I hear that with unbroken spirit, more fervently than ever, you are busy, teaching, in the assembly of ministers, and in the pulpit . . ."[87]

WITH A SMIRK on his face, Pierre de la Baume, the bishop of Geneva, exiled by the Reformation, rubbed his hands when he heard the news of the expulsion of the preachers. Already he saw the moment approaching when, once again taking possession of his diocese, he would celebrate the first Mass in St. Peter's. Calvin's and Farel's presence would remain only an episode in the eventful history of the city by Lake Geneva . . .

Cardinal Sadolet, his colleague, the bishop of Carpentras, came to his aid. He was not the very best Cardinal. He was a friend and connoisseur of antiquity, a scholarly humanist, an excellent speaker. And yet with all this he was no blind follower of Roman doctrine. It was said of him that he valued Melanchthon's writings. He objected to the Reformation primarily because it seemed to impede the intellectual movement which posterity would call the Renaissance.

Cardinal Sadolet planned nothing less than to lead the heretic city at the mouth of the Rhone back to Rome through the power of his word. He addressed a message to the mayor, the councils, and the citizens of Geneva:

"Peace be to you, most faithful brothers in Jesus Christ, and with us, the Catholic Church, namely your and our mother; love and unity through God, the Father almighty, and his Son Jesus Christ, our Lord, and the Holy Spirit . . . Amen."

"Pax vobis et vobiscum"—a beautiful evangelical beginning! But not only these initial words were to be pleasing to the recipients of the letter. He told them the most flattering things: "I love the noble manner of your city, the order and form of your free state, the excellent characteristics of its citizens, and above all this rare humaneness towards strangers . . ."

In apt and well-chosen words he gave utterance to his grief that several crafty men, enemies of Christian unity, had carried the seed of discord into other cities and villages of this "pious and mighty confederation" as well as into Geneva.

His exposition was discreet and must have caused doubt in many a one in whom the Reformed faith was not yet firmly grounded. He praised the Word of God, he praised the work of the Redeemer, indeed he even succeeded in praising justification by faith, a doctrine which his Roman associates usually damned outright: "The eternal salvation is offered to us solely by faith in God and Jesus Christ. When I say 'solely by faith' I do not mean, of course, that works of mercy and the duties of a Christian are to be neglected . . ."

The exposition culminated in a passionate invitation to return to the fold of the Catholic Church, now five thousand years old, against whose eternal standard the cunning innovators of a few years represent a vain attack.

Rome knew why it sent a man into this battle who came from a small evangelically minded group. The Church tolerated them in its midst so long as it had hopes of winning the apostates back.

The City Council of Geneva gladly accepted the letter of the prince of the Church as well as the flattering words which were dedicated to the city. For the rest, they wanted to think it over and give answer at a later date. The messenger left and brought word to the Cardinal that, in his opinion, everything was in fine shape.

Rapidly the news of the message spread through Geneva. The disguised followers of Rome, still to be found numerous among the citizens, rejoiced. They had good reason, for had Bishop de la Baume sounded such notes five years before, the Reformers would hardly have been able to get a foothold.

Disquieted, the Evangelicals took counsel. None of the Geneva pastors felt sufficiently adequate to refute the scholarly mouthpiece of the Pope. However, if his message went unchallenged, then the whole Roman party would triumph. One, indeed, would have been able to give the Cardinal a rough welcome. But this one lived in faraway Strasbourg.

And only two days after the Council in solemn meeting had received the invitation of the Cardinal to sacrifice the Reformation, a delegation of citizens demanded to be freed from the oath to the Confession which had been taken at St. Peter's on July 29, 1537.

Danger! Danger for the pure Word!

Soon, however, to those who kept their eyes open it became evident how they were to understand the "Christian kindness which is moved by a neighborly love of double mercy," which the Cardinal exalted in his message. Not quite a month had passed since its arrival when news reached the city that Curtet, one of its respected citizens, had been burned alive because he had interpreted God's Word to a few country people on his estate in Annecy in Savoy. A week later a second Genevan, Jean Lambert, was burned at the stake without trial because of his Evangelical convictions. Everybody knew him. Was it possible that the joyful youth prior to the gruesome execution preferred to have his tongue pierced than to deny his faith with a Hail Mary?

With heads held high, the supporters of Rome walked the streets of Geneva. Between them and the expelled Bishop de la Baume—the Pope consoled him with a Cardinal's hat—rode mounted couriers. The Evangelicals looked with worry into the future.

Then, suddenly, there came an open letter from Calvin to Sadolet. It was a firm, passionate answer to the latter's message. Everyone clamored for a copy. In no time the supply of the book dealer was gone. If the arguments of the Bishop of Carpentras seemed good, those of his opponent were of a superiority which reduced them to naught:

"Not long ago you wrote the Council and the people of Geneva; soft words in order not to embitter those whom you needed to accomplish your goals. You attacked violently only those who, as you say, have caused disturbance in this poor city with their craftiness. Be it known to you, Sadolet, I am one of those whom you slander and, although at present I am not pastor of the Church in Geneva, I hold to her with fatherly love.

". . . You who took your apprenticeship at the Roman Court, in this workshop of astuteness and craftiness, you who, so to speak, were nursed in the arms of Pope Clement, who were made Cardinal with a fresh horse, you have intentions that make you suspicious. It is the pastor's duty to lead souls straight to Christ. Your most important design is to bring them into the power of the Pope.

"In order to sow discord among us you accuse us, against better knowledge, of ambition and love of money. Well, were I looking out for myself I would probably never have cut myself loose from your party, not to speak of Farel who, coming from a well-to-do noble lineage, would never have been in need of assistance. Would not the shortest route to wealth and honor have been to accept from the beginning the conditions which you offered us? What sum would the Pope have paid in order to buy the silence of some of us, and what would he pay today? Did we not demand that the wealth which with you is swallowed up in chasms be divided among the poor as in the early Church? Our only goal is to increase the Kingdom of God by our smallness and humility. To assert the contrary is highly unbecoming to the respected gentleman of science, the prudent, wisely calculating Sadolet.

"Where is there with you the Word of God, the true mark of the Church? . . . If a man belongs to the forces of God, then he must be equipped for battle. The enemy is at hand; he attacks, he fights, he is so powerful that no earthly power can resist him. What weapons, therefore, does the poor Christian possess in order not to be overcome? What else than the Word of God? The soul deprived of it is helpless against the Devil. Therefore the first concern of the enemy is to wrench the sword of Jesus Christ from the warrior. The Pope prides himself on possessing the Holy Ghost; it is written, however, that to blaspheme the Holy Ghost is to sever him from the Word of God.

". . . You touch upon justification by faith. Yet in this phrase, the most important in our confession, has it not been extinguished from the memory of mankind by you? You assert that we disparage good works. If only you took the trouble of going through my catechism, the very first word would disprove your claim. We verily deny that works serve for righteousness, for Scripture gives us no other hope than the grace of God. Still if we allow no works for righteousness, we give them a place in the life of the children of God. Christ wants a people which performs good works."

There followed comparisons between the ruinous Church of Rome and the beginnings of the Christian Church, and the Reformed doctrine which strove to follow the latter. There were clear words about the Lord's Supper, confession, the veneration of saints. Sentence after sentence refuted the opponent, until the author assumed the summons of the other before the judgment throne of God and freely reported concerning his own conversion, concluding with these words:

"We demand a peace in which the Kingdom of the Redeemer reigns—you believe that everything which has been won for Christ is a loss for you. May the Lord grant, Sadolet, that you and your people will finally come to realize that there is no other bond of our Church than Christ the Lord who offers us His communion so that His words and His spirit unite our hearts and thoughts."

The eyes of the Evangelicals in Geneva were filled with triumph. Calvin had spoken the last word. The prince of the Church would not be able to make answer.

And they were right. He remained quiet. Perhaps because the arguments of his superior opponent had inwardly disarmed him. At any rate, he was not anxious to cross words with him again.

Adherents of the Reformed faith elsewhere rejoiced with their brethren in Geneva. Above all, Luther, who saw in the opponent of the Cardinal the continuer and finisher of that which he himself had undertaken against the Anti-Christ. The Wittenberger smiled grimly, "Would that Sadolet might recognize in God the Creator of mankind—outside of Italy as well . . ."[88]

THE EXILE of Calvin and Farel did not bring the hoped-for calm in Geneva. The city chronicles during those three and a half years that followed report stormy events. The opponents of the Reformers put in their place four straw men, weak preachers, who blindly followed the dictates of the ruling party and thereby lost all respect. However, the wheel of time seemed suddenly to turn more quickly. Those in power made mistakes in their foreign relations. They granted the much feared Berne special privileges which might mean loss of Geneva's independence. The friends of the Reformers—they are called the Guillermins after Farel's first name—urged caution. During elections they unexpectedly won mandate after mandate. The losers were banned from the city as traitors for a hundred and one years. Those accused most severely were beheaded . . .

Yesterday still laughed at and persecuted, today the Guillermins were in control of the city. The four puppet preachers were snubbed. Two of them departed from Geneva without taking leave.

And now the wish which had been lying dormant in the hearts of many began to take form. Calvin, so rudely expelled, was to be recalled to direct with a strong hand the destiny of the Genevan Church.

At once cordial invitations were sent to him at Strasbourg or in Germany where he might have been attending religious discussions, to return to his former place of labor. The Council itself decided to commission Sir Ami Perrin to find ways and means to make Master Calvin's return possible.

The letters showed overwhelming joy concerning the change in attitude. "Triumph, come quickly, brother, come, come, that we may rejoice in God our Redeemer . . ."[89] Viret, who had been called to Geneva until Calvin's expected arrival in the city, entreated his friend, "Don't linger, come to build up and to gladden the church which lies in misery, grief, and sorrow."[90] Even one of the two pastors who co-operated with the former Council and then left Geneva, urged, "Do not say 'No.' You would resist the Holy Spirit, not men. Remember the fruits waiting to be harvested in France. The Genevan Church is important . . . no mortal man is able to direct it with such force, so wisely and so ably as you."[91]

But the one so entreated was deeply frightened at the thought of having to return to the place of his humiliation. Better the gallows or into the ocean, but not back to this place of agony. He trembled for fright to think once more he would have to accept the yoke which, as long as he bore it, he dared not throw off because God Himself had placed it upon him.[92] Here in Strasbourg, where the citizenship conferred upon him offered him a sense of home, he could labor undisturbed, maintain fruitful contacts with scholars of all lands, primarily Germany. In Geneva there would be battles, nothing but battles.

The requests did not let up, rather they became more insistent. "Come, honored father in Christ, you belong to us, the Lord Himself has given you to us. Everybody sighs for you . . ."[93] These are the words of one of the pastors who remained. He wrote in his helplessness.

Several times the Council sent emissaries accompanied by heralds. In its letters, bearing on its seal the words, "Post tenebras spero lucem," the burning desire which prompted their origin broke through every line of the official document. In translating it I have attempted to preserve this candid mixture:

"We, the mayor and the Council of the city of Geneva, to Doctor Calvin, our good brother and our distinguished friend.

Inasmuch as we know that your desire is none other than to further the growth of the honor of God and the extension of His Word, we wish sincerely to commend our request to you, and to beg you most decidedly in the name of our Small and Great Council, also our General Council (which earnestly instructed us to make this known to you), to betake yourself hither to your old office . . . inasmuch as our people want you the worst way. We shall deal with you in all things in such manner that you will have no cause to find trouble and grief." [94]

The clergy of Zurich were asked for their word of support and they urged with insistence. The Council of Strasbourg, too, received a pressing request from the Council of Geneva to release the preacher so necessary to them.

Everything seemed to be in vain. The answers to Zurich and to Farel and Viret bespoke real horror at the idea of having to return to the place of eternal discord. Calvin feared no place on earth more than this one. When he received a new respectful message from the Geneva Council presented in person by the emissary in Worms, he broke out in tears and could not suppress his sobbing. He was moved so much that twice he had to leave the room. [95]

FAREL AGAIN BROUGHT about the decision. His letter of February, 1541 [96] is lost. But it must have been of the same convincing force as the decisive entreaty in Geneva five years before. We deduce this from Calvin's answer: [97] "You have been of unspeakable distress to me with your thundering and lightning . . . Is it necessary that you make me so bad and almost renounce our friendship?"

But the old daredevil accomplished his purpose. His letter gave the oppressed no peace. It disturbed his conscience incessantly until his resistance was broken. Soon he answered, "I yield, I surrender!" [98]

Thus he assumed for the second time against his will, in obedience to God, the heavy burden against which his whole being struggled.

"If I had a free choice, I would prefer to do everything

else in the world than to do your will," he wrote later to the unyielding Farel. "But I know that I am not my own master. I offer my heart to the Lord in sacrifice. After I have overcome my soul and control it, it shall be subject to Him alone."[99]

"Cor mactatum in sacrificium offero." These words are his motto. He carried them on his seal next to a picture of a hand which grasps a heart.

This time he did not come to Geneva as an assistant to an older man. And obviously, he did not come solely as the pastor to serve a city church. He was prepared—this can be gleaned from letters of Bucer, from preachers in Strasbourg and Zurich[100] —as its head to lead the Reformation movement which was to begin its triumphal march from the city on Lake Geneva which was destined for this task because of its location.

The thirty-two-year-old, sickly and shy.

V.

The Years of Struggle

(1541-1555)

"FINALLY HE COMES TO YOU, this incomparable, this rare instrument of the Lord. Our century knows of no other like him—indeed, if beside him one can still speak of another . . ."[101] In this manner the people of Strasbourg announced to the Genevans the coming of the long-awaited one. They assured the departing Calvin they would consider him their fellow citizen for life. They even offered him the continued income of his theology professorship. But without reflection, Calvin rejected it. It smelled too much of a beneficiary-living business. It was enough that his departure was made more difficult by their devotion to him.

The trip was not without incident. In Neuchâtel, Farel's passionate hot-headedness once again got him into trouble. From the pulpit he had denounced a public scandal which the daughter of a high official had raised. Therefore he was supposed to leave the city. Calvin was able to settle the matter. In Berne, where at the time the relation with Geneva was tense, he got the cold shoulder.

More than the external events, the pressure of being forced to sacrifice the activity which was so much to his liking for one such as this at the scene of his most painful experience, weighed upon him. Every step was accompanied by a sigh.

"When I returned to the flock from which I had been torn, I did so with sadness, tears, forebodings, and anxiety of heart. God and a few good friends are witnesses of this. And they would like to have spared me this sorrow . . . For although I would have offered my life for the welfare of the Genevan Church, my shyness continued to whisper good reasons into my ear why I should not carry this burden again," he confessed later in the Preface to his commentaries on the Psalms.[102] The account of his Catholic biographer,[103] "Triumphantly he now traversed in part the same regions through which three years ago he had strayed as a stranger seeking help," is refuted by this and other testimonies. Not a triumph, but a bitter road of suffering.

THE COUNCIL and the people received the former outlaw with open arms. They were waiting for him as the savior in need. In readiness stood a roomy house on Canon Street, the top floor of which offered a view of the landscape around the lake. It was late in summer, the beginning of September, 1541.

The first reception before the Council proceeded in the most promising manner. Tensely two dozen pairs of eyes looked upon the new arrival of whom such great things were expected. Five years before he still had looked somewhat young as a Reformer. Now he was thirty-two. His stay in the Alsace, his association with scholars from everywhere, had made him even more mature, more secure in the world. Master over all his repressions, he stood before the members of the Council, medium in height, pale countenance slightly tanned, his animated eyes addressing one then another. Something fine, a winsome quality, radiated from his being. It was this particular, indescribable trait which constantly won him new friends. Really, a number of Councilmen were quite embarrassed. They were glad not to have to stand alone before this earnest-looking minister, for their bad consciences called for a severe penitential sermon. Farel at least would not have spared them. Others, who belonged to the present majority party, were actually hoping for such a thing. They enjoyed the humiliation of their colleagues. But nothing came of it. Modestly he said,

"I am here to serve Geneva. And to enable me to perform my service the Church must be established in accordance with the

Word of God." Heads nodded in agreement. The settlement of the Church regulations was the first condition of his return, laid down in Strasbourg. So the Council named six laymen from its body who were to work out a Church constitution with the preachers.

They felt relief, for this peculiarly excellent man seemed to have it within his power to create quiet and order in this city which had been severely torn by civil strife. Because of his importance and the efforts he expended in providing lodging for strangers passing through the city, he received a higher remuneration than his colleagues. He was honored in the joy of welcome with a trimmed cloth suit costing eight Sonnentaler, and the Council decided to transport his family and his goods from Strasbourg with public funds. This is sufficient for Kampschulte to conclude, "With almost creeping submission we saw the representatives of the people pay homage to their leader. A government which subjected itself so deeply before him wrote the death sentence over its own authority . . ." From this he concludes Calvin's conception of how he obtained the right to rule over Geneva.[104] This matter of "creeping submission" is certainly wrong. That is not the Genevan. He was not like that then. After all, it will not do to explain the free Genevan spirit of Reform from the standpoint of monastic submission. Calvin had to wait another eighteen years before he was even offered citizenship. However, Kampschulte's description will influence the writing of history for decades, which is why I am detaining myself to take issue with him. A sentence like the one above cannot but lead astray and can cause great harm in the understanding of Calvin. Especially when its author—who incidentally after the publishing of his work entered the Old Catholic Church, not the Reformed—is praised even by Protestants as an exemplarily objective reporter and who is considered the crown witness.

When Calvin mounted the pulpit of St. Peter's, the people crowded the wide nave. Eagerly they waited for the first sermon and hoped it would cause a sensation. Anyone who came for this, however, was disappointed. But there was a surprise. The pastor who had come back opened the Scriptures and began by con-

tinuing exactly where he left off three years before. He wanted
to show that he had been forced to interrupt his preaching office
but that he never gave it up.[105]

That was the only revenge on the congregation which had
expelled and exiled him like a criminal. Not a word of the past,
nothing about his adversaries. That would be ignoble, an insult
to the losers. These feelings he expressed in letters. He showed a
loving attitude also toward the two ministers who stayed on. He
did not let them feel how low they had fallen because they had
permitted themselves to be used as instruments in the hands of a
God-estranged party. And yet it would have been easy for him to
remove them from their offices. In time his magnanimity earned
him nothing but ingratitude.

The Guillermins, who with such persistency worked for and
accomplished his return, expected him to handle their opponents
quite roughly. But he did not please them in this way. He wanted
to show himself "not as the revengeful party head but as everyone's pastor, instituted by God." Kampschulte, who cannot but
discover these facts to be literally so, is forced to admit, "Such
a moderation was something absolutely new and unusual in the
community which had been torn asunder by the most violent
party fights and feuds. And this moderation could not but make
a fine impression upon the great majority. This mild, recon-
cilable position after his return constitutes one of the most beautiful pages in the life of Calvin . . ."

That is fine. But it is too much praise already. The "impar-
tial" biographer feels constrained to modify this statement in the
second part of this sentence, ". . . and posterity would praise his
merit even more if he had been less conscious of it himself." This
he says because Calvin reported freely about his actions to Farel
and Myconius, intimate friends, who with trembling hearts were
waiting for the first news from Geneva. He was happy and grateful over the victory which the voice of the Saviour of peace had
won in his heart over intentions of revenge!

In his exposition of the Sermon on the Mount, Calvin com-
mented on the words of the Lord concerning the meek (Matthew
5:5): "That the meek who instead of flaring up excitedly at each

insult rather bear it all than to become like the godless; that these meek are promised the possession of the earth, may seem quite strange. For precisely those take possession of earthly power who are ready to fight at the slightest provocation and who quickly raise their hand in revenge when they suppose themselves injured. Do not the infidels rage more furiously, the more they are borne with meekness? Is it not said that 'one must howl with the wolves' because the wolves devour him who makes himself the meek lamb? Christ, however, who places His power and His Father's protection against the unbridled power of evil, elects the meek as lords and heirs of the earth . . . Contradiction? Yes; notice in what constant unrest the proud and haughty live! Though in their restless existence they may be called the lords of this world a hundred times over, in reality they have nothing, even if they possess all. In the name of the children of God I say, in quietness they may enjoy their earthly life even if they may not call a foot of land their own. This is not a presumptuous possession. They possess the earth and know that it is given by God . . . Exposed to all the darts of fate, at the mercy of the wickedness of infidels, surrounded by dangers, they are trusting pilgrims under God's protecting hand, and now already have a foretaste of the grace of their God. This is sufficient for them until at the Last Day they gain possession of their world-wide inheritance."

These words are fitting here. One or another reader may, with the author, see in them an explanation of the Reformer's truly great attitude of magnanimity after his return to the city in which so many with their insults had given him cause for hatred and revenge.

Calvin was a man of meekness and of peace who avoided all dissension so long as it pertained to private affairs. This statement is out of tune with the picture which his secret and open opponents among historians have painted of him. But when God and His Kingdom were attacked, it was different. Then he felt himself the instrument of the Most High and became relentless. All gentleness disappeared. Did not the Son of God who promised the meek and peaceful so much, swing the whip to cleanse the desecrated temple?

The amazing, moving fact in the life of this man is this humanly observable split personality which psychologically has perhaps no counterpart. Only he who has experienced to a small degree with close friends how decisively the resignation to the will of God can change the nature of man, will be able to solve this riddle.

His contemporaries had perhaps more understanding for such a process than our century which is so proud of its science of the soul. "Animum immutare divinum opus est" ("To change the soul is the work of God"), said Oekolampad, the Reformer of Basel.

PERHAPS this is the place to touch upon Calvin's maladies. They alone provide a satisfactory explanation of the excitement which at times appears in the expressions of the tormented man, even if his lack of sleep and his indefatigable labors are not taken into consideration.

As a consequence of his privations and vigils during his youth, early in his life he was afflicted with a headache concentrated on one side which hardly ever left him during his life. These pains were wont to enhance his emotional excitement to such an extent that during many a night he was "inhumanly" tormented by them.

Subjected to maladies of the trachea, he had with pains in his side to spit blood when he had used his voice too much in the pulpit. Several attacks of pleurisy prepared the way for consumption whose helpless victim he became at the age of fifty-one. Constantly he suffered from the hemorrhoidal vein, the pains of which were unbearably increased by an internal abscess that would not heal. Several times intermittent fever laid him low, sapping his strength and constantly reducing it. He was plagued by gallstones and kidney stones in addition to stomach cramps and wicked intestinal influenzas. To all this there was finally added arthritis. It was no exaggeration when he parenthetically wrote in a letter, "If only my condition were not a constant death struggle . . ."

THE CUP of suffering was not exhausted with these maladies that accompanied him to the end of his life. We have already mentioned the constant sickliness of his wife, who passed from his side after nine years of happy marriage, and the early death of his three children. Torments of another kind in his household were added which wounded him deeply in the course of time. The wife of his brother Anton, who lived in Geneva as a book dealer, was caught in Calvin's own house committing adultery with Peter Daguet, his factotum. What a scandal this incident was for the whole city and what a feast for gloating enemies; and at that in a house which wanted to offer to Geneva a pattern of exemplary living! The court proceedings brought to light something else. The unfaithful factotum had for years stolen from his master, who trusted him implicitly. "These things nearly crush me," he groaned.[107] His friends had difficulty encouraging the deeply humbled and depressed Calvin.[108]

And there was more. The Reformer's own stepchild, Judith, the daughter of Idelette de Buren, brought new sorrow into the life of the man who lovingly had assumed guardianship over her. After the death of her mother she, too, committed adultery. One can feel that the words would scarcely leave his pen when he had to write to Bullinger, "Still abed with fever, I got the news of the disgrace of my stepdaughter. It forced me to go to the country for a few days . . ."[109] How upset and how torn up must have been the inner life of this strong man who did not even interrupt his sermons and lectures at the death of his wife, when now he had to flee into solitude . . . And after such experiences in his own home, with how much feeling would he have written at about the same time (1562) to an evangelical congregation in France from which serious moral misconduct was reported to him! It is truly an Apostolic letter, concluding:

"It is wrong for you to bear the name of God while you lead a life of disgrace and shame. Put away all uncleanness! Let each of you keep his life pure and arouse no suspicions of immorality . . . I shall pray to the Lord that the grace which He gave unto you be not extinguished or brought to naught. Rather, despite your falling, may He renew you in such a way that you

may become a mirror of His immeasurable love, and that thereby
His name be praised more than ever before."[110]

I HAVE INTENTIONALLY mentioned here
what in part should come later in the proper chronological order.
No Reformer, not even Luther, was at all times exposed to more
furious attacks than Calvin. Rome as well as irreligion recognized in him the most dangerous enemy. He was accused of
harshness, lust for power, self-righteousness and cruelty, and the
attempt has been made to substantiate these assertions with
expressions torn out of their context. Even more disastrous to his
memory than the open enemies are those who write about him
from the so-called non-partisan point of view. They copy "collec-
tions of evidence" from one another. Yes, often even his followers, after superficial examination, regretfully feel they have to
admit various things all of which show only their misunderstand-
ing and ignorance concerning details and relationships. In order
to arrive at a fair judgment, one has to put one's self into the
spirit of an age long past, an age which cannot be measured by
our current concepts. And one must remember that he who
fought against a world of deadly enemies was a very sick man.
He was tormented by much domestic grief. Occasional irritation
may well be pardoned him when his most sacred convictions were
attacked. And it may be done without branding him thereby
inhuman. Especially when one evaluates his tremendous work.
Besides his daily sermons and lectures and the pastoral duties
which he took very seriously, and in addition to the administrative
responsibilities of the Church, there is added the long list of his
literary activities and his extensive correspondence in which many
a reply contains judgments and conclusions which must have been
the fruit of deliberation.

Considering all this, one becomes truly aware of the lonely
greatness of this man who, standing in a place he inwardly
despised and bleeding from a thousand wounds, fought still
another twenty-four years as a heroic general for his Lord.

HIS FIRST JOB in Geneva was the com-
position of the new Church ordinances, the "Ordonnances ecclesi-
astiques." During the five years since the earlier draft had been
confirmed by oath, his horizon had been broadened and he had
received new insight through the thought exchange with Melanchthon and Bucer. Viret was a useful helper and the six Council
members who had been chosen worked with him in the completion of the ordinances. Everything thus far went better than he
had feared.

He expected the Councils before whom the ordinances were
placed piecemeal for adoption not always to be of one mind.
After all, it was not child's play—first to get twenty-five, then
two hundred Councilmen to agree with each other, and that upon
a Church ordinance. Some did not appear for the sessions to
avoid getting mixed up in spiritual affairs. They were frightened by the serious content of the articles and feared the consequences to their comfortable ease. They had to be asked to appear
for voting. But the majority won, and it was the overwhelming
majority this time which, tired of perennial unrest, was favorably
disposed toward the new ordinances.

Some of the sections called for debate. They were considered,
the wording changed, and sometimes even a regulation. The
Council was not happy with the monthly celebration of the Lord's
Supper. Therefore it was reduced to four Sundays in the year.
And in the end, in order not to give the spiritual rulers too much
power, an important sentence was added: ". . . And that all this
take place in such a manner that the preachers have no secular
jurisdiction and use the spiritual sword only as the Apostle Paul
commands them. That the Council of the Presbyters in no way
infringe upon the power of the Magistrates nor upon that of the
judges. Rather the secular power is to remain fully intact. And
if punishment is to be pronounced or pressure to be brought upon
parties, the ministers and the Presbyters are to report to the Council, which, upon investigation of the case, will judge and decide."

Still the structure with its cornerstones remained standing.
Concession spent itself on non-essentials; it did not affect the
balanced whole. All in all, it was a victory. It cost tremendous

labor, many sleepless nights, many drops of sweat. But the victory was won.

On November 20, 1541, the sound of horns and the clang of the big bell at St. Peter's called the citizens together for a town meeting. They voted unanimously to accept the Church constitution:

"In the Name of God, the Almighty!

"We, the mayor, the Small and Great Councils of the city of Geneva, have according to ancient tradition gathered with our people.

"Realizing that it is more important than any other thing that the doctrine of the holy Gospel of our Lord be well preserved in its purity, that the Christian Church be duly protected, that our youth be faithfully instructed, that the hospital be kept in good condition for the poor and the invalid, we are pleased to have the spiritual supervision, as our Lord teaches it through His Word, brought into good order so that everyone may live in accordance with it. We have recognized this and resolved to introduce in our city and surrounding country the Church ordinance necessary to accomplish these things, according to the Gospel of our Lord Jesus Christ."

CALVIN WANTED a pure people, sound in body and soul. He envisaged making of Geneva what it was truly to become, a citadel of evangelical truth. From here it was to conquer those lands which were yet under the power of Rome. Preaching was not sufficient for this purpose. The seed sown in the hearts of men must be cared for so that it would bear fruit. He wanted the whole of Christianity which is manifested in faith and works. His unceasing challenge to a truly Christian life is his particular characteristic in comparison with other Reformers.[111]

"The goal of our new life is that in the life of believers there exists an accord, a harmony between the righteousness of God and our obedience, whereby we seal our calling as children of God."

These are the opening lines of a new chapter in the *Institutes*.[112] These words may be taken as the motto for the Church ordinances. Since history generally has called these ordinances too severe, it is well to quote verbatim what Calvin added with respect to admonitions and reproofs for transgressors: "Nevertheless, all this be so modified that no one be injured by any kind of severity. The punishment must not be harsh, so that sinners will find their way back to the Lord."

AND NOW for the content of the famous Church constitution. It was established on the grounds of the Gospel. What could be taken over from the early Church, Calvin incorporated. That which had to be supplemented he did in the spirit of the example. This spirit, he decided, must reflect itself in the laws and customs of a people. The living Word of God must accomplish more than what the lawgivers of antiquity achieved, when the Christian state elevates as laws those things which can serve the growth and preservation of the Kingdom of God on earth.

The authority which was to guard the Church constitution was divided into four classes: preachers, doctors, elders, and deacons. The duties and responsibilities of these units were clearly set forth.

Strict demands were made upon the preachers, whose selection and installation were regulated in detail: "Let no one assume the office of a servant of the Word without an inner call." The preachers had to confess the faith of their Church. Above all, they were to proclaim the pure doctrine of Christ. But it had to be the living doctrine, not a dry scholastic dogma: "Let the proclamation be such that it will uplift the people." The word spoken from the pulpit was to correspond with the life lived. The preacher was also to teach through his deeds, "to have good manners and to keep himself unspotted." He listed the sins individually which made a preacher impossible. He who succumbed to them must be removed from his office, a lesson for all Christians. Sins other than *these*—also mentioned—they had first to try to overcome through brotherly admonition.

The creator of the constitution was particularly concerned with the instruction of youth. Here, too, everything was set forth in detail.

The second unit, on the doctors, included scholars and teachers. Their duty was to take an active part in the life of the Church. They were to renounce the vanity which had overcome many of their colleagues and submit to the simple Gospel. And behold, everywhere where Calvin and his doctrine gained influence, one can see the fruits of this part of the constitution as well: It was an educated people which held learning in honor.

Twelve elders were to be chosen. They were to be "honorable people with good manners, without blemish and beyond any suspicion; above all, God-fearing and wise." After their election the names would be read from the pulpit and everyone had four days in which to express to the mayor any objections. They promised before the Council to report every wrong which should come to their knowledge "without hate or partiality, but solely that the Church be kept in good order and in the fear of God." Each elder had a certain territory in which he visited the church members to strengthen them in the faith.

The deacons, finally, were designated to receive and distribute the daily church contributions, to administer the possessions and the income of the Church, and to look after hospitals. A physician and a surgeon were called to the hospital—not a matter of course in those days. Both were to serve the poor along with their other duties. A hostel was founded for strangers passing through and also an infirmary for people infected by the plague. Prisoners were to be called together every Saturday afternoon and the Gospel preached to them.

The preachers and the elders formed the Council of the elders or the Consistory,[113] which convened every Thursday in order to discuss all matters concerning the Church. At this time the elders made their reports about observations and disorder or about stiff-necked sinners. Such sinners were called before the Council and in brotherly fashion questioned. If they showed understanding, they were dismissed in a friendly way. But if they persisted after having been arraigned three or four times and repeatedly reprimanded about their evil deeds, then they were expelled from the congregation. For secret sins an account in secret was to be given.

No one because of them is to drag his neighbor before the Consistory unless he has previously attempted to lead him aright.

The phrase "expulsion from the congregation" overcomes the modern reader who thinks of the Roman ban and the Inquisition with a slight shudder. With Calvin, the sentenced person could not appear at the Lord's Table so long as he did not reform. This was the excommunication practiced in the early Church.

No doubt, the much-damned Church discipline is strict and represents strong interference in the life of the individual. Yet it was necessary if its creator wanted to reach the goal of making out of the immoral, greedy citizenry a strong and faithful people for God. Merle d'Aubigné cites here a spoken word of the historian August Cramer who is well known for his moderate and unbiased judgment: "Without the transformation of morals, the Reformation in Geneva would only have been a change in the form of worship. The foundations for a more serious struggle would have been lacking. Nothing less than Calvin's genius was needed in order to inspire a people, to transform it completely and to infuse it with new life. In order to accomplish the transformation of faith, as he understood it, it was unavoidable to subject all external actions of life to a severe discipline. Just the same the pressure of this discipline in the sixteenth century must not be measured with nineteenth century attitudes. Everywhere at that time there existed the principle of unqualified obedience, and subjection was more bearable in Geneva precisely in the realization that no one was exempted, no matter how high his position."[114]

To what pains have Kampschulte and others gone to sketch the severity of the criminal procedure in Geneva and then to blame it on Calvin! Everyone acquainted with history knows that this entire century is to be criticized for its criminal procedure, not *one* man. In Geneva, as an imperial city, the Carolina, the punctilious rules of the court of Charles V, had had validity since 1532. The commission of 1541 revised essentially only the existing judicial order. The penal law in this century was generally influenced by religion, and that not only

in Geneva. And it is incorrect to say that criminals were spied
out more severely in Geneva than elsewhere. The death penalties
were those of the Carolina, which even specified the precise ap-
plication of the tortures. Games and lavish apparel were subject to punishment in other places too. The Carolina punished
adultery; poisoning was threatened with the wheel or drowning,
but the poisoner was defined as one who spread the plague. That
from 1542 to 1546 proceedings were brought against such un-
happy persons was not Calvin's purview, but went back to the
Carolina. And Calvin had no power to remove such laws. It was
the age which was harsh, cruelly harsh, and in it man's life had
trifling worth.

Nevertheless, everything in it must be held out to calumniate
the Reformer who steppped into conditions which had run completely wild.[115]

IT IS CUSTOMARY to describe Calvin-
istic Geneva as a theocracy. Insofar as the word is translated as
the priest's reign, this judgment does not correspond with the
facts. Indeed Calvin, like Zwingli before him, aimed at a theocracy. In reality it was the Reformation in Geneva which completely supplanted the secular power by the spiritual. From then
on only did the state become concerned about things which heretofore pertained to the Church only. The state went so far as to
establish the number of worship services and to specify the meeting hours. A preacher was not allowed to publish anything without the approval of the Council, nor might he leave the city even
for a few days.[116]

Depending upon the changing relation between Calvin and
the Magistrates, he possessed great or small or no influence at
all upon their resolutions. Thus his repeated efforts wrought
nothing to achieve a more lenient penalty for Servetus upon
whom the death sentence had been pronounced.

All in all, the execution of the Geneva Church discipline is,
apart from the *Institutes,* his most important work. The congregation received from this document a far-reaching blessing. "A
period begins which stands unique in the history of the Christian

Church as the heroic daring of faith, the unbending will power and the tremendous self-denial of him who brought the church into being . . . Nothing did he do for himself, but everything for God, and the secret of his power and his firmness was the certainty that his whole being and action stood in the service of God. He was doing His work." [117]

The light which had been lit in Geneva would soon begin to illumine the darkness elsewhere. Its glow would continue through many generations; yea, from this flame innumerable torches would be flaming in France, in western Germany, Holland, Scotland, in the New World, in Hungary, and in Transylvania. The leaven of Christianity with a Calvinistic stamp remains active in the churches of these countries to this day.

WITH CEASELESS LABOR Calvin attempted to bring to life the letter of the Church discipline. He was a relentless preacher of the Word. In addition to the Sunday worship service, every second week he held the daily weekday services.

More than two thousand of these sermons are preserved. Their clear, fresh presentation is still gripping. Verse by verse, as his custom was, he went through a Prophet, a Psalm, a Gospel, or an Epistle. There was not a word in disagreement with Scriptures, no digressing inferences, no evasion of difficulties. He renounced everything which might bring him personal glory and placed his genius, his scholarship, his rhetoric, wholly at the service of the Gospel. This inflexibility with himself was the great fact in his proclamation. And with the fiery power of the expression of his conviction he succeeded in arousing the masses for God as they crowded around his pulpit. More and more followed him inwardly also—so he himself related with rejoicing to his friends Farel and Myconius.

Besides his preaching he delivered three lectures on theology during the week. He visited the sick and lackadaisical members. On Thursdays he conducted the Council of the elders, and on Fridays the preachers' meeting in which Holy Scripture was discussed. There was not a day when strangers did not visit him to receive his encouragement. The nights were devoted more to writing than to sleep.

In other than spiritual matters his counsel was also sought. He was a member of the executive committee for examining physicians, actively supported efforts for the improvement of public health, and even did useful work for the economic advance of the city. He fought against unproductive lines of business and when after the plague and famine in 1544 there existed unemployment among the poorer people, the Council received a plan worked out by him to bring in a cloth and velvet mill.

The execution of the Church discipline, which took time to lay hold on all spheres in its ramifications, gradually met with resistance on the part of those for whom the severity of its clauses thwarted old customs and inclinations. At the beginning the few who resisted did so in secret. Only two years after Calvin's return did it break out into the open. A party of dissatisfaction was formed. The Libertines, whose pantheistic-mystical teachings deviated from those of the Church, gained adherents among them and were soon in control. And again he who despised all battles found himself daily involved in party squabbles and nasty dissension. They ruined his weak health and kept him from fruitful labors.

CALVIN'S SECOND STAY in Geneva lasted twenty-three years, closing with the end of his own life. Doumergue, his most famous student, divides this era into two parts: fourteen years of struggle, and nine years of triumph.

Biographers treat the years of struggle with greater detail than the years of his growth. If, then, I have done it the other way in my sketch of him, it is because the growth of this will appears to me basic, this will, firmly grounded in God, which was developed in constant struggle against a timid disposition, broken health, and a host of enemies. And with both followers and opponents, even down to our own day, this unfolding of his will has made him famous for his iron obstinacy.

The struggles which henceforth occupied this strange life

will only be indicated where I do not choose individual encounters which seem to me characteristic as episodes for the description. Here and there it is hoped that my presentation will help to refute repeatedly copied lies.

BEFORE MEN were able to oppose the work of the Reformer, a higher power interfered.

After an initial flare-up the year before, in the spring of 1543, the plague once again broke out in Geneva with tremendous fury. The unlucky victims were crowded into an infirmary which every healthy person avoided as the first step to a terrible death. The alleys of the city were desolate, the highways which led to it, deserted. Shops were closed and school discontinued. In small numbers the faithful came to church, each looking upon the others with suspicion and seating himself at some distance from them. Carts with gruesome loads rattled over the pavement. Among the corpses with which they were filled, the groanings of this or that one about to die could be heard. The Corbeaux, black-clad servants, also called ravens, made short work. Terror gripped the minds, paralyzed the spirit, and brought life to a standstill . . .

Pastor Blanchet, who had already assumed the care of the diseased the year before, once again took over this dangerous duty.

During these days Calvin wrote to his friend in Lausanne (he had long since been recalled from Geneva), "I fear that if something happens to Blanchet it will be up to me to take his place. For we belong to every member of our flock and cannot withdraw ourselves from those who most need our assistance."[118]

This was characteristic. In the first sentence he spoke as the man, afraid by nature, as the young husband whose tender wife was perhaps just now anticipating a mother's joys. He spoke as one beset with physical affliction who knows for certain that his condition would not withstand the plague, and who was also aware that to assume this terrible task would be detrimental to and mean the premature end of his great life work. In the second sentence he spoke as one in whom the command of the bitter duty had overcome all hesitation. He did not boast of courage nor laugh at danger. There was only the quiet expression of inner distress, "I fear . . ."—But, "we cannot withdraw ourselves."

Opponents among his biographers enjoy themselves in this "Vereor ne"—"I fear that"—which they have pulled out of the context of a long letter to his friend and not designed for the public. What a find it is to brand the supposedly strong man a coward![119] They make no great fuss about his submission to duty.

No, he would have undertaken this duty without losing many words, as he had cared for Farel's sister's son in Basel until he died of the plague, and as he afterwards cared for the latter's friend. Likewise in Strasbourg, he and his brother attended faithfully those in his congregation who had been stricken with the plague.[120]

Blanchet became the victim of his sacrificial courage. But the Council was determined not to endanger the head of the Reformation who had been obtained with so much difficulty. It ordered the preachers to convene and to select the most suitable for the ministry to the victims of the plague. "Master Calvin, however, is barred because the Church needs him."[121]

The preachers were fainthearted. Because they appeared before the Council with Calvin, it was explained to them once again that he was beyond consideration. Calvin himself was not in agreement with the exception which they wanted to make of him. But it was of no avail. The Council persisted.[122] The others trembled and refused to walk right into the arms of death just as is reported of the priests and monks in the Old Church in Geneva during the fifteenth century.[123] In the city which was to become its bulwark, the Gospel still lacked the power, unafraid of death, which later on would be revealed at every opportunity. Indeed, at the beginning of his work the Reformer was dependent upon deplorable co-workers!

Finally de Geneston, a French pastor, volunteered to serve in the plague-hospital. His despondent brethren, with the exception of one who proved his life in devoted service to the church, were to be eliminated from the Geneva Church during the next years for lack of ability.

VI.

Antagonists of Calvin

FROM CASTELLIO TO SERVETUS

CALVIN'S CHOICE of a rector for the College was a spiritually active and self-reliant young Humanist who, won to the Evangelical faith through the *Institutes,* had in Strasbourg been a temporary boarder in Calvin's house. The new rector arrived in Geneva shortly after him. He was twenty-six-year-old Sebastian Castellio from Savoy.

Soon, however, the Reformer repented of his choice. The youth's disputatiousness and quarrelsomeness made enemies. He had been in Geneva only a year when there developed between him and his wife's brothers such animosity over her dowry that the scandal arising out of it injured the prestige of the school. No sooner had the difficulty been resolved than he became involved in a new quarrel with one of his teachers, also a relative. Calvin did his best to patch up the differences, but each newly settled dispute gave rise to another.

The ambitious Castellio wanted to translate the New Testament into a popular realistic language, in which dialect would receive due recognition. The task was difficult. Where an expression was lacking, he coined it himself without hesitation. He sent a few chapters to Calvin, and in the joy of creativeness he could hardly wait to hear how his work had impressed the head of the Church. "Hm," replied the latter, "this is in need of a number of improvements. Look, instead of 'The Holy Spirit *dwells* in us,' you translate 'He visits us.' "

A long discussion ensued over the expression until the visitor

understood his mistake. Before leaving he obtained from the busy
Calvin the promise to look over his work. The latter was not
altogether easy when he agreed to do it! The translator's wish
to create something new led him to make things worse, to distort.

Thus quite soon the young author was no longer satisfied with
the promise to have his manuscript checked. He begged Calvin
to specify the hours during which they would be able to read
the translation together. But it was impossible for him, overbur-
dened with a thousand things, to concede this. For the sake of
a single word they would be arguing back and forth for hours![124]
The offended author was greatly disappointed. From this moment he bore within himself a growing resentment against his
benefactor.

By the end of the second year, because of his quarrelsomeness
and because he thought his salary too low,[125] Castellio had to resign his rectorship. A pastorate for which he applied was denied
him because in doctrinal questions he deviated from the teaching
of the Church. Calvin himself admitted they were modest devia-
tions. The matter dealt with such things as the conception of
the Song of Songs, and the words "descended into hell" in the
Apostles' Creed. More important is that, as his biographer and
eulogist himself notes, Castellio "placed his feeling, his reason,
his conscience above the doctrine of the Church."[126] To give him
a pulpit meant to start a dispute in Geneva which would endanger the uniformity of the Reformation movement. It might
well have thwarted its victory.

But Calvin wanted to help to a continued livelihood the
youth whose honesty and great gifts he acknowledged. On several
occasions he recommended him to friends abroad. He wrote to
Viret, "I have great sympathy for him, for I fear he will hardly
find with you what he wants. Help him according to your
ability."[127]

Yet in the heart of the disappointed Castellio there had
grown a deep rancor against him whom he considered the cause
of his misfortune. In May, 1544, when Calvin spoke in a Bible
class for preachers before some sixty persons on the words of the
Apostle, "But in all things I prove myself at all points a true min-

ister of God,"[128] suddenly Castellio who was seated among the lay
visitors rose and interrupted the exposition: "Servants of God,
like Paul? Don't make me laugh! Paul was obedient, you obey
yourselves; Paul was very patient, you are very impatient. Paul
devoted his nights to the building of the Church, you spend them
with playing; he was sober, you are guzzlers; he fought against
temptations, you create them; he was chaste, you are licen-
tious . . ."

The excited man worked himself into a fit of anger. A
scandal! In order not to add fuel, Calvin remained silent. He
closed the Bible and left the room. The only punishment for the
attacks upon the Genevan clergy, which Castellio did not even
attempt to prove, was that the Council relieved him of the re-
maining offices he still held. A month later Castellio left Geneva.

The hotheaded youth had thrown away a fine and blessed
activity. In extreme poverty he was to spend many a year in
Basel. And in order to earn a scanty livelihood in a laborious
manner, he eventually had to collect driftwood from the Rhine.
One may pity this basically decent man whom quarrelsomeness
and false ambition robbed of his entire happiness in life.

From now on he belonged to the most embittered enemies
of Calvin. He it was who after the execution of Servetus directed
sharp accusations against the Reformer of Geneva. These writings
have brought to Castellio the glory of a pioneer for religious liberty. And the fact of the matter is that in many of his views he
seemed to be ahead of his intolerant century. Only one goes
wrong in assuming that his tolerance applies to *every* unusual
conviction. In an illuminating chapter of his work on Calvin,
Doumergue has expressed this contradiction.[129] The words of
Castellio are quoted, "Calvin in his writing *De Haereticis* calls
heretical teachers those who urge forsaking the only God. Far be
it from me to defend such monsters. *I readily admit they are
worthy of death.* Yet I do not believe that those whom Calvin
considers heretics belong to them."

The argument, therefore, is: Who is a heretical teacher?—
and not, Should a heretical teacher be judged? The teacher of
heresy, as Calvin defined him, is worthy of death—says Castellio.

Something of the halo with which he has been glorified as the Apostle of Tolerance fades thereby. There is nothing to the reputation that Castellio alone was not a child of his century. And anyone in the future who wants to equate him once again as the preacher of freedom of conscience with Bayle and Voltaire[130] will, therefore, have to do it with some qualifications.

THE DISCONTENT of the citizens over the Church discipline grew steadily stronger. It was no respecter of persons, not even of the nobility. It was known that the Libertines and others complained much and misinterpreted the facts. But the offenders were rarely caught. Only with severity could loose tongues be checked in their derogatory talk about the discipline. One had to keep his eyes open.

A Councilman, Peter Ameaux, a playing-card manufacturer, felt that the strict mandates impaired his business. He also had to bear a hard domestic cross. His wife had embraced Anabaptist doctrines of most hazardous hue. She considered herself sinless and understood by the communion of saints things which her husband, because she practiced them, considered conclusive cause for divorce. Despite the fact that in view of the peculiar case, Calvin recommended separation, the Council decided otherwise. Peter Ameaux had to take his man-crazy wife back. Only when, after repeated warnings, she continued the scandal, was she imprisoned for half a year and the husband permitted to marry someone else. The long-drawn-out proceedings lasted a year and a half. Is it any wonder that with the declining business and the domestic troubles the good man's blood boiled over?

One day when he had invited four good friends, he opened up. "What do you think I hold of the new doctrine?" He wagged his finger and used the strong word which almost three centuries later made Cambronne at Waterloo historic. "So much, now you know it! And this foreigner from Picardy, this liar and seducer of the people, who wants to make himself bishop—it's a laugh, were it not so tragic! No one in the Council any longer dares to speak his frank opinion,[131] without having first inquired about his views. Look out! If things continue to go that way, the city will yet be played into the hands of France . . ." And his complaints continued until God and the whole boring Church were included.

To show their gratitude for the hospitality received, the four good friends ran straight to the Council and gave a red-hot report of the edifying words of its member. Next day, half the city knew about it. Those opposed to the new discipline winked at each other and rubbed their hands. "He certainly told them off! Yes, Peter doesn't mince words!"

If he had aimed at Calvin only, the perpetrator might have come off unhurt. But the taunts against the Council of which he himself was a member, what a disrespectful thing . . .

Peter Ameaux was seized. Calvin wanted to visit him in order to speak to his conscience, but he was not permitted. He entreated the judges not to employ the full severity of the law.[132] Only let the punishment be public, a warning to all mockers.

Instead, to spite the Reformer, the loud mouth was to be acquitted if he would apologize before a closed session of the Council.

This produced holy anger in him who had for five years now given his entire strength to win the city for God. The blasphemies and the slanderings against himself were known throughout the city. And for that, Ameaux's act of acquittal was to take place in secret? Never! All the preachers supported Calvin.

The opponents of the Church discipline got together. They wanted to exert pressure upon the Council's decision to reconsider the decision in the light of the letter of the law. The excitement took on a dangerous character. In serious sermons Calvin called for reason. Farel and Viret, who answered his cry in distress, assisted him therein. They were partially successful. But the enemies of the clergy excited and fanned the passions of the populace. Only after, in the presence of the Council and police, a gallows had been erected on the main square of Saint-Gervais, which was the center of the unrest, did the excitement subside.

They realized now that Calvin, who did not want any halfway measures, was right. And now the Council reached its verdict. Peter Ameaux who pleaded guilty to having spoken ill of God, the Council, and Master Calvin, had, clad in a penitential garment and carrying a torch in his hand, to be led through the streets of the city and in an open place, kneeling before the judges, ask pardon.

Once again there is an opportunity to deal the Reformer a blow. And none of his biographers, unfriendly toward him, lets this chance pass. The material is especially suited to their purposes. From the point of view of religious liberty which has become so much a matter of course today, and which even rejects legal apology for blasphemy, it is cheap to put Calvin in the wrong. I cite Doumergue: "One ought not to criticize Calvin's attitude towards Ameaux alone, but his entire attitude, his concept of state and of religion. A priori, Calvin was always wrong. He should not have had to carry out the Reformation in the sixteenth century. He should have waited for the 'true philosophy' of the eighteenth or the customs of the twentieth in order to accomplish it.—That can only mean to place one's self outside of history . . ."[133]

FIRST CASTELLIO, the ambitious opponent in thought, next Ameaux, the noisy, narrow-minded fellow. Now a third type: the sneering literary Epicurean.

Strictly speaking, Jacob Gruet does not even belong in a short biography of Calvin, for the Reformer had almost no active part in his destiny. Letters to Calvin's friends touch upon the incident as a matter in which he is present as a spectator only. I mention it briefly so as not to be reproached for having hushed up an unpleasant matter concerning Calvin's reputation. For that is what the incident has been called.

There was found on the pulpit of St. Peter's a libelous pamphlet, written in Savoy dialect. Gruet, who had in addition been seen suspiciously sneaking around the church, was one of the few who knew how to write in this dialect. With it he had often swayed laughter to his side. When his house was searched, large stacks of peculiar stylistic exercises were found which showed the bachelor, heretofore known only as an immoral person, from a new angle. Infamous slanders were here made against the Council, the Church, the clergy, primarily against Calvin, of course.

Everything was filled with blasphemies of things which are sacred to every Christian. There were also outlines of mysterious letters which smelled of state treason. In short, a scandal of the worst sort. They requited him in 1547 by beheading the libeler.

It is a sentence which at that time any other power would have pronounced as severely. Catholic judges would without hesitation have prepared the stake for him. Nevertheless, the incident gives occasion to the afore-mentioned biographers of Calvin to wash the dirty linen. A judicial murder—perhaps the man was not the author of the pamphlet on the pulpit at all!

At any rate, three years after his death, a piece written by him was found in a crack in the wall of the house in which he used to live by himself. Leo Taxil later on did not write anything more lewd than what could be found here. Gruet called Christ a crazy good-for-nothing, an evil seducer and a wretched visionary, a conceited churl, a drunkard, hypocrite, and traitor who was rightly executed. The Apostles were rogues and rascals, the Virgin Mary a harlot.[134]

This man, offended by the constraint of his habitual loose living, did psychological groundwork for the hoped-for Libertine revolution which was to free him and his party from uncomfortable Church discipline.

AND THERE is one more enemy whom I cannot neglect to mention: Jerome Bolsec.

A former Carmelite friar from Paris wheedled himself into the good graces of the Court of Ferrara where the Duchess Renate took him for her Evangelical pastor. In reality he was a spy of the duke. He cooked up much mischief; without his tittle-tattle the noble Olympia Morata would not have been expelled from her native home only to meet a miserable death abroad. Finally, when his double-dealing was discovered, the ground in Ferrara became too hot for him. We find him in 1550 and 1551 in the vicinity of Geneva and in the city itself pretending to be a traveling physician.

Here he was pleased to play the part of a theologian, attacking the doctrine of election by grace. The belief was that he

had been induced to do this by political opponents of the Reformer. Perhaps. Or it was conceit in play, the desire to attack the
Reformer in his own bailiwick and in his favorite doctrine. One
day, as a visitor at the Friday meeting he began to draw his sword.
He called election by grace a preposterous heresy which made God
a tyrant and idol. It was a new invention based on distorted
Bible passages. Just then Calvin entered the room, unnoticed.
No doubt it was his absence that had given Bolsec the boldness to
speak so freely. As soon as he had concluded, Calvin rose and
refuted the attack with Scripture passages and citations from
Augustine so convincingly that the disconcerted aggressor lacked
words to defend himself. Once again the phenomenal memory
of the Reformer, which held in readiness for him every necessary
proof, won him a splendid victory. The impression of this victory
upon his hearers was tremendous. A judge-advocate who was
present in the assembly ordered the immediate seizure of the
Parisian. He saw in his address a revolt against religion and the
Church.

A trial followed which resulted in the quack's exile. The
sentence was mild, for he was not a Genevan and therefore had
nothing to lose. Later we find the former Carmelite as a Reformed
preacher in France after having recanted his errors. However,
he was forced to resign the position in shame and rebuke as an
"infamous liar." Finally, in 1563, the restless spirit returned to
the fold of the Roman Church. He settled down in Autun as a
physician and in his old age wrote a "History of the life, the
customs and the teachings . . . of John Calvin."

If one wants a friendly judgment of the "Carmelite, learned
in Scriptures and firm in conviction, and of the irreproachable
scholar,"[135] the "poor man upon whom Calvin, with the superiority of his rich biblical and patristic knowledge, pounced,"[136] then
one ought to read the corresponding sections in Kampschulte's
book. If one is interested, however, in forming an independent
opinion of Bolsec, then one ought to leaf through his works. The
servants of Rome have repeatedly cared for new editions and
their distribution. Even to the ignorant in history, the lies and
slanders found in these pages are so tangible, as big as a fist,

that even decent opponents of Calvin are disgusted. The baseness of the author goes so far as to accuse his irreproachable enemy of unnatural unchastity! [137]

Of all the Reformers, Rome hated none worse than Calvin; for among them he was the pre-eminent theologian and the most logical thinker. Therefore the defenders of the Papal chair have thrown themselves with voracious appetite upon these "memoirs" of one of Calvin's contemporaries. And where Calvin is mentioned in an anti-Reformation writing the reference is spiced with Bolsec's coriander. A priest has molded these "memoirs" under false colors into a Calvin novel which has also been translated into German and may cause confusion in many minds.

Galiffe, a Genevan Protestant, followed in the footsteps of Bolsec in order rightly to make room again for a Catholic. Nevertheless, the biased yet earnest historian Kampschulte is not to be compared with his backbiting first predecessor.

EVEN BEFORE the starring performance of Bolsec, at about the time of the execution of Gruet, the party of the Libertines was so strong that in the Council of the Two Hundred it equipoised the supporters of the Church discipline. In the Council hall and in the assemblies, on the street and everywhere, the Libertines fought the innovators and above all Calvin, their leader. The dissatisfied were the old Genevans who called themselves patriots. They saw in the preachers, who had mostly immigrated from France, foreign oppressors of their personal liberties.

For many years, until 1555, the Reformer had to swallow so many humiliations that a healthier one than he would have had to become sick of them. His propositions were rejected, his warnings scorned. He could not walk across the street without being mocked, "There he goes, neighbor. I prefer to hear three dogs barking than to listen to him preach." "Did you know, hell has only two devils, and there goes one of them!" Children called after him, twisting his name, "Cain, Cain!" More than one dog answered to the name "Calvin". . .

Ami Perrin, his former friend in high position, the same who traveled as ambassador of the city of Geneva to Strasbourg in order to convince him that he should return, joined the Libertines and became their leader. He was not able to take it. His wife and his brother-in-law, Franz Favre, were punished. She had taken part in forbidden dances; he had committed adultery. It was clear the Church discipline respected no persons. The Mayor, Corne, had found that out. Because he danced at a wedding, he was summoned. However, different from the conceited Perrin, he humbled himself and "gave due thanks for the admonitions received according to the Word of God and the law."

But Perrin's wife wanted to dance now more than ever to spite the clergy. She behaved like a dragon before the Council of the elders. "You pig,"[138] she screams at Calvin, "you low-down liar!" Her sister-in-law was no more reserved.

Calvin remained firm. No halfway measures, no giving in, or breaking down. "So long as they are in Geneva, they try in vain to defy the discipline; even if this house contained as many devils as raving heads, that would not impede the victory of the Lord."[139]

But the rift cut deep. As zealously as Ami Perrin once supported the demands of the Reformer, so he now stoutly opposed them with the entire weight of his influence.

Having laid himself open to attacks during an ambassadorial trip to Paris, he was even temporarily placed under arrest. But soon he was on top again. The son of a small crockery dealer, as the people's leader he bore all the signs of those rising to fame.

"Our comical Caesar," so Calvin referred to him in letters to friends. Philibert Berthelier, a son of a martyr for the freedom of the city, and Peter Vandel who, according to the report of a contemporary, must have been deuced in his mother's womb, formed with Ami Perrin a triumvirate. It was a sort of side-government which sought to cross all decrees of the Elders' Council.

ONE DAY the glowing spark in the Council of the Two Hundred exploded. Calvin, coming from the Elders' Council, perceived confused screaming in the City Hall. He ran to the scene and found the Councilmen with drawn swords in an ugly scuffle in the courtyard. And now the unimaginable took place. He who by nature was timid, withdrawing even at the thought of battle, without thinking of himself plunged with outstretched arms into the thickest knot. Petrified, they all moved back. Immediately he was surrounded by his supporters who, frightened to death, wanted to protect him with their lives. He motioned them away. "I am here to place myself between your swords. If there is to be blood, begin with me!"

The words worked wonders. The fighting cocks were cooled off. They returned to the Council chamber. Calvin was even asked to sit in on the deliberations. Again minds clashed and again he had to mediate and settle the dispute. Finally he made a stirring, heart-searching address. With the exception of a few, they were marvelously moved by it. Even his worst enemies congratulated him for his intervention, which avoided great bloodshed. But he was deeply discouraged. The letter to Viret[140] in which the event was described—it is also found in other contemporary reports—closed with these words: "Wickedness has grown to such proportions that I scarcely hope that an orderly condition of the Church can be preserved, particularly through my service. I am a broken man if God does not stretch out His hand to me."

But he persevered through all trials and tribulations. Another eight years had to pass after this moving incident in the court of the Geneva City Hall before the biographers terminate the years of struggle and note the beginning of the era of triumph.

In 1549, Idelette de Buren died. Through the death of his life partner his life not only became lonelier, but again and again he showed the need of the assuaging, steadying encouragement of a gracious wife.

MERLE D'AUBIGNÉ makes a remarkable comment about the Reformer: "The man of God has been charged with despotism. That is quite understandable: because he was an enemy of excess he has been made an enemy of freedom. No one opposed the ethical and social anarchy which threatened the sixteenth century, and which has infested every century that did not know how to defend itself against it, more resolutely. This courageous battle of Calvin is one of the greatest services he performed for freedom. For freedom has no more dangerous enemies than immorality and anarchy.

"Of course when it comes to the means to check these evils, he does not stand above his century, which in all communities with one accord attacked them with the heaviest penalties. One who errs in the knowledge of God is accountable to God alone. When man makes himself God's avenger, our conscience revolts. Three hundred years ago people had not advanced this far—the most superior spirits in some ways are always subject to human frailty. Nevertheless, during a famous affair when a wretched individual, whose doctrine threatened the community, stood before the secular court of Geneva, one lonely voice in all of Europe was raised on behalf of the accused, demanding mitigation of the sentence of Servetus. It was the voice of Calvin."[141]

I am glad to place this comment ahead of that part which for every Protestant of our time is the most painful and shameful in the life of the Reformer. Perhaps the famous Church historian is considered biased—I do not think so. At any rate he is far less so than the propagators of the customary, factually incorrect assertion that Calvin ordered Servetus burned.

WE ALREADY ENCOUNTERED Michael Servetus in the year 1534, when he avoided a debate with Calvin which he himself suggested. This foresight continued to pair itself with the passion for introducing daring ideas into the religious movement. As early as at the age of five he had been emasculated. Perhaps therein lies the explanation of his divided personality.

In one of his works[142] Servetus discussed the mental disposition of his fellow countrymen. "The spirit of the Spaniard is restless and dreams great things. He knows by dissimulation and a certain verbosity to pretend a greater erudition than he really has. Sophistry appeals to him more than is profitable. Among all mortals, he is the most superstitious." With this he may well have characterized his own nature.

Without any doubt, in the realms which he tried to penetrate, Servetus was a blusterer averse to the conventional. As successor to Vesals he became assistant to the famous Paris physician Jehan Winter and soon was an esteemed physician and teacher of medicine himself. A passage in his later published principal work gave temporary recognition to him as the discoverer of the circulation of the blood. Of late, however, a question mark has been placed there. He wrote an astrological apology in which he described astrology and medicine as inseparable. Since the doctors got off poorly in this work, he was sued and yielded, humbly asking pardon. This brought his stay in Paris to an unglorious end in 1537.

Then he practiced in French country towns under the name of Michel de Villeneuve, first in Charlieu, then in Vienne, where the Archbishop made him his physician in ordinary. In the mornings he attended Mass; in the afternoons, in the habitation which the prince of the church had prepared for him in a side wing of the palace, the alleged Catholic wrote about the Roman Church, "O monster, most despicable of all animals, most shameless of all wenches . . . Synagogue of Satan!"

And the good Archbishop, who was particularly concerned with preserving the faith unspotted, had no idea what an arch-heretic had settled down in his quarters, and he was not aware of the giant cuckoo egg which was being laid here in all quietness. Flattered, he accepted the edition of Ptolemy, made by his doctor and dedicated to him. It praised him as a benefactor and friend . . .

Oh, the good Archbishop!

In complete secrecy his guest was writing a work which was supposed to make an end to the teachings of Rome as well as those of the Reformation.

CALVIN HAD WRITTEN the *Institutes.* Servetus wanted to outwit him with the *Restitutes,* "Christianissimi Restitutio"—a restitution of Christianity. The preface itself reveals the fantastic mystic: "We endeavor to reveal the secret of faith from the earliest times, a faith which stands above all disputation. We will take away the veil from the countenance of God that we may behold it and it may illumine us."

The work is divided into five books and two dialogues on the Trinity, followed by three books on faith, justification, and the kingdom of Christ, and three more books on regeneration and the kingdom of the Anti-Christ. The closing chapters contain twenty open letters to Calvin, sixty "signs of the power of the Anti-Christ," and a polemical treatise against Melanchthon. For the author, the Trinity was a red flag. No word was strong enough for him in deriding this hallowed concept. He opposed justification by faith and infant baptism. All the arguments were presented with such bluntness that Rome, Wittenberg, and Geneva would feel equally injured. His speech was not without the sweep of the prophets: "Already heaven and earth are moving against the dragon and Anti-Christ, already mankind, which heretofore slumbered in the dust of this earth, is being awakened to eternal life, already the lamb that was slain begins to open the book which has been closed with seven seals!"

All Servetus' hopes, an almost superstitious confidence, were set on the transformation which his work was supposed to bring about in the entire Christian world.

He prepared the printing with special care. A publisher from Basel whom he had contacted returned the manuscript to him at first—he did not want to get into any trouble. He was, however, able to win two printers in Vienne to this rash enterprise. To each he promised one hundred Taler in addition to their regular wages. During the winter of 1552 the book was printed in all secrecy in a remote house outside of the city walls. The author's name did not appear in print. He was careful, however, to identify himself later on as the author of this work. In the middle of the volume, which has seven hundred and thirty-four pages, in one of the dialogues, a certain Peter greets his friend Michael with these words, "Look, here is Servetus for whom I am looking—!" One may also discover at the end of the volume, above the year of publication, the letters M.S.V. (Michael Servetus Villanovanus.)[143]

A FEW of the thousand copies of the *Restitutes* found their way to Geneva. And from here out fate overtook the author, for he was recognized. For many years he had corresponded with the preachers of that city and returned to the author of the *Institute* his work filled with mocking marginal notes. He wrote to Abel Poupin, a minister, "Your Gospel is without true faith, without good works; instead of the one God you have a trinitarian Cerberus, instead of the true faith an imagined fate . . . Woe to you, woe, woe!"[144]

No one was in doubt as to the author of the book, which was received with horror. And when Guillaume de Trie, a religious refugee from Lyon, was admonished in letters by his cousin in France, who had remained a Catholic, to return to the bosom of the only saving Church because the Reformation was creating nothing but disorder, confusion, and moral and religious depravity, he answered him: "I see that vice is punished here better than where you are! And concerning the faith, no one allows the name of God to be abused. Let me speak frankly; it is a shame that the men who confess the one God and Jesus Christ are cruelly burned at the stake, while Michael Servetus, living in your midst, in Vienne, calls Christ an idol and destroys every foundation of the faith, yet he is not punished for it . . ."[145]

One has to understand this man. The prisons in Lyon were overcrowded with Evangelicals, all of whom were waiting to be burned at the stake. He had friends there. Among the prisoners were five students from southern France. They were trained in Geneva and Lausanne as Reformed preachers and their fate was now awaited with anxious concern. People hardly talked about anything else, and yet he who was held the most godless was unmolested by the forces of the Pope. The writer of this letter aired his honest indignation.

His cousin did not believe him and answered that for such a terrible accusation proof was needed, otherwise he knew what to think of it. Immediately after the first report, the personal physician of the Archbishop of Vienne was given a special hearing. He angrily denied every charge and swore to being a faithful

son of the truth. Ory, the inquisitor, was behind the demand for
such a hearing.

What proofs might de Trie be able to give? Only Calvin was
able to confirm the evidence. After much hesitation, against his
will, he gave him several of the Spaniard's letters. De Trie sent
them to his relative, writing: "It took a lot of pain to get these
letters from Calvin. He wishes that the blasphemies by Servetus
would be punished; but he says it was not in his province to
wield the sword of judgment. Rather he would prefer to check
the erroneous ideas by teaching than by persecution. He finally
gave in when I told him that without his help I would be accused of blackmailing."[146]

The entire mob of Calvin's despisers concludes from this
incident with delight that the Reformer gave his opponent over
to the Inquisition. Such accusations are not only found among
those who despise him, but even in unbiased writings. With
shaking of the head one reads in the biography of a Reformed
author, "At least Cardinal Tournon laughed heartily that here
one heretic was denouncing another. We do not have to apologize."[147] No, not to apologize, but to contest. The lone star witness whom the Bernese theologian has for the hearty laughter
of Cardinal Tournon, who reports it, is—it is amazing—the
slanderer, Bolsec, the same whom the Reformer describes as im-
moderate and immoral, a thief of funds for the poor, afflicted
with shameful diseases, who invoked the Devil on his deathbed.
Calvin's greatest student has written eighteen folio pages,[148]
filled with a discerning historical and psychological investigation
of the entire matter, the perversion of which has done so much
damage to the memory of Calvin. After examining all sources and
after carefully weighing the pros and cons, he arrived at the
rejection of this malicious interpretation. The French scholar,
Bossert, indifferent in matters of faith, arrives at the same conclusion, "Calvin has been accused of having handed the letters
over to de Trie. It is sufficient to read them in order to be convinced by the untenableness of this opinion."[149] Finally, Calvin
knew for years Servetus' whereabouts and his assumed name.
Therefore he could have done away with him long before by

giving his name to the Inquisition. Swiss and German biographers of Calvin may henceforth cease repeatedly to copy this fairy tale from each other, even though most of them state that Calvin himself declared, "Nothing is true of this slander."

Can one really know Calvin and think him capable of a cowardly lie? His word ought to be sufficient even if all proofs in circumstantial evidence spoke against it. But these "proofs" cannot withstand rigid examination, and thus another stain has been effaced with which the picture of the great seeker of truth has been marred.

THE PHYSICIAN, Villanovanus, was now seized and put on trial. One has to read how masterfully he attempted to lie himself out of the difficulty. He claimed not to be Servetus, but since Calvin called him Servetus by mistake— as a boyish trick he had accepted this name and answered him as Servetus. He must have been fifteen or sixteen years old at that time and somewhere in Germany . . . As a precaution the letters had not been dated. For the rest, with tears of outrage he pretended to be no other than the staunch Catholic doctor who was a friend of so many clergymen.

The court was only partially convinced. At any rate, one morning when the prison warden and his helpers left for work in the vineyards, the opportunity was at hand. Servetus, who was not closely guarded, jumped from a balcony to a roof and from there into the court whose door was luckily unlocked. His subsequent flight into the territory around Lyon was also successful. After the disillusioned people of Vienne had condemned him to a fiery death, nothing remained for them except to pronounce the sentence of execution in front of his picture, under which they had piled five bales of his books.[150]

SERVETUS WAS FREE. The five students who had equipped themselves in Geneva and Lausanne to preach the Gospel in France languished in the prison in Lyon. They returned to their home country as enthusiastic followers of Calvin, meeting a citizen of Lyon not quite three hours beyond the border. The fellow traveler invited them into his house where they were immediately apprehended. He had betrayed them. Merchants from St. Gall, Hans Liner, and the brothers Zollikofer, took care of their room and board and helped them as much as they could. Zurich, Basel, and Schaffhausen intervened on their behalf with the king of France through a legation because, having lived within the confederacy for some time, these men were recognized as half citizens. Berne undertook special steps and Geneva, too, sent an ambassador to Paris. Archbishop de Tournon of Lyon, on his way through Lausanne, gave assurance after pressing entreaties to do his best in the matter, without giving any thought to keeping the promise which he had made to a heretic government. Henry II remained under the influence of his mistress, Diana of Poitiers, and that of the Guise, who fanned his zeal for persecution.

Steadfastly, the five young men confessed their faith. Their example did not induce backsliding, but on the contrary strengthened the congregation at Lyon inwardly and outwardly. Even a highway robber imprisoned with them renounced his wild and evil ways and because of their witness became a confirmed follower. Such was the strength of the seed sown by Calvin.

The Reformer himself left nothing undone to save these unfortunates; his letters of consolation belong to the dearest and most precious testimonies from his pen. In May, 1553,[151] when their fate appeared already sealed, he wrote them, ". . . our heavenly Father has so expressly proved by action how much His strength is mighty in you that we doubt not that He will perfect His work. You know that in leaving this world we do not go away on an uncertain venture; in addition to the confidence of eternal life, you have the assurance as children of His gratuitous adoption to enter your inheritance. That God should have appointed you His Son's martyrs should be an added sign of this . . .Beloved brethren, act according to the word of David, 'My soul is continually in my hand: yet do I not forget Thy law,'[152] and be ready to give your life at any time. Seeing that the Lord employs your life in so worthy a cause as is the witness of the Gospel, doubt not that it is precious to Him. The hour draws nigh when the earth shall disclose the blood which has been hid, and we, after having been disencumbered of these fading bodies, shall rise. Meanwhile be the Son of God glorified by our shame. Let us be consoled with the sure testimony that we are persecuted and mocked for no other reason than that we believe in the living God. This is sufficient cause to despise the whole world with its pride, till we be gathered into that everlasting Kingdom where we shall fully enjoy those blessings which we now only possess in hope." [153]

A few days after receiving this last letter of their master, on May 16, 1553, the five young martyrs were led to the stake which had been erected on the Place des Terreaux in Lyon. Clad in gray shirts and chained, they began joyously to sing the Ninth Psalm as they were riding on the cart which carried them to the place of execution, "I will praise Thee, O Lord, with my whole heart; I will show forth all Thy marvelous works. I will be glad and rejoice in Thee, I will sing praise to Thy name, O Most High . . . for Thou hast maintained my right and my cause; Thou satest in the throne judging right." Harshly they were commanded to cease, whereupon they called out passages of Scripture to passers-by so as to sow the good seed even until their last hour. Then they began with the Apostles' Creed, each taking a portion, so that it could be seen that they were of one faith. The one who came to the sentence, "Conceived by the Holy Ghost: Born of the Virgin Mary," spoke even louder that people might perceive how wrongly they had been accused of having denied the miraculous conception.

Joyfully they mounted the faggot pile. While the four younger ones were stripped of their clothing and tied to the stake, Martial Alba, the oldest, prayed on his knees. When the hangman grabbed him also he turned to the royal procurator, "Sir, grant me one wish still!" The other raised his eyebrows, asking, "What?" "That I may kiss my brethren once more before death." The procurator could not refuse the petition. Then Martial stepped to each one bound to the stake, saying, "May God keep you, my brother!" They followed his example, stretching their necks as best they could to the front and to the back in order to give the parting kiss. They too said to each other, "May God keep you, my brother!"

The oldest having now been tied to the stake as well, all five of them were bound with a heavy chain around their bodies. Then the fire was lit. It leapt into the air. Those consecrated to death stood fast. And for a little while longer they could be heard mutually consoling and strengthening each other, saying, "Courage, brother, courage!"[154]

Thus died Calvinists.

This is one example. History knows thousands of its kind. Only two months later there was a letter of Calvin to Farel reading, ". . . Last Saturday a merchant was burned at Lyon who marched to the place of execution full of courage and self-control although his relatives and the people were trying to make him recant by every possible means. Even his mother approached him three times, falling down upon her knees and begging him with tears in her eyes to save his life. In vain . . ."[155]

This digression seemed to me important in this connection: not because in the bloody acts of Rome there lies a justification of the sentence pronounced upon Servetus, but to prove that the Calvinist who desired unflinchingly to bring about the rule of the Word of God was himself ready, at all times, to give his life for this cause. Moreover, no Catholic was ever executed in Geneva for the sake of his convictions.

MICHAEL SERVETUS hid himself. No one knows anything about the four months which lay between his flight from Vienne and the day on which he was recognized in Geneva. What he himself testified in the course of his trial hardly shed any light upon the matter, for as one could observe in Vienne, he was never at a loss for false evidences. Castellio and Bolsec, enemies of Calvin, reported that Servetus had been seized in Geneva on his way to Italy the morning after his arrival in the city. Most of the biographers accept this theory without question. Other biographers figure that he must have hidden himself for a month before he was discovered in the city. To know the truth would be important to evaluate the intention which brought the Spaniard to Geneva! To presume, as it has been a favorite way, that he came here by chance, is untenable. The way from Vienne or Toulouse, where he may have gone first, leads through Grenoble, Modane, and Turin. Why then such a wearisome detour? Moreover he had every reason to avoid Geneva because Calvin had warned him for many years. As early as 1546, he wrote to Farel that should Servetus come to Geneva he would not leave alive, provided his authority was still respected.[156] From the connection of the letter, I conclude he must have written to Servetus in like manner. According to the documents of the trial, Servetus seemed to be of the opinion that Calvin himself served notice on him in Vienne. Did this man really have so much self-confidence in his so frequently successful craftiness that he moved into the territory of him whom he considered his deadly enemy?

One suspicion lies at arm's length. One of the pair of Vienne printers of the *Restitutio* was a Libertine from Geneva. Is it otherwise possible than that the Spaniard frequently conversed with him about the conditions in his native city? He found out that the Libertines, Calvin's fierce opponents, for the time being held the majority in the Council and that they had the upper hand among the citizens. He heard of the many hardships that Calvin daily experienced. How would it be, then, if he who was himself far superior in knowledge and mind to the Reformer, would take his place, and then, getting hold of the threads already stretching from this city into distant lands, he could substitute for the Reformation his own system of beliefs, exchanging the *Institutes* for the *Restitutes!*[157]

Calvin had no doubt whatsoever as to the danger that threatened his life work from this angle. He was about to make the city entrusted to him a fortress for the pure doctrine. Servetus was intent upon undermining this structure. Calvin was well acquainted with the ambiguous plans which the former had written to him in letters for many years. He knew that the fantastic doctrine had already gained a foothold in Italy. From there he had been entreated, "to be the hammer which would crush the proud, devilish Servetus."[158]

As soon as he found out that the dread man was actually in the city, he anticipated everything which the other might want to carry out. He had him apprehended and put on trial.

IT IS STRANGE that in Vienne the defendant, Servetus, behaved like a coward, a liar, and a hypocrite. His eyes filled with tears, he submitted to the Church and desired henceforth to believe nothing else than what it commanded him; he wanted to live and die like a good Catholic Christian. A few months later as he stood before the judges of Geneva this submissive humility changed into a daring joy of confession. He would rather die than retract one sentence!

The answer to this noticeable change of mind is easy to find, in spite of the fact that certain historians are unsuccessful in it. In Vienne, the heretic found himself before a closed Roman court which knew no mercy for a heretic; in Geneva he found a strong party under the leadership of Ami Perrin, Berthelier, and Vandel, who were intent on overthrowing the head of the Church. He got assurance that this party would back him up and out of it there would come defenders and persons to go bail for him, willing to help him as if they were "his real cousins."[159]

In Geneva it never occurred to him to deny his name or his work. On the contrary, during the first hearing he assumed a challenging stand and pretended to be the indicter. He was aware of the fact that Calvin was just then in the most difficult position he had experienced in Geneva since 1538, the time of his exile. Calvin also knew that everything hung in the balance.

And since Berthelier took the matter of the one under arrest into his own hands and defended him personally before the court, the Reformer, despite initial hesitation, had to enter the battle himself, a battle which would either bring victory or defeat to his Church. Orally and through the written word the two opponents daily fought. Servetus spared no words: "Simon Magus, criminal, killer . . . wretch who judges things which he does not understand . . . liar, evil wrangler . . . Your impudence is so great that you dare to contest that snow is white . . . Ridiculous dwarf . . . Do you believe yourself able to deafen the ears of the judges with your canine barking?" "Wretch, wretch," he repeated again and again. One must not blame him too much for his recklessness of expression. Strong words among ecclesiastics of that day were common. That he dared to use them in his position shows, however, that he had great confidence in final victory.

Modestly, humbly, as if he were the prisoner who had to defend himself for his doctrine, Calvin frequently stood before him. In spite of the invective he kept his peace; in fact, many times he preferred to be silent. He and the other clergymen had done everything to assure the Spaniard a free discussion of his teaching, so much so that voices were already heard charging him with too much yielding and weakness. Only rarely did the attacks of the frantic Servetus make his blood boil so that he lost his temper, branding the other's "deceit, ignorance, a wild assumption, ugly stupidity." [160]

And yet the battle was fought solely for the cause, not the person of Servetus whom he did not hate. He testified to this several times. Even during the first days of the trial, Calvin wrote to Farel that he wished to spare the people's seducer from a painful death. [161] And he did everything to lead the mistaken man to the truth. He was certain that, motivated by external reasons only, he would grasp the saving hand, did he not live under the presumption of soon being free, honored, and a leader . . .

One would think that this exciting battle with his rabid opponent and the powerful party behind him would demand of the tired Reformer, so averse to fighting, his whole attention. The fact of the matter is, however, that none of his activities was neglected. He watched the progress of the Reformation in France and England, wrote to the martyrs the glorious letters of consolation which are still a comfort to us today, and everywhere used his influence on behalf of those in danger.

The Libertines were not idle, either. Calvin had to fight against constant threats to place the trial upon another basis. For this reason the attempt to take it before the Council of the Two Hundred, where their majority was even greater than in the Small Council.

THE OPPONENTS of the Reformer sought to injure him most decisively where he and the elders had the authority, placed in them by the people themselves. That would cut an opening in the iron wall of the Church discipline. Philibert Berthelier, the main patron and attorney of Servetus, was under the Church ban. This many-talented and quarrelsome man who wielded his great influence and popularity on behalf of the prisoner, had not been found worthy to receive the Lord's Supper because of moral and other offenses. For during a mighty drunken brawl he and some armed fellows with threats pursued a preacher right up to his home. His friends resolved at this very time to obtain his rights.

Calvin was called to meet with the Small Council where it was decided, in spite of his pleas, that Berthelier was not to be prohibited to receive the Lord's Supper. Ami Perrin chaired this memorable meeting. With the encroachment upon the rights of the congregation, the entire discipline which had been established with so much labor was shaken. The legislative body showed open disrespect for its author.

Once again Calvin was summoned and brought before the Council opposite Servetus—who could now witness for himself the dissension between his despised opponent and the Council members. The Spaniard could now laugh in his sleeve.

The next day—it was the day before the Lord's Supper— the Council gathered for a special meeting. In a deeply moving speech, with the whole power of his conviction, Calvin spoke for the reconsideration of the resolution passed the day before. He trembled in agitation as he said, "I swear rather to die than to have the Lord's Supper defiled . . . I would rather be dead a hundred times than to commit such terrible mockery to Christ."[162]

To no purpose. Perrin anticipated the stormy protest and attended to its failure. The majority of the Council decided to leave the resolution as it stood. Calvin was dismissed.

His words, however, had not fallen under the table, and his features revealed an unflinching determination. On the other hand, everyone knew Berthelier was a daredevil who was not afraid to cause an uproar in the House of God. A few of the Council members suddenly became worried. And Perrin unexpectedly hit the table heavily with his fist, "Once and for all, let us have a purifying thunderstorm at St. Peter's. Only thunder and lightning can free us from this pressure. Geneva belongs to the Genevans."

This time, however, he could not muster a majority. The cautious among Perrin's followers agreed with the followers of Calvin. They did not want a repetition of the events of 1538 with the ensuing confusion. The result of the meeting was that Berthelier was secretly ordered not to partake of the Lord's Supper.

Calvin knew nothing about it, when, overtired yet with rapid steps, he ascended the pulpit on Sunday morning. The news of the decision of the Council and the opposition of the Reformer had spread through the whole city like wildfire. The large sanctuary was filled to the last place. And in view of the rows of Councilmen whose faces stared at him malevolently out of the Gothic choir stalls, after a powerful sermon he began a very serious address: "I asked that God would give me firmness and my prayer was answered. Therefore know that whatever may occur, I shall act according to the clearly revealed command of my Master. Should there be anyone during the Lord's Supper which we are about to celebrate approaching the table of the Lord who has been denied this privilege by the Elders, I shall take the stand that is required of me."[163]

The emotion of the preacher was conveyed to all the people. In hushed silence they awaited the next move. "Slowly he descends the pulpit and places himself before the Lord's table. There he stands, the sickly, pale, slight, and exhausted man whom any breeze threatens to blow over and whose eyes with a feverish glow search for him who, unworthy, will be pressing himself to the Lord's table. The congregation, moved by the solemnity of the hour, is searching with him. Berthelier is not among them . . ."

Doumergue to whom we owe the picturesque description of this scene rejoices, "Let Ambrose be celebrated who bars the

Emperor from entering the Cathedral of Milan; let Luther be celebrated who defied Charles I at the Diet . . . My admiration belongs in like manner to him who at St. Peter's in Geneva hurls against the alarmed Council members and the frightened people, 'You may kill me, but you will not force this hand to administer the bread of God to an unworthy man.' " [164]

Calvin had obeyed God. He acted, however, against the express order of the authority of the state and he was convinced after the last Council meetings that he would be expelled from the city for the second time. His heart was almost breaking because his leaving meant not only a triumph for Ami Perrin, Berthelier, and Vandel, but was at the same time a victory for Servetus. The heretic would reap what he himself had sown.

With a heavy heart he ascended the pulpit for the afternoon sermon, his parting sermon. He read the passage of Paul's address to the elders at Ephesus;[165] expounded it with stirring words and ended as he closed the Bible, saying, "You, however, remember, that for years I have labored day and night, often under tears, for the salvation of your souls. Remain faithful to the pure doctrine which I have preached unto you. And now, beloved brethren, with the Apostle I commend you to God and to the word of His grace."[166]

It did not come to that. The Council, convinced of the firmness of the head of the Church for whom a great part of the congregation had boundless respect, was more divided and undecided than ever. The members were not anxious to press the matter to extremes. Kampschulte the "objective and unbiased" twists his thumbs, "the sense of honor and dignity . . . seems to have left the first city government."[167] The battle for the maintenance of the discipline continued and became a terrible problem for the Reformer who refused to compromise.

FOR THE LIBERTINES the attacks upon the Church discipline constituted ways and means: Calvin had to be overthrown. The means seemed to fail. The ways, however, the acquittal of Servetus, was to humiliate the despised head of the Church and bring his downfall.

Clear-eyed, Calvin realized the danger threatening his work. The letters of his friends were full of sympathy and lovingly sought to console him in his distress. Theodore Beza, the young French scholar and poet who after Calvin's death became his successor, wrote during these difficult days to Bullinger, the prelate of Zurich, "His enemies are so many, they press upon him in such manifold ways, that I can hardly understand his power of resistance . . . He suffers it all with an amazing constancy. Nevertheless, if the Lord does not intervene, then his labors and his sorrows will take him from us. What would become of us! He needs our prayers and our encouragement."[168] The darker Calvin saw the situation, the more jubilant was Servetus. The certainty of the coming triumph gave him strength and new encouragement for ever new attacks. Despite the decree of the Council that he was not to have contact with the outside world, he must have been well informed about the desperate condition of his enemy. Not in vain was his prison warden a Libertine who transmitted information so well that he had to be replaced.[169] The letters of the prisoner were written according to the mood and condition in which he found himself, sometimes haughty, challenging, the next time eliciting sympathy. The poor man suffered from cold and noxious insects. Now, however, he saw himself at the threshold of the fulfillment of his wishes. Soon he would stand in the place of the one whom he so bitterly despised. It was the twenty-second of September when the Council received Servetus' famous writing:

"Therefore, gentlemen, I demand that my false accuser be punished, *poena talionis,* and that he, like me, be imprisoned until the trial be decided either by his or my death or by some other punishment."

He demanded even more—that the property of the opponent be adjudged to him. At the reading the Councilmen lost their seriousness. The Reformer's poverty was known throughout the city. He kept nothing for himself, absolutely nothing![170]

SERVETUS' friends in the Council unswervingly labored in his behalf. The latest plan was to ask the opinion of the Reformed Swiss states. During Bolsec's trial they advised moderation, and it was believed that in this case they would again dampen the fiery spirit of the Reformer. This applied especially to Berne, which was favorably inclined toward the Libertines and let slip no opportunity to play Calvin a trick. It seemed, therefore, quite plausible that with the opinion of the confederates the desired direction might be given to the trial.

This time, however, the enemies of the Reformer miscalculated. The answer from Zwingli's city was clear-cut: "No severity is too great to punish such an offense. Our preachers are in total agreement with what Calvin thinks of his doctrine." Schaffhausen followed, "Stop the evil, otherwise his blasphemies, like a crawfish, will eat away the members of Christ!" Basel wrote, "Do what lies in your power to convince him of his error. If he persists in his folly, then use the power which is entrusted to you by God to prevent him by force from any further injury to the Church of Christ."

There still remains Berne, the most powerful neighbor state, bound to Geneva by treaty. It would certainly not answer to please Calvin. The Libertines placed their entire hope upon its influential reply, which counted as much with them as the other three combined. But the people by the Aare judged no differently. "We pray that God may give you wisdom and courage to expunge this pest from the churches, from yours as well as from others."

These opinions, accompanied by supporting letters of individual personalities from the cities to which inquiries had been sent, gave the matter a sudden sharp twist. Since all of them with one accord condemned the doctrine, the Council did not trust itself to make an independent decision. An acquittal would not be understood anywhere in all Christendom. That he who had been stigmatized from all sides should become the Reformer's successor was now absolutely out of the question. It was the opinions of the German-Swiss confederates which, although they shrewdly circumvented the word execution, sealed Servetus' death sentence. Down in the mouth, the Libertines had to acquiesce.

IT WAS STRANGE how rapidly every-thing now happened. On October eighteenth the last opinions arrived and were translated by the twentieth. Ami Perrin, none the less, was attempting to gain time; he pretended to be ill. On the twenty-sixth, the Council members were called under oath to the meeting in which the destiny of the prisoner should be decided. Twenty of the twenty-five members were present. Under the leadership of Ami Perrin the meeting proceded with excite-ment. He opened it with the cold-blooded proposal to let Servetus go scot-free, and when this was not accepted, put forth a second, to leave the decision up to the Council of the Two Hundred. But that, too, was rejected. The Small Council was jealous of its rights and had once before refused to bring Servetus' case before the Two Hundred.

As any parliament of today, so the Council of Geneva consisted of three main groups. Between the left wing, the Libertines, and the right wing, the Calvinists, stood the center party. This last group had shown itself hostile to the Reformer in the delibera-tions thus far. However, it could not reject the opinion of all the sister churches of the country. Even the conservatives among the Libertines may have been frightened by the fact that their city might be brought under the influence of a heretic who was gen-erally despised. They feared a civil war would be the inevitable consequence if no sentence were pronounced.

Thus the decision was made by a secular court the majority of whose members were opposed to Calvin. This is the decision which after almost four centuries is the only familiar fact in the life of Calvin to countless "educated" people: ". . . Inasmuch as you, Michael Servetus of Villanueva in the Spanish kingdom of Aragon, have been accused of terrible blasphemies against the holy Trinity, against the Son of God and other principles of the Christian faith, whereas you have called the Trinity a devil and a monster with three heads, whereas you went about to destroy poor souls by your horrifying mockery of the honor and majesty of God, too wicked to be mentioned, whereas refusing to be taught in any way, you called faithful Christians atheists and magicians, whereas, whereas, whereas . . .

"We, the mayor and judges of this city, having been called to the duty of preserving the church of God from schism and seduction, and to free Christians of such pestilence, decree that you, Michael Servetus, be led to the place Champel and be bound to a stake and with your book be burned to ashes, a warning to all who blaspheme God."[171]

CALVIN WAS DEEPLY PERPLEXED by the harshness of the sentence. With his faithful contemporaries he held that the death of this violent enemy of the Reformation was necessary, but that the execution by fire was an unnecessary severity. He remembered the burning of the martyr Pointet at Paris which made such a terrible impression upon him as a youth. Should Geneva imitate the thousandfold example of Rome, should it give to the world the spectacle of a stake upon Evangelical soil?

He made every possible effort, gathered the preachers in order to bring about by unanimous petition a moderation of the death penalty.[172] They showed the Council that the old canonical law which demands the fire penalty for heresy was a hangover from the Catholic era. Yet their efforts were vain. In the evening, Calvin wrote hurriedly to his friend in Neuchâtel, "We endeavoured to change the manner of execution; why we achieved nothing, I shall tell you orally."[173]

It is not difficult to discover the reason for this. Resentful at Calvin's disobedience in not admitting Berthelier to the Lord's Supper, piqued at his firm stand in regard to the discipline, perhaps also angry about the justification which would be his because of the sentence pronounced, the Council showed not the slightest intention of granting the Reformer his wish. God forbid!

THE NEXT DAY when Servetus was informed of the decision, he was speechless, stunned. To this very hour, having been strengthened by the Libertines in his opinion, he not only believed that he would be acquitted but that Calvin would be sentenced.

The outburst of despair lasted for hours until he recovered

his senses when Farel spoke with him. This old man had come in haste to stand at the side of his friend during these difficult days, before he had received this short letter. Upon his entreaty, the condemned agreed to see Calvin. The Council gave its permission but not without sending along two of its members as witnesses.

Now there came a change in the life of the Spaniard, a change which the certainty of impending death frequently produces in man. Having abandoned his conceited, injurious ways, he asked him who entered for forgiveness. Filled with emotion, the other spoke lovingly to him, "Believe me, never did I have the intention to prosecute you because of some offense against me. Do you remember," he spoke now with a tender voice and not in a tone of reproach, "how, in danger of death, I wanted to meet you in Paris sixteen years ago in order to win you to our Lord? And afterwards when you were a fugitive was I not concerned to show you the right way in letters until you began to hate me because you were offended by my firmness? But let's not talk about me, nor of the past! Are you thinking of asking forgiveness of the everlasting God whom you have blasphemed on so many occasions? Are you thinking of being reconciled to the Son of God? If you deny that He became man as we are, you are destroying the bond of brotherly union which binds us to the Saviour, you are destroying our only hope . . ."[174]

Calvin looked expectantly into the eyes of the one doomed to death—now, now the moment must come in which the angels in heaven rejoice!

But Servetus shook his head. Indeed, he spoke a different language now. Not one more unkind word could be heard from him. But he retracted nothing . . .

His dying could not be compared with the joyful going home of the Evangelicals for whom in all the surrounding Roman lands stakes had been set ablaze; yet greatness belongs to such dying. The last twenty-four hours of his life were climaxed by his exclamation, "Jesus, Son of the eternal God, have mercy upon me!" These words made up for many things in the restless life of this highly gifted man whom fatal ambition led to the obstinacy of a heretic.[175]

Calvin went to see him again. It must have been an extremely bitter walk for this sensitive man. Ami Perrin did not again visit Servetus, who through his promises had come to ruin. Early the next day the sentence was executed. It was impossible for Calvin to be present at the execution which he so desperately tried to prevent. He was spending the hour on his knees, collecting the thoughts which broke powerfully in on him. In his stead, Farel accompanied the condemned on his last walk.

IN HIS OWN CENTURY—aside from Calvin's personal enemies, like Castellio[176]—the execution of Servetus was generally approved. Among these many voices we mention only one, that of Melanchthon who wrote to Calvin: "The Church of Christ will be grateful to you today as well as in the future . . . your government has proceeded in the death of this blasphemer according to all laws."[177] In other words, Calvin objected to the cruel death sentence; the gentle Wittenberger found it just.

Our age is of a different opinion. Still it sounds strange when of all people Catholics in this connection turn so sharply against the "cruelty" of Calvin. His Romanist contemporaries politely refrained from such criticism. Had Servetus been burned in Vienne exactly according to the sentence pronounced, à petit feu, the little smoke from his stake would hardly have been noticed among the tens of thousands of stakes which continually caught fire in Spain, in the Netherlands, in the England of the bloody Mary, in France the land of immoral bigoted kings, for the followers of the pure doctrine.

Moreover, had Calvin's wish been granted and the fire penalty mitigated to an execution by sword, little fuss would have been made about it. Even in the Lutheran Church, and much later, beheadings for the sake of belief took place.[178] It is the stake taken over from Rome, which Calvin did not want, to which Servetus' case owes its tragic fame. The Libertines inflicted far greater injury to the Reformer by denying his wish than they dreamed of. They have thereby seriously vilified his memory.

And as a conclusion to this painful section:

It is wrong to accuse Calvin of intolerance. Scattered every-

where throughout the *Institutes* are edifying passages which prove
the contrary. Book IV, chapter twelve, paragraph 8, begins with
these words: "The severity becoming the Church must be tem-
pered with a spirit of gentleness. For there is a constant need of
the greatest caution, according to the injunction of Paul[179]
respecting a sinner; lest such a one should be swallowed up with
overmuch sorrow; for thus a remedy would become a poison."
And the tenth paragraph in the same chapter concludes with
this admonition:

"Count him who has become disobedient to the Word not
your enemy, but admonish him as a brother, says the Apostle."[180]
Calvin did not want the Church to be overly severe, to go to
unmerciful extremes; but to anticipate the offender and extend
its arms to him. "Unless this tenderness is diligently observed by
the congregation and its members, there exists the danger that
we make of the Church a hell and we ourselves become hangmen
instead of monitors."

It is wrong to call Calvin an enemy of freedom of instruction,
which in his writing against the Council of Trent he expressly
defended.[181] He was intolerant only about blasphemy and the
determined destruction of the faith. If one calls his Genevan
Reformation intolerant, what then will one call the French Revolution, this "cradle of freedom," which squeezed everyone's neck
under the guillotine who did not agree with the people's benefactors?

Michelet, the great historian who has been quoted once before,
himself a free-thinker, confessed, "I went to Geneva myself to
form an opinion. As a follower of freedom of thought I was
inclined toward Servetus and his friends, the Libertines. However, research in the Geneva archives shows the matter in a different light from what I had conceived it to be through historical
works. I gained the conviction from the Council meetings that
the Libertines would have surrendered the city to France. This
would have been an immeasurable misfortune for Europe"—says
the Frenchman, Michelet!—"Servetus counted upon the victory
of the Libertines; therefore his stay in Geneva which became his
doom. No doubt, Calvin was determined to save the faith, the

homeland, the European transformation of the spirits . . . This was the most burning moment of the school of martyrdom. In an unpublished letter which was at my disposal, Calvin describes his embarrassment at having to choose among the petitioners who are crowding in front of his door and who are quarreling. What about? To be sent into certain death as messengers of the faith!"[182]

Thus the honest scholar who investigates the sources corrects his prejudice. While a Jewish author, absolutely incapable of comprehending the Reformer, draws his wisdom out of muddy waters and serves it to his well-meaning readers in these words, "Calvin, God's bloodhound, to whom Melanchthon, Bucer, and other proclaimers of the German Gospel bark their approval . . ."[183]

Let us not be disheartened! In four hundred years our own leaders will also find critics who will be ignorant and imaginative about the spirit of a past age. At that time will conscientious historians be able to match them with as much genuine greatness as the experts on Calvin and his time are able to do today?

ON THE PLACE of Champel where the stake was set afire for the unfortunate Spaniard there stands today a monument of reconciliation. It was inspired by Doumergue, the great admirer of Calvin. He it was who drew up the following inscription:

"As reverent and grateful
sons of Calvin,
our great Reformer,
repudiating his mistake, which was the mistake
of his age,
and according to the true principles of the
Reformation and the Gospel
holding fast to the freedom of conscience,
we erect
this monument of reconciliation
on XXVII October MCMIII"

It is placed here not to please or hurt anyone, but in keeping with Calvin's Reformation, although or rather because it confesses an error which violated its spirit.

Protestantism has erected a stone of reconciliation at the place where its only stake stood. When will the first stone of reconciliation of the Roman Inquisition follow?

I have allowed an unduly large space for the Servetus episode in this biography. Other, more edifying, incidents lose out thereby. It is really a shame that he who wants to make the Reformer known in his true nature has to undertake a vindication in order to eradicate from the world prejudices which by this time have become deeply rooted. A Reformed Swiss pastor was greeted during a meeting of the Gustaf Adolf-Association by a Lutheran colleague with the following friendly suggestiveness, "In which year was it now that Calvin burned Servetus?"

TOWERING WITH RAGE, the Libertines experienced the collapse of the plan which they had tied too closely to the destiny of the Spanish heretic. Instead of crushing the Reformer, they had made his position stronger than before. Once again they attacked the discipline; should they succeed in shaking it, then they would be rid of him with one blow. The introduction of the discipline had been the condition under which Calvin was won for the second time to come to Geneva. He stood or fell with its continuation. Openly and in secret Berthelier pushed forward his admission to the Lord's Supper, and in this act he was fully supported by his party. But Ami Perrin who led the movement was frustrated in all his efforts by the iron inflexibility of his opponent.

The common man with his own scent began to realize that he had to make a choice between the Reformer and Berthelier who was constantly getting into difficulties with the police and whose victory would bring to the people nothing but restlessness and disturbance. Therefore, the people turned more and more toward the man behind whom, in their discerning understanding, stood God. His influence through daily preaching reached almost unnoticed into the hearts of those who were lukewarm or opposed to him.

The minority in the Council which was constantly inclined toward Calvin kept itself well informed about these incidents. It did not lose sight of the fact that public opinion was daily more strongly backing it. And the minority showed itself with increasing self-confidence. Perrin and his party, too, were not unaware of the turning of the tide. New elections were at hand and they deemed it wise to climb down. On January 30, 1554, they pleaded with their enemy for reconciliation and came to agreement upon the promise never again to defend a bad matter. The following day a solemn peace meal united the opponents. The Small Council attended in a body. And the Council of the Two Hundred with fingers raised for an oath resolved in its next session to be faithful from now on to the Reformation and, forgetting all former quarrels, to live in unity.

Only the squabbler, Berthelier, stood aside, pouting his lips. His friends had dropped him.

On February fourth the new elections brought a shift in the parties as had been anticipated. The Calvinists gained a majority in all governing bodies; they had elected three out of the four mayors.

But had they won the game? Calvin was too wise to believe it. About this time he wrote, "The Church of Geneva is like Noah's ark, bobbing up and down on the waters of the flood." [184]

In fact, the quietness of the new year seemed almost like the calm before the storm. The Council Records and letters report subversive activities against the Reformer, spiteful poisoned arrows shot from ambush. No means was too low for his enemies to achieve their end. Even love letters without name or date were smuggled to him to undermine his reputation.

The most evident reason for discontent among the older generation of Geneva was the heavily increasing immigration of French Huguenots. What rabble cannot be incited by pointing to the dangers of too many immigrants? No day went by on which there were not refugees, almost starved to death, dragging with them wife and children, and having passed through unspeakable

hardship and trials, now appearing at the city gates. With tears
of joy they fall upon their knees, singing psalms as they kiss the
dust of the ground upon which they may now live according to
their faith. Full of mercy, Calvin and his followers stretched out
their hands to those who had been saved from the terrible persecution of Cabrières and Mérindol and favored their becoming
citizens. With sympathy for the lot of the refugees there rose in
the preachers the wish to win citizens who had been purified
through hard trials: Evangelicals who had proved they loved the
faith beyond wealth and blood, seven times sifted Reformed,
dependable Church members.

From now on the question of naturalization became the apple
of discord between Calvinists and Libertines. The latter had no
easy task, for those who had moved in were predominantly people
of good social position [185] who brought profit to trade, rented
vacant apartments, and offered to the city treasury large sums of
money to purchase their citizenship papers. These noble aristo-
crats and scholars filled the humble city of yesterday with a refined
spirit and gave her outward recognition and standing. This flattered the self-consciousness of one part of the "old guard" as it
engendered indignation in the other part. The enemies of Calvin
were also those of the strangers because the immigrants showed
their frank veneration for the Reformer; for his sake they had
come here. Each new citizenship certificate meant a new, dependable party member. Naturalizations continued. Full of anger, the
Libertines followed the growing strength of the party which they
opposed. Where they still possessed influence or were able to win
new men—popularity suddenly favored them again during the
election of the city manager—they sought to thwart naturalizations into the community. In vain. Month after month new
Huguenots swore the oath of allegiance to the city.

The January elections of 1555 brought new success to the
Calvinists. This time all four mayors were members of their party,
headed by Jean Lambert, a friend of the Reformer and an ardent
protector of the immigrants. And the victorious party made good
use of its position. Two years before, a motion by Berthelier
became law according to which anyone elected who lacked certain

qualifications was eliminated from the Councils. Thanks to this law the Libertine majority was able to get rid of annoying Council members, and replaced them by conscious nepotism with relatives of their leaders. Now the law proved itself advantageous for those against whom it was intended. Some thirty followers of Perrin in both Councils were replaced by staunch Reformed, and, what is more, they chose primarily young men "who were not born and reared in the godless old days but saw the light of the world shortly before the arrival of the Gospel,"[186] and who from their youth had been instructed in the Evangelical faith. This young guard was expected to become a good support of the theocracy which they intended to establish.

More and more Perrin and Vandel saw their influence upon public affairs waning. Their suggestions before the Small Council to stop naturalizations were unheeded.

Thus the dissatisfied grasped a last desperate means. What they were unable to achieve by legal means should now be accomplished by an armed insurrection. They expected the success which surprise readily brings to a resolute minority. And since they no longer possessed sufficient following among respected citizens they sought it among the common folk, inviting sailors, fishermen, and tavern owners, even tenant farmers, to meals where, by abundant free drinks, the heads of the saturated guests grew hot and daring.

During the night of May sixteenth, the plan was executed. But perhaps the leaders themselves had too enthusiastically imbibed and proceeded without due caution, or perhaps their plan leaked out; the fact remains that instead of the expected isolated resistance, they found the entire city watch at hand, which made an inglorious end to the whole enterprise almost without bloodshed.

The newly naturalized Huguenots who had been threatened with a massacre were sleeping unsuspecting in their beds and were informed only the next day that they were saved by a miracle. Calvin, too, regarded their protection as such and after a detailed report concerning these events he wrote:

" 'Kill the Frenchmen, those traitors,' was sounded through the streets. Yet the Lord Himself in unbelievable manner kept watch over these refugees and put them into a sound sleep . . .

Not one of them left his house. This miracle of God brought the plot to nought. For, as was later discovered, they tried to pretend at first to fight against armed Frenchmen and to kill them, then they planned to attack the rest in order to create the belief that the insurrection had been started by the refugees. However, not only were they threatened but their benefactors' lives were also sought. The foolhardy tried even to punish the Council members . . ." [187]

The collapse of the insurrection was decisive for the cause of the Reformation. The Calvinists, now in the majority in the Council, were tired of exposing themselves and their master to the temerity of a clique which for more than a year, by day and by night, had been disturbing the peace of the city. Their leaders were put on trial and those who had not fled across the border to safety like Ami Perrin, Vandel, and Philibert Berthelier, were beheaded. Calvin himself was not involved in the quick proceedings. "I was not present when the accused were tried. Slanderers say that I was the leader of the entire proceeding and they consider me the most wretched man, even though I was involved merely as an advisor. The only reason why I went to the prison was that these men had begged me to come, and not to influence the judges." So he testifies. [188]

An era had come to an end which constantly drew the Reformer into repugnant and malicious battles. It is amazing that he was not crushed by them. Without interruption he was active in the pulpit. It has been figured out that he preached two hundred and eighty-six sermons and gave one hundred and eighty-six lectures each year during that time. Whoever wrote to him, and wherever he might be, he would always receive a well-weighed, truly apostolic reply. During the critical year 1554 we find especially valuable letters, such as those to the king of Poland, to the Churches of Strasbourg, Frankfort, and Wesel, also the dedication of his commentary on Genesis to the three sons of the electoral Prince Johann Friedrich of Saxony which they declined at the instigation of Lutheran theologians. [189] In the same year, seventeen of his books were published, including republications and translations.

Even his Catholic biographer cannot deny admiration for this tremendous energy for work. He writes: "It is almost unbelievable how a man who had to fight continually against serious bodily infirmities was able to unfold such a many-sided and fatiguing activity. Contemporaries have well compared him with a bow that is always strung. He robbed himself of sleep in order to devote his time to work and wearied even his secretaries with constant dictation. His home was always open to anyone seeking advice. At all times he was informed about all affairs of Church and state, even down to the most insignificant details. Although he had little contact with the outside world, he knew almost every single citizen."[190]

It is astounding when one considers this profusion of spiritual work of one man who was sick and harassed. And—again I must emphasize it—after such reflection one will judge less harshly occasional outbursts of irritability for which he has been so severely criticized.

VII.

The Years of Triumph

(1555-1564)

WITH THE OVERCOMING of the Libertine resistance in 1555 began the last and outwardly clearly marked chapter in the life of the Reformer which his biographers entitle "Le triomphe." The end of the opposition in Geneva did actually make an end to civil battles as far as the existence or non-existence of the work of the Reformation was concerned. But even now struggles were not wanting. In place of the internal came external ones. Berne, recognizing in the Libertines compatriots, interested itself vigorously in those who had fled from Geneva into its territory. For its resistance to the wishes of the mighty city on the Aare, the Geneva Council had to fight for its independence and suffer disadvantages relative to the renewal of castle rights and other things as well. The conflict, which lasted for years, was to become so intense that Viret and the Calvinistic preachers of the Vaud lands were expelled. The ever increasing propaganda for the Gospel originating in Geneva antagonized the governments in Catholic countries. And then: Luther was dead. His less worthy descendants had begun to war against Calvinism as an enemy power.

Battles in all directions, battles . . .

BUT IN GENEVA itself the Word of God ruled. Therefore this dawning era—it included Calvin's last nine years—has been called the "era of triumph." The battles had brought him to his life's goal: the city had been won for the Lord and became the "cité calviniste." The honor of God became the first principle of the state; the honor of God, salvation for the individual as well as for all citizens collectively.

Prior to the Council elections in 1558 Calvin recommended to the citizens, "Choose wise men who fear God. Remember your experiences and how much you formerly had to suffer because of culpable governments. All of us need to recognize our insignificance and that unless God is for us we count little or nothing in the fight against the convulsions and dangers which fill this world. The honor of God and good order, this be our motto . . ."[191]

Words which could serve as a program for the government of existing states.

In the last paragraphs I have occasionally called Calvin the head of the Church. This is true in the sense that he guided the church of the city. Not only the church in the city: but he guided the rise of the Reformed Church movement in all countries and as such was recognized as its leader. In his public appearance he never put himself above other preachers and refused every outward recognition. The Church of Geneva had no prelate as other Reformed cities of Switzerland had. Calvin did not want a higher salary than his colleagues,[192] and gifts of the Council had persistently been refused by him for a long time.[193] In his public position he wanted only to be known as the preacher of St. Peter's and teacher of theology.

An opinion that is quite common but which has long been rejected by initiated historians is that Calvin had now become the absolute lord of Geneva, the dictator. He has been called Pope, Caliph, the "protector" of Geneva. This opinion is untenable for the simple reason that after the defeat of his opponents, Calvin remained as simple and humble as before. Fearfully he avoided the glitter of sovereignty; he was the servant of God, nothing else. His flatterers had no success because anyone who even tried to use his influence offended the unassuming man.

And yet this influence was astonishing, not only in matters pertaining to the church, but also in the city's state and foreign politics. Calvin was recognized as a superior lawyer, manager, diplomat, and it became customary to make no important deci-

sion without his advice. Foreign powers soon realized this. First
of all Berne, which saw in him the soul of the opposition to its
wishes. Then also Savoy, France, and Spain became aware that a
superior mind put its stamp upon the affairs of the city. Important diplomatic writings often referred to him as "the man of
Geneva." Alardet, bishop of Mondovi, whom the Duke of Savoy
sent to Geneva as a spy, was of the opinion that so long as Calvin
was alive, any attempt to overthrow the city was in vain because
he seemed to possess "devilish means" to bring all plans to
nought. He proposed to the duke, therefore, "to massacre Lucifer,
for which everything has been put in readiness as for the most
beautiful and holy work which had been done in a hundred years,
a work which would not be done again for another hundred
years."[194] The assassination which was to take place on the road
to a village three miles from Geneva came to nought. But its
scheme illumines like lightning the fear which the prelate, and
with him the threatened Roman Church, had for the towering
spiritual power of the Reformer.

It would be a subject for an artist of outstanding ability to
picture the pale, frail, modestly clad Reformer as he passed
through the alleys of the old city, a spiritual prince and a bond-
slave of God, going either to church to preach or to the Council
meeting of the elders. Hodler's attempt[195] is not altogether satis-
fying; it is too anecdotal. If only this artist with his monumental
plastic faculty had been gripped inwardly by his task, we would
indeed possess a moving, true monument of Calvin.

It was as if his strength increased in proportion to the tasks
laid upon him. He overcame the opposition of an easygoing
people which fought the Church discipline and completed the
laws with supplements which incorporated the "Ordonnances" of
1541, primarily by eliminating all ambiguity so that they corresponded to his original intentions. In place of the old Geneva
which was hit on the head with the suppression of the revolt of
1555, there stepped a new community which by its faith and its
walk became as the holy city of God. A powerful religious zeal
which laid hold on rich and poor left its imprint on the entire
population. The Small Council met before every celebration of

the Lord's Supper; the behavior of its individual members was discussed and he who through indifference, enmity, or in any other way had failed, was admonished in brotherly love to make amends. Despite the increased number of worship services, the churches were so much overcrowded that plans for a new building were discussed. The sermons formed the center of the spiritual life. Religious questions, and the progress of the Gospel near and far, constituted the main topics of conversation. Everyone was in a position to give an account of his faith, "like a doctor of the Sorbonne."

The forces of the Gospel, working from within, produced a visible renewal which was also evidenced in the outward conduct of life. The population became industrious, sober, and thrifty, and laid thereby the foundation for economic progress.

In 1556, John Knox, the subsequent Reformer of Scotland, wrote from Geneva to his home, "Here exists the most perfect school of Christ which has been since the days of the Apostles on earth. Christ is preached elsewhere too; yet nowhere did I find that morals and faith have been improved more sincerely than here."[196] And Farel exclaimed, "Better to be the last in Geneva than the first somewhere else."[197]

Countless contemporaries expressed the same judgment. A German historian put his impressions into the following words: "Geneva, saturated with the piety of Calvin, became the spring from which Calvinism in its extraordinarily vigorous expansion in all the countries of Europe ever drew new strength. Those who fought against the Counter-Reformation, the martyrs, thought with longing of the things they had seen in Geneva or what they perhaps only knew from descriptions. The ideal, embodied in Geneva, inspired them to hold out until death."[198]

ONE THING was lacking for the final development of the city as the bulwark and postern-gate of Protestantism; as yet her sons had to be sent abroad for their education.

Two hundred years before, when the Emperor Charles IV offered the city a university under the protectorate of the Count of Savoy, it refused the gift, so as not to make new concessions to the enemy whose yoke it was about to throw off. Now, however, there arose a university as a monument to the political and spiritual freedom that had been won.

With all the tenacity and perseverance of his being, Calvin furthered the plan. This city of hardly more than fifteen thousand people was first of all devoid of means. He understood how to arouse the people. Voluntary gifts laid a solid foundation for the capital which would make the realization possible. Poor and rich competed in their sacrificial willingness. From the printer Mathieu de la Roche, who endowed it with a quarter of his fortune, down to Jenon, the baker's wife, who contributed five Sols, everyone gladly assessed himself for it. Soon the collection was so far advanced that the erection of the college building could be begun. And as the walls were slowly rising the Reformer could be seen, in disregard of the fever which shook him, dragging himself to the building lot, watching with satisfaction the progress of the edifice and speaking words of encouragement to the laborers. Above the entrance the mason chiseled the words: The fear of the Lord is the beginning of wisdom.

The indefatigable Calvin had already been looking for teachers for his school. The best ones were just good enough for him. We are still in possession of the letters in which he unsuccessfully tried to win the scholars Mercier and Tremelius from Paris. They show the zeal with which he undertook this as every other task. To Mercier he wrote that from a famous place of activity he would come into a dark and humble corner of the earth. For this reason, however, God would offer him the opportunity to complete a work whose immeasurable usefulness would have far-reaching effects. "May the Lord grant that some day I may become your associate in the work for which I have the greatest longing!"

At this juncture conditions in the Bernese Lausanne unexpectedly added to the founding of an excellent staff of scholars. The professors of the academy in Lausanne were confirmed Calvinists. Berne was hostile to Calvin. The antagonism became so sharp that Viret and with him the best teachers left the city in the Vaud land. Chevalier, Bérauld, Tagout, and Randon occupied with Calvin the first chairs of the new Academy in Geneva whose rector was Theodore Beza, scholar and poet. Numerous students from Lausanne followed their professors and thus the existence of the new school was assured. On March 5, 1559, the opening was solemnly celebrated at St. Peter's.

The Reformer himself devised the "laws of the Academy of Geneva." It consisted primarily of a theological and a philosophical faculty. His ingenuity was evident in the clear-sighted division of the curriculum. This school was devoted to the holy service of the highest Lord and its task was to further the true knowledge of God and to serve to the honor of God. It was to train warriors for the Lord and to be primarily a seminary for servants and preachers of the Divine Word.

A brief digression. A few decades later when Acquaviva, the general of the order, devised the curriculum for the Society of Jesus, he borrowed much from Calvin's academic regulations "in the conception and the treatment of scholastic affairs." In fact, he "followed the same principles." "In regard to the organization proper and in fundamental principles, the two institutions are much alike, so that they are related to each other as the blueprint and the completed work." The Catholic biographer, who with these words refers to the surprising similarity, offers for it a number of illuminating proofs which he concludes with the collection of evidence, "the approbation and recognition which have been voiced concerning the curriculum of Geneva's Reformer, even by his acknowledged enemies, are at once the best testimony for its usefulness and timeliness."[199]

Thus originated the Academy of Calvinism. From the very beginning it was crowned with marvelous prosperity. Even in the year of its founding some nine hundred youths, coming from many different countries, matriculated as regular students, and almost the same number were being trained in Calvin's lectures to become Evangelists and teachers of the Bible in their respective lands.[200] The Academy was soon the heart of the Evangelical life of Western Europe. From it flowed the forces which carried its founder's knowledge of God abroad. The Academy became a model for future school and university affairs in France, Holland, Scotland, and even in the New World.

ON CHRISTMAS DAY, 1559, Peter Viret and the other Lausanne preachers submitted a petition to the Council to be accorded Geneva citizenship. Their wish was granted and their purchase-money refunded. Suddenly it occurred to one of the Council members that all the preachers and all the teachers were citizens of Geneva—with the exception of the head of the Church. It was then that the Council proceeded to do something which is contrary to all customs. The Minutes report this in their brief, legal style, "Therefore, Mr. Calvin is also asked to become one of the citizens . . ." In other words, it was a formal invitation! He was called to a Council meeting where in solemn tone the presiding mayor made the proposal. Calvin, visibly moved, responded, "Do not think it unkind, noble Sirs, that I myself have not long ago asked to become a citizen. My only reason was to avoid any false pretense." And he found words of sincere gratitude for the honor which brought him visible happiness.

Herein lay the only reason why he was afraid to become a citizen of Geneva: not to be suspected of seeking his own interests. And he refrained from doing it in the city for which he had been praying and laboring for the last twenty-two years, *his* city, he whom the Courts of Paris and Madrid had long since called "The Man of Geneva" because he embodied the character of this city . . .[201]

This belated recognition was not premature! On that same Christmas Day, Calvin was stricken with that ailment which had recently caused him to suffer more than any other infirmity. The day before he had used up more energy and strength during the Communion service in the overcrowded St. Peter's Church, so that he might be understood by the many who had to find places in the far corners of the side chapels. Now, just as he was returning from the City Hall where he had been made a citizen, he suffered a terrible coughing fit which was followed by vomiting of blood. "An artery has burst!" was the physician's diagnosis.[202] But we know better. Tuberculosis had broken out in the body weakened by work and privations.

He was advised to rest for a month. Yet he could not bear to remain more than a few days within his own four walls. And once again he resumed his indefatigable activity in the pulpit and as a lecturer.

FROM NOW ON it was a slow death. Not that it could be marked in his endeavors. Once more he revised the French as well as the Latin edition of the *Institutes* and daily wrote long letters. He advised the Council of Geneva as well as foreign powers and heard the many who thronged to see him, finding for each the fitting word. Above all, he continued his expositions of Holy Scripture. These expositions constitute his precious legacy to this day. A German theologian judges, "Calvin's commentaries will remain for all time the best that have ever been written on Scripture." [203]

To the joy of watching the triumph of the Reformation in France, the Netherlands, and across the Channel, there was added the daily grief over his followers who were persecuted with fire and sword. And there was more grief: Luther, that great and admired man, was dead. Those who called themselves after him frustrated in petty party passion Calvin's fervent desire to cultivate relationship with the German Church, and to bring about uniformity in the principal beliefs of Evangelical Christendom. "Along with the proscription of Melanchthon's interpretation of the Lord's Supper, that of Calvin is also condemned, and when he finally established his full agreement with the Swiss in the Concensus Tigurinus, the Lutherans' hatred knows no limitations." [204] Their spokesman was the Rev. Joachim Westphal of Hamburg, who, beginning in 1552, published spiteful writings against the Reformer of Geneva. The campaign launched by him bore disastrous fruits. Suffering Protestants who, under the leadership of John a Lascos, after the death of King Edward of England, fled the cruelties of the Inquisition under the rule of Catholic Mary, were mercilessly rejected by Danish and German seaside towns. [205] Only he who knows the reconciling spirit of Calvin can realize how such incidents embittered the end of his life.

ON FEBRUARY 6, 1564, for the last time Calvin ascended the pulpit of St. Peter's to preach on the harmony of the Gospels. Breathing difficulties were so great that he was almost unable to finish. A few days before he also concluded his teaching activity at the Academy with a lecture on the Prophet Ezekiel. Then the mouth which from the day of his calling gave all honor to the Word became silent before the public.

Soon he was only able to lie outstretched on his bed. The physicians were helpless. The net of his maladies was too entangled. In his suffering he could be heard to whisper, "O Lord, how long?" Still he continued to labor on unfinished work, and orally and by correspondence he took part in the affairs of the Church. Those who visited him begged him to give himself a rest. He shook his head, "Am I still working? Bear with me that God will find me watching and busy at His work until my last sigh . . ."

The love and veneration that everyone had for him was daily manifested in moving ways. On March tenth, prayers were requested for him. The Council made a gift in the form of money and in order that he would not refuse it, it was conveyed through his brother. But even this was in vain. He refused the gift like earlier ones intended for him, explaining that it was too embarrassing already to have to receive his salary now that he was no longer able to work for it.

Two weeks later he asked once more to be carried to the door of the City Hall and, supported by two friends, he ascended the stairs with difficulty. Holding his cap in his hands, he stood for the last time on the place from which, called or uncalled, irrespective of applause or disapproval, he had expressed his frank opinion. He found words of kindness for every kindness shown to him. How inwardly moved the clerk of the Council, otherwise so dry in style, must have been to record on this day, "He talked with exceeding breathing difficulties and with such marvelous graciousness that the gentlemen were hardly able to hold back their tears . . ."[206]

The following Sunday—it was Easter—he could not resist the desire once more to celebrate the Holy Communion with his congregation. He was carried into the church, stayed through the entire sermon, and sang with the rest the hymn, "Lord, now lettest Thou Thy servant depart in peace." His voice was frail and trembling but upon his countenance there rested such quiet joy that those around him were deeply moved.

On April twenty-fifth he dictated his will. It is reproduced here in its most important aspects as an exalting testimony of a humble Christian:

"In the name of God. I, John Calvin, servant of the Word of God in the Church of Geneva, weakened by many illnesses . . . thank God that He has shown not only mercy toward me, His poor creature, and . . . has suffered me in all sins and weaknesses but what is much more that He has made me a partaker of His grace to serve Him through my work . . . I confess to live and die in this faith which He has given me, inasmuch as I have no other hope or refuge than His predestination upon which my entire salvation is grounded. I embrace the grace which He has offered me in our Lord Jesus Christ and accept the merits of His suffering and dying that through them all my sins are buried; and I humbly beg Him to wash me and cleanse me with the blood of our great Redeemer, as it was shed for all poor sinners so that I, when I shall appear before His face, may bear His likeness.

"Moreover, I declare that I endeavored to teach His Word undefiled and to expound Holy Scripture faithfully according to the measure of grace which He has given me. In all the disputations which I led against the enemies of the truth, I employed no cunning or any sophistry, but have fought His cause honestly. But, oh, my will, my zeal were so cold and sluggish that I know myself guilty in every respect; without His infinite goodness, all my passionate striving would only be smoke, indeed the grace itself which He gave me would make me even more guilty; thus my only confidence is that He is the Father of mercy who as such desires to reveal Himself to such a miserable sinner.

"As for the rest, I desire that after my passing my body be buried according to the customary form in expectancy of the day of the blessed resurrection."[207]

Instructions followed about his possessions. One is amazed at the insignificance of the legacy.

Besides the notary there were seven witnesses who signed the last will so that no doubt might arise concerning it. Calvin may have been aware that his enemies would spread slanders about the last days of his life, something which happened frequently to well-known men during that time. The attempt was actually made.[208] Luther received no better treatment from his Roman historians.

TWO DAYS LATER Calvin received a visit of the Small Council, later that of the clergy. It was a moving picture to see the dying Calvin, emaciated to bare bones, extending his small hands out of the white sheet to bless. Only his eyes still glowed with the old fire as he spoke to the members of the Council.

". . . If our state is to continue, then the house of God which He has erected therein must not be dishonored, for He says He will honor those who honor Him and despise those who despise Him. There is no higher power than that of the King of all kings and the Lord of all lords.

"I say this that we may serve Him truly according to His Word and become ever more established in it. Each of us has his weaknesses; let each examine himself carefully and fight against them. Some are cold, devoted to their business but show no concern for the church. Others are slaves of their passions. Again others whom God has endowed with gifts use them not.

"You older ones be not jealous of the gifts which the younger generation has received, but be glad and praise the Lord who has given them.

"And you younger ones, be humble and seek not to achieve greater things than you can do; for youth is seldom void of ambition and tends to despise the opinions of others . . ."[209]

The death struggle began on the second of May. Beza wrote,[210] "From here on until the last breath, in spite of the terrible pains, his sickness was a constant prayer and often the words from the 39th Psalm, 'I opened not my mouth because Thou didst it,' could be heard from him."

Many were anxious to see him; to let all those who wanted

to come in, one would have had to keep the door open day and night. His followers came to Geneva from distant places in order to look once more in the face of their venerated master. The eighty-year-old Farel was not deterred by the difficulties of the long journey on foot to take leave of his friend. A French nobleman begged to stay with him and received permission to eat a meal in the room of the dying. In all churches, even those of distant Zurich, people prayed for him. In the entire city of Geneva there prevailed a depression as before a national calamity; it was evident how much he had won the hearts of all. The high and the lowly felt a faithful, loving father was going to be taken from them. And in these warm-blooded people there rose a deep-felt grief and love for the dying Calvin who had given everything for them.

The emaciated body seemed almost transparent but the spirit glowed mightily in the pale countenance of the sufferer. His gasping breath gave him unspeakable distress, his prayers and his words of consolation were more sighs than understandable words. But his eyes shone and his features revealed to everyone the directives of his life: a sure hope and a firm faith.

It seemed as if he regained speech once more on the twenty-seventh of May. But it was the last flicker of life. When Beza, who had shortly before left him, was called back at eight o'clock in the evening, he found the master departed. "He was more like one who slumbers than a dead person. Thus it happened that at the same moment the sun was setting and the great light of the church of God was taken heavenward. It has pleased God to show us in the life of a single man of our time how to live and how to die."

Beza wrote these simple words.[211] They are, judged on comparison with other testimonies of that day, an expression of the prevailing feeling. "During the night and the following day," he continued, "there was great lamentation in the city. For its government mourned for the prophet of the Lord; the poor flock lamented the loss of its faithful shepherd. The Academy deplored its true doctor and head, and all in common wept over the departure of their father and chief comforter next to God."

And again the clerk fell out of his customary official style as he summarized the speeches about the deceased which were given in the special session of the Council, "Dieu lui avait imprimé une caractère d'une si grande majesté . . ."[212] Freely translated—one must do so in this case—: "God had impressed upon his being such loftiness . . ." Like lightning this half sentence catches the popular feeling. Majesty, loftiness—it may also be rendered "glory": to his surviving fellow citizens these were the outstanding characteristics of the deceased leader who was shy, slim, and worn out with infirmities. And God Himself, they felt, had endowed him with this loftiness, this glory. Thereby had the Lord made him radiant for all to see. It is a tremendously impressive testimony, this echo of many voices from men who lived and labored with the Reformer, voices which for four centuries have been imagined silent, which spiteful historians like to suppress, voices, however, which shall resound so long as the memory of this man of God exists in Evangelical Christendom, "Dieu lui avait imprimé un caractère d'une si grande majesté!"

In Berne, the grieved Haller exclaimed, "My Father, my Father, the chariot of Israel and its horsemen!"[213]

CALVIN HAD GIVEN definite instructions for his funeral. Nothing must distinguish it from that of any other citizen. His body was to be sewed into a white shroud and laid in a simple pine coffin. At the grave there were to be neither words nor song.

The wishes of the deceased were scrupulously carried out. But although in accordance with his will all pomp was avoided, an unnumbered multitude followed the coffin to the cemetery Plainpalais with deep respect and silent grief.

He who was averse to all ambition did not even want a tombstone. Just a few months later when foreign students desired to visit the place where the Reformer's earthly remains rest, the place could no longer be pointed out among fresh mounds.

THE CLOSING WORDS belong to Doumergue, the great student of Calvin:[214]

"Zwingli, the devout Christian and hero with the mind of a Hellenist, the statesman with large-scale plans which only subsequent centuries came to value fully; he whose destiny grips the imagination like the end of a classic tragedy, dies on the battle field in ominous defeat. The clouds in the sky gather over his place of death, over his home land, his life work.

"Luther, the champion of the German epic, the hero of Worms, who has enriched the piety, the language, and the poetry of so many Protestant generations to this day, dies tired and filled with anxious forebodings, without a successor who could fully replace him. Again the clouds in the sky gather over his grave, his country, and his life work.

"Calvin dies and one is hardly aware of his passing. Everything remains quiet. In peace and absolute order he takes leave of state and Church, and his successor, even if he had been less prominent than Beza, might equally well have taken his place. Everything remains quiet and continues to go its way . . .

"The dough is kneaded. He who kneaded it is no more. But irresistibly the dough rises. The leaven works in many lands, for years, for centuries, even yonder in the New World.

"Thus Calvin has proved, as he did not cease to testify, that his work and his words were not his own. Does he who kneads the dough have even the smallest share in the life of the ferment which he adds? Reassured, justified, the Reformer of Geneva may lay himself into an unknown grave which no stone will ever reveal to the eye of man. For brightly shines the only epitaph which he might have desired, the humble, triumphant epitaph:

"SOLI DEO GLORIA"

NOTES

Notes

My dear, honored friend, the Rev. Director Rudolf Grob in Zurich, has assisted in this work with valuable suggestions and references for which I thank him heartily.

1. *Institutio*, Bk. I, ch. 16, paragraphs 8 and 9. (I am translating from my French edition of 1562.)
2. Florimond de Raemond, *Histoire de la naissance, progrès et décadence de ce siècle.*
3. See also Doumergue, Vol. I, p. 532. Zahn writes, "I can only warn seriously about Kampschulte. Every one of his sentences ought to be checked with the sources. He understood nothing of the *real Calvin.*" (*Studien*, p. 17.) Again, "It is surprising that Catholics occupy themselves so much with the history of the Reformation. They do so in all countries. The history of the sixteenth century is treated with painstaking method, frequently with the definite intention of destroying its radiance." (*Op. cit.*, p. 19.)
   In his *Church History* (Leipzig, 1896, 2nd ed., Vol. III, p. 194), Hase writes: "A Catholic theologian in Bonn has undertaken a complete history of Calvin, so thorough and objective that it could not have been written better and less prejudiced by any one of us."
   In other words, the Protestant, Hase, in his conception of Calvin is completely guided by the "so thorough and objective" Catholic theologian. And his conception is in accordance with it. This is only *one* example, and there are many, to show what havoc Kampschulte has wrought in the evaluation of the Reformer.
4. "L'oeuvre d'un humaniste d'une précocité merveilleuse." (Doumergue, Vol. I, p. 213.)
5. Epistle to Cardinal Sadolet. See Lang, *Die Bekehrung Joh. Calvins*, Leipzig, 1897.
6. The title page of one of the tracts distributed by de la Forge is reproduced in Doumergue, Vol. I, p. 340.
7. Some, not all, among the more recent students of Calvin question the Reformer's authorship of the Rectorial address of Cop, and therefore also Calvin's flight. Their reasons are not convincing. Calvin's contempo-

rary and successor, Theodore Beza, has reported both incidents as facts in his, the oldest, Calvin biography. On the MS. fragment of the address by Cop which the Geneva Library guards, there stand the words written by an old hand, "Haec Johannes Calvinus propria manu descripsit, et est auctor." Doumergue, who is over-accurate, has not the slightest doubt. (Vol. I, pp. 331f.)

8. Beza describes this incident in detail in his *Vita Calvini*.

9. *Bezae Icones.*

10. Florimond de Raemond, *Hist. de l'Hérésie,* II, p. 246; and in the French edition, Bk. VII, ch. 9.

11. Florimond de Raemond, *Hist. de l'Hérésie,* II, p. 272.

12. Beza, *Vita Calvini.*

13. Some biographers report an imprisonment of Calvin in Noyon. Doumergue, who also mentions it in Vol. I, p. 426, proves at the end of Vol. VII that it is a mistake in identity. Calvin never was in prison.

14. *Institutio,* Bk. I, ch. 5, par. 2.

15. Ch. 12:2.

16. *Corp. Ref.,* II, p. 600.

17. "Perdat Dominus omnes ecclesiae tyrannos! Amen." (*Christ. Restitutio.*)

18. Calvin, *Opera* VIII, p. 511.

19. Critical research has been able to show errors and poetic license in the work but never such as would injure the inner truth of the whole. Here and there I have gladly followed in my treatment his vivid descriptions where I did not find them refuted by later scholarship.

20. Florimond de Raemond, *Hist. de l'Hérésie,* II, p. 272. Wernle (*Calvin und Basel*) thinks a meeting between Calvin and Erasmus impossible. Already A. Bayle questioned it in his Lexicon (article on Calvin); Merle d'Aubigné thinks, "Bayle porte partout son esprit sceptique . . . nous croyons authentique le récit de cette visite." (*Hist. de la Ref.,* III, p. 204.) Doumergue does not believe in the meeting.

21. Wernle, *Calvin und Basel,* p. 1; Doumergue, I, p. 488.

22. *Institutio,* Bk. I, ch. 1, par. 1.

23. I am not following the first Basel Edition, but the complete work. (See footnote 1.)

24. *Instituio,* Bk. I, ch. 1, par. 2.

25. *Institutio,* Bk. I, ch. 1, par. 3.

26. In this case, Judges 13:22; Isaiah 6:5; Ezekiel 1:28; 3:14.

27. II, pp. 374f.

28. See Zahn, *Studien,* pp. 56f. "Paul strove as much against heretical teachers as Calvin and when the Lord calls James and John sons of thunder, He then gives them the spirit of Elijah, which is sufficiently revealed in the Epistle of James and in Revelation which is Old Testament in nature through and through."
Wernle repudiates convincingly (*Calvin,* pp. 27f.) the notion that the Calvinistic God looked "like a variant of Jehovah in Isaiah or Ezekiel" in contrast to the Father of Jesus Christ, or that Calvinistic Christianity

represented a relapse into pre-Christian Jewish form: "It is lamentable that nothing lay so far, so unreachably far, from late Judaism as personal assurance of grace. This assurance of grace was not something especially entrusted to Calvin which he might then confer upon others individually. His Christianity is, after all, no more and no less Judaistic than that of Paul, who comes in every respect out of his own faith in order to overcome it. Paulinism seems to me to be the strongest and most characteristic factor in Calvinistic theology . . . The dogmatics of the *Institutes* grew out of the Epistle to the Romans; the glory of God the Creator, God the Redeemer, and the God of Providence stands in the center with Paul as with Calvin. Their entire faith rests in the trust and obedience of forgiven sinners which they have in this God . . . That, for instance, to mention only one thing, he presents the entire doctrine of the law under the heading of 'God the Redeemer' in the *Institutes,* is purely thinking according to Paul and it should prohibit the attempt to assert too much for Calvin the motto 'the religion of the law.' "

29. Zahn, *Studien,* pp. 66, 79.
30. *Institutio,* Bk. III, chs. 21-24.
31. Rudolf Grob, *Die Prädestinationslehre Calvins Und Ihre Bedeutung für unsere Zeit.* MS. of an address made in the Cathedral Church of Zurich, May 9, 1917.
32. Heinrich Hoffmann, *Johannes Calvin.* "It was to him [Luther] an inevitable consequence of justification by grace alone. But it did not belong to those to which his faith was predominantly attached. Conscientiously he turned his eyes from the hidden God of Predestination to the God of Mercy. Zwingli related it to speculation (which probably ought to read: consequence) concerning the omnipresent activity of God . . ."
33. Wernle, *Calvin,* p. 26.
34. Zahn, *Studien,* p. 90, *op. cit.,* p. 91. "Two factors will always guard Calvinism, one, that the Gospel is preached only to a small number of nations, the other, that among them, it is the few again, who believe. Whither are they and what decree rests on the others?"
35. Rudolf Grob (*Die Prädestinationslehre Calvins,* see footnote 31) says: "If it is concluded, however—as a host of the ignorant has done—that Calvin, proceeding from the thought of eternal election, had developed, so to speak, as a consequence the doctrine to which he gave such impetus so that there is no chance, and every good or evil act—as a matter of fact, every event, even the smallest one—has been predestined by God, then this is gross distortion. When Calvin speaks of the doctrine of predestination, he does not refer in any way to his doctrine of Providence, which has determined all events of the world for all times. And as much as we are tempted in little penetrating studies of Calvin's writings to understand the doctrine of predestination only as a particular part of his doctrine of the providence (*providentia*) of all things, just as carefully does the Reformer separate the two dogmas in their description. He is almost afraid to draw relations between them."

36. *Institutio,* Bk. III, ch. 23, par. 4.
37. *Histoire de France,* 1865, Vol. 8, p. 196.
38. *Histoire de France au XVI Siècle,* Bungener, p. 83.
39. Why is it that this Preface is lacking in the German translation by Karl Mueller? Even the oldest German edition (Heidelberg, 1572) has it. Surely, not only as a historic document, but as an important part it belongs to the whole. It is found in Schwarz and in Matthias Simon, *Um Gottes Ehre,* Munich, 1924.
40. I remind the reader I always translate from the old-French edition. (See footnote 1.)
41. "The most Christian Majesty" was the title belonging to the King of France.
42. Cesare Cantù, *Gli Eretici d'Italia,* 1866, II, p. 90.
43. All details are found with Bartolommeo Fontana, *Renata di Francia,* Rome, 1893. Concerning Renate's imprisonment see Vol. II, pp. 337f.
44. Franklin, p. 26.
45. Tiraboschi, *Storia della Letteratura italiana,* VII, p. 358.
46. "Natura subrusticus" (Preface to the Commentary on the Psalms).
47. This observation is made by the Eastfrieslander, Udo Smidt, after having read through Calvin's letters. (Festgabe für Adolf Schlatter, Berlin, 1927.)
48. *Opuscules français,* pp. 84, 92.
49. "Mon très doux ami."
50. *Opuscules français,* pp. 108, 124, 128, 129.
51. Micah 3:8.
52. Letter of Mathieu Cogniet of July 15, 1537, Herminjard, IV, p. 259.
53. See Calvin, *Commentaire sur le Livre de Psaumes,* 1859, p. IX, "Je me recognoy estre timide, mol et pussillanime de ma nature."
54. "Ac si Deum violentem mihi e coelo manum injiceret." (Calvin.)
55. *Leçons ou Commentaires . . . de M. Jean Calvin sur les . . . Revelations du Prophete Ezechiel . . .* 1565, p. 50.
56. See Doumergue, II, p. 215, *Ibid.,* footnote 3, "Les connaissances patristiques de Calvin étaient célèbres, même parmi les plus savants Réformateurs, comme Mélanchthon."
57. The Small Council consisted of twenty-five members and among them the four mayors (Syndics).
58. Calvin demands on principle the separation of Church and state—this is shown in subsequent battles with the Geneva Council. The combination between state and church authority is a compromise which was not made in those places where Calvinistic ideas were able to gain a free foothold (i.e., in the Calvinistic refugee congregations on the lower Rhine).
59. I Peter 2:2; 3:15.
60. Calvin, *Instruction et Confession de Foy,* 1878, p. 58.
61. Quotation from Merle d'Aubigné, VI, p. 497, from Farel and Calvin's letter to the gentlemen of Berne. Calvin, *Opera,* X, p. 189.
62. Merle d'Aubigné, VI, p. 501, according to Rozet, *Chronique msc. de Genève,* 1. IV, ch. 18.

63. Of course, Kampschulte has to say, *"Seemingly* with great quiet and composure."

64. Council Minutes, April 23, 1538; Beza, *Vie de Calvin,* p. 35.

65. Printed in Henry, I, Appendix, p. 81.

66. Calvin, *Commentaire sur le Livre de Psaumes,* 1859. Preface, p. IX.

67. Wernle, *Calvin und Basel,* p. 18.

68. Calvin's letter to Viret, Henry, I, p. 203.

69. *Ibid.*

70. Herminjard, V, p. 43. Schwarz, *Calvins Lebenswerk in seinen Briefen,* p. 40.

71. Bonnet, *Lettres françaises,* I, p. 19, and Schwarz, I, p. 40.

72. Wernle, *Calvin und Basel,* p. 19.

73. Merle d'Aubigné after Roehrich, *Mitteilungen aus der Geschichte der Ev. Kirchen des Elsasses,* III, p. 133.

74. New edition in German translation by Johannes Kiefel in Barmen-N., 1909.

75. Henry, II, pp. 502f., with a reference to the sources and authorities for this incident.

76. Luther, *Epistulae,* V, p. 211. De Wette, *Luthers Briefe,* V, p. 210.

77. Letter of Calvin to Farel, Nov. 20, 1539, see Henry, I, p. 267.

78. Merle d'Aubigné, VI, p. 577. *Opera,* X, p. 332.

79. A Gulden corresponded to about 4.30Frs. (roughly $1.00).

80. Staehelin, I, p. 253, with reference.

81. In a letter of Calvin to Farel of Jan. 31, 1541, details are found concerning the tenacious adherence of Melanchthon to his person.

82. Letter of Nov. 25, 1544. Schwarz, I, pp. 200f.

83. Merle d'Aubigné, VI, p. 633, after Bonnet, *Recits.*

84. Merle d'Aubigné, VI, p. 631, after Calvin, *Opera,* X, p. 348.

85. Doumergue, II, p. 463. According to this reference, chronological and other data of the Calvin biographers are incorrect concerning the marriage.

86. Doumergue, II, p. 475.

87. The letter is printed in Staehelin, I, pp. 281f.

88. Luther, *Epistulae,* V, p. 211; Calvin, *Opera,* p. 402.

89. Letter of Mathurin Cordiers, October 1, 1540, Herminjard, VI, p. 319

90. Herminjard, VI, p. 329.

91. Letter of Antoine Marcourts, Herminjard, VI, p. 318.

92. Letter to Farel of Oct. 21, 1540, Schwarz, I, p. 104.

93. Letter of Jacques Bernards, of March 1, 1541, Herminjard, VII, p. 42.

94. Herminjard, VI, pp. 331, 332.

95. Doumergue, II, p. 702. Henry, I, p. 397.

96. Doumergue, II, p. 702.

97. On March 1, 1541. Herminjard, VII, p. 41.

98. Herminjard, VII, p. 23.

99. Henry, I, pp. 397, 398.

100. Herminjard, VI, pp. 242, 243, 358; VII, p. 77. Doumergue, II, pp. 706, 7(7.

101. Herminjard, VII, p. 231.

102. Paris Edition, 1859, p. IX.
103. Kampschulte, p. 381.
104. *Op cit.*, p. 385.
105. References in Doumergue, VI, p. 3.
106. Doumergue, III, pp. 509f.
107. *Opera*, XVI, p. 406.
108. See letters by Viret and Farel, *Opera*, XVI, pp. 382, 386.
109. Doumergue, III, p. 574.
110. Schwarz, II, p. 421.
111. Merle d'Aubigné, VII, p. 84.
112. *Institutio*, Bk. III, ch. 6, par. 1.
113. What is now known in Geneva as consistory has only the name in common with the original institution.
114. Merle d'Aubigné, VII, p. 98.
115. Zahn, *Studien*, pp. 11, 12. *Ibid.*, the remark, "In a description of the morals court in Geneva, every individual case ought to be examined in the most careful manner. It is a favorite pursuit to bunch these glaring cases together until terrible caricatures emerge. As soon as the individual case is reported with the precise facts [see the author's treatment of the cases of Castellio, Ameaux, Gruet, Bolsec, and Servetus], it loses something of its horror."
116. Roget, *L'Eglise et L'Etat*, Geneva, 1867, p. 7.
117. Rud. Staehelin, *Prot. Realenzyklopaedie*, III, p. 665. Of course, when the author further explains (p. 667), "The ethical order not only shows the ethical earnestness of Calvin, but also the thorough misconstruction of that which is the task of a Christian government and the goal of the formation of a Christian people, indeed of that which is the will of God for the Christian congregation," then he will have to be answered by another student of Calvin and his age, who has entered more deeply into the intentions of the Reformer than have most. "I am always quite concerned when I hear that Calvin has misunderstood the will of God. Everywhere in Scriptures it is the will of God that the powers that be have the responsibility to uphold the two tables of the law in equal manner . . . The New Testament also expressly recognizes the right of the law. What severe law could not be set up from Matt. 5:21 and 22, when children curse their parents! . . . The Lord Himself in His death sentence is the most stirring example of the eternal validity of the law. The entire age of the Reformation has the conception that the powers that be have to stand for the honor of God with every possible means. The Church cannot accomplish its 'heavenly purpose' when it stands among a people which transgresses the laws of God and thus cuts off every one of His blessings. The powers that be must punish that which goes against the law of God. Thereby they prepare the way for the Church and surround it with a protective fence . . . Thereby the Church retains its independence, for in the reclaiming of souls it can only work through the Word. The state as the authority to punish must maintain the whole law of God; the Church

cares for the souls and exercises over them spiritual discipline and exclusion from spiritual gifts." (Zahn, *Letzte Lebensjahre,* pp. 25, 26.)

118. Letter to Viret, October 25, 1542, Schwarz, Vol. I, p. 160.

119. Kampschulte allows himself the spiteful remark, "The author of the *Institutes* did not combine to the same extent the courage to enter into the unfathomable depths of the Christian faith with the courage of everyday Christian love." (Vol. I, p. 484.)

120. Doumergue, III, p. 150, with references.

121. *Op.* cit., p. 148.

122. Zahn, *Studien,* p. 14, after Beza.

123. Bugener, p. 297.

124. Doumergue, VI, p. 10.

125. He received 450 Gulden, only fifty less than Calvin.

126. F. Buisson, *Seb. Castellion, sa vie et son oeuvre,* Paris, 1892, I, p. 200. Doumergue, VI, p. 12.

127. Doumergue, VI, p. 14.

128. II Corinthians 6:4. (See Moffatt's Translation.)

129. Vol. VI, p. 438f.

130. Buisson, I, pp. 411, 412.

131. Doumergue, VI, p. 84, after Gautier.

132. *Op. cit.,* p. 89, with references.

133. *Op. cit.,* p. 87.

134. *Opera,* XIII, p. 568. Doumergue, VI, p. 128.

135. Kampschulte, II, pp. 136 and 151.

136. *Op. cit.,* II, p. 128.

137. Doumergue, who goes to the bottom of everything, did not refuse to refute even this sad slander with all the means of scholarship. (See Vol. I, ch. 3.)

138. Pouacre, which the *Nouveau Petit Larousee,* Quarantième Edition, 1949, p. 814, explains as, "sale, dégoûtant, vilain." (The German equivalent chosen by the author is "S..kopf" [Saukopf]).

139. Doumergue, VI, p. 197, with references.

140. From December 17, 1547, see Schwarz, Vol. I, p. 294.

141. Merle d'Aubigné, I, pp. 8, 9.

142. In the Preface to the second edition of his geography of Ptolemy, Vienne, 1542.

143. Barth, p. 11.

144. *Op. cit.,* p. 10.

145. Doumergue, VI, p. 282.

146. Barth, p. 12.

147. Barth, p. 13.

148. Doumergue, VI, pp. 276-294.

149. A. Bossert, *Calvin,* Paris, 1906, p. 163.

150. Doumergue, VI, pp. 301-305.

151. According to Schwarz, at the end of April, 1553.

152. Psalm 119:109.

153. Bonnet, I, pp. 384-386.
154. Volume 40 of *Voigtlaenders Quellenbücher* offers a description and a series of contemporary reports concerning this moving episode in R. Schwarz, *Die Hugenottischen Martyrer von Lyon und Johannes Calvin*, Leipzig, n.d.
155. *Op. cit.*, p. 83, Schwarz, Vol. I, p. 484.
156. Schwarz, Vol. I, p. 237.
157. I have expressed this view earlier already in my volume *Reformation* and received the approval of Prof. E. Doumergue, who wrote me concerning it, "Vous animez l'histoire, vous ne l'inventez pas."
158. Letter of the Veltline pastor Paolo Gaddi of July 23, 1553, *Opera*, XIX, p. 557.
159. Words of Calvin, *Opera*, XXVII, p. 262; quoted by Doumergue, VI, p. 320, where four similar testimonies of other contemporaries are printed.
160. Brière réfutation des erreurs et impiétés de M. Servet, *Opera*, VIII, p. 798. Staehelin, I, p. 449.
161. Schwarz, I, p. 484. The response of Farel is characteristic of the thinking of the sixteenth century: "When I read that Paul did not refuse to die if he had injured someone or had acted worthy of death, I frequently offered my life, if I had taught something against the Gospel, and I added that I would be worthy of the greatest torments if I had made some disloyal to the faith and the teachings of Jesus Christ. Consequently I can demand of others no less than I demand of myself." (Doumergue, VI, p. 355.)
162. *Opera*, XIV, p. 606; Doumergue, VI, p. 332.
163. J. A. Gautier, *Histoire de Genève des origines à l'année 1691*, Geneva, 1896-1911, III, p. 506. According to a footnote, the paper on which was written this sermon of Calvin's along with others seems to have been repulped around the middle of the eighteenth century! See Doumergue, VI, p. 334.
164. Doumergue, VI, pp. 334, 335. Even the panegyrist of Castellio who is hostile to Calvin must confess, "Calvin's act would have as much dramatic greatness in a less crowded place, and on a more widely visible stage, as any one of the tremendous episodes in the century-long struggle between spiritual and secular power." (F. Buisson, *Seb. Castellion, Sa vie et son oeuvre*, Paris, 1892, I, p. 340.)
165. Acts 20:17-38.
166. Beza, pp. 100, 101.
167. Kampschulte, II, p. 212.
168. *Opera*, XIV, p. 607.
169. Henry, III, Supplement, p. 57, according to the Minutes.
170. *Opera*, VIII, pp. 804-806.
171. The entire judgment is found in Henry, III, Supplement, pp. 75-78.
172. Henry, III, p. 188, and Staehelin, I, p. 453, report this petition by the preachers according to the second edition of the *Vita Calvini* by Beza. I have in my possession Kampschulte's private copy of Henry (*Das Leben Johann Calvins*, 3 Vols., Hamburg, 1838). The Catholic biographer put

a question mark next to this place. The editors of the *Opera Calvini* (XIV, p. 657) are also critical of this fact. If the witness, Beza, is not trustworthy, then Farel's letter of October 26, 1553, is a valid testimony; for certainly in the presence of Farel, if he had been capable of an untruth, Calvin would least have dissembled himself!

173. Schwarz, I, p. 493.

174. Calvin recorded in detail this conversation which I have abbreviated. Besides being in the *Opera* (XIV, p. 693) it is printed in the original in Henry, III, p. 193, footnote 1. A further report forms Farel's letter to Blauer, the Reformer of Constance, dated December 10, 1553. (*Opera*, XIV, pp. 692-696.)

175. Early legend has already woven over the unfortunate stake an incombustible yarn. It is reported that a strong wind had separated the flames so that the unfortunate one had to run around in them for hours (!); long theological talks which he is supposed to have given from out of the fire are being printed; green, still leafy oak wood which did not want to burn for a long time had been used. This last item was presented by the prejudiced Castellio. It cannot be supported by any other report. However, if one wants to accept it as true, then one ought not to overlook the fact that the use of green wood along with the other was not considered to make the sentence more severe, but to make it milder because of the dense smoke—this has been proven through physiological experiments with animals—which stops breathing and in many cases the heart as well (Syncope!). The victim suffocates before he would have to endure the pains of being burned.

176. Even the mocker, Bolsec, agrees to the execution of Servetus.

177. Letter of Melanchthon to Calvin, October 14, 1554. *Melanchthon Opera*, VII, p. 362; Henry, III, p. 216.

178. In 1601, the Calvinist, Nikolaus Krell, was executed in Dresden; in 1687, the Socinian, Peter Guenther, in Luebeck. And how many Anabaptists had to pay with their lives for their convictions, until deep into the seventeenth century!

179. II Corinthians 2:7.

180. II Thessalonians 3:15.

181. Henry, III, p. 224.

182. Michelet, *La Ligue et Henry IV, 1856*, pp. 55, 464. Doumergue, VI, p. 363.

183. Thus verbatim in Mauthner, *Der Atheismus und seine Geschichte im Abendlande*, I, p. 598.

184. *Opera*, XV, p. 40. Doumergue, VII, p. 4.

185. "L'élite de la France intellectuelle et morale," says Doumergue, VII, p. (30), after recounting the names of new citizens.

186. Bonivard, *Anc. et nouv. pol.*, pp. 97, 98. Kampschulte, II, p. 257.

187. Letter to Bullinger of July 15, 1555, Schwarz, II, pp. 89-95.

188. Letter to Bullinger, October 18, 1555, Schwarz, pp. 106-111.

189. Wernle speaks (*Calvin*, pp. 17f.) of the missionary and conquering zeal which Calvin possessed more than Luther, "The expansion of Lutheran-

ism, however great it has been, was more a matter of chance, at any rate, not Luther's direct work. His mission was to preach the Word which then, without human assistance, would conquer the hearts of men." Calvin's life work was the furthering of Christ's Kingdom in all of Europe in the sense of a united Protestantism. "An international air moves through his whole work of reform the farther it is extended . . . With this agrees also the logical character of his church constitution which is devoid of all particularity and thus could be accepted at once in France, Scotland, and Holland, and which created a new community of thought and life. One has to go down as far as the more recent political liberalism and socialism until one meets again similar doctrines and forms of life which ignore national peculiarities. And with all that, Calvin was not wholly theoretical in details. No one knew so well how to value the peculiarities of the individual countries and how to distinguish between the inevitably necessary reform and that which was at the discretion of freedom, with the ability to compromise . . . A world historic political figure of the first rank stands here before us with all the characteristics of a real politician, with the art of being able to give in and to overlook less important matters, as well as with iron firmness in everything which is of primary importance. With these gifts he organized the Reformation of Western Europe and created, beyond his death, a fighting organization on which the attack of the Counter-Reformation was to break itself."

190. Kampschulte, II, pp. 381, 382.
191. Council records, p. 685. Doumergue, VII, p. 113.
192. Doumergue, VII, p. 119, after Gautier; Kampschulte, II, p. 382, after the Council records.
193. When Pope Pius IV heard of Calvin's death he said these words: "The influence of this heretic consisted in this, that money had no enticement for him at all. If I had such servants, my empire would stretch from ocean to ocean." (Zahn, *Letzte Lebensjahre*, p. 298.)
194. Letter of Alardet to the Duke, May 12, 1560, Doumergue, VII, p. 163, with references.
195. In his painting, "Les Réformateurs de Genève," in the Geneva Museum.
196. F. Brandes, *John Knox*, Elberfeld, 1862, p. 133.
197. Letter of Farel to Blauer, April 13, 1557. *Opera*, XVI, p. 446.
198. A. Lang, *Johannes Calvin*, Leipzig, 1909, pp. 169-173.
199. Kampschulte, II, pp. 337-340.
200. Staehelin, I, p. 494.
201. Council Minutes, Vol. 55, Fol. 163. Doumergue, VII, pp. 168, 169.
202. Letter of Beza to Bullinger, January 1, 1560. *Opera*, XXI, p. 89.
203. Zahn, *Letzte Lebensjahre*, p. 185. See also Tholuck's beautiful statement. Wernle (*Calvin,* pp. 29f.) writes: "Clearly and concisely. These are the standard commentaries of the entire age . . . The critical freedom of Calvin over against tradition has rightly been praised, all the more because later Protestant exegesis remained so far behind it . . ." In a

special instance, the exegesis of the parables, Wernle cites Jülicher as an authoritative judge, "All in all, Calvin is the greatest exegete of parables in the sixteenth century. The break with Catholicism, with all of tradition, produced marvelous fruits. Freedom from prejudice and a historical sense, linguistic knowledge and the ability to keep a firm grasp on all of the analogous material in the exposition of the individual part, worked together to bring about a tremendous advance beyond Erasmus and Luther."

204. *Prot. Realenzyklopaedie,* III, p. 680.
205. P. Bartels, *Johannes a Lasco,* Elberfeld, 1860, pp. 46f.
206. Doumergue, VII, p. 456.
207. Bonnet, II, pp. 563-566.
208. Bolsec, p. 40.
209. Bonnet, II, pp. 568f.
210. Beza, p. 193.
211. Beza, pp. 197, 198.
212. Council Minutes, dated June 8, 1564. Staehelin, II, p. 372.
213. Zahn, *Letzte Lebensjahre,* p. 296.
214. Doumergue, VII, p. 470.

Employed Literature

Calvin's Works in first editions in French.

P. L. Jacob, *Oeuvres françaises de J. Calvin*, Geneva, 1842.

C. O. Viguet and D. Tissot, *Calvin d'après Calvin*, Geneva, 1864.

Jules Bonnet, *Lettres de Jean Calvin*, 2 Vols., Paris, 1854.

Rudolf Schwarz, *Johannes Calvins Lebenswerk in seinen Briefen*, 2 Vols., Tuebingen, 1909.

A. E. Herminjard, *Correspondance des réformateurs dans les pays de la langue française*, 9 Vols., Geneva, 1864-1897.

E. Doumergue, *Jean Calvin, Les hommes et les choses de son temps*, 7 Vols., Lausanne and Paris, 1899-1927.

————, *Iconographie Calvinienne*, Lausanne, 1909.

Théodore de Bèze, *Vie de J. Calvin,* published by Alfred Franklin, Paris, 1864.

Hicrosme Hermes Bolsec, *Histoire de la vie . . . de Jean Calvin*, Paris, 1577.

Paul Henry, *Das Leben Johannes Calvins*, 3 Vols., Hamburg, 1838.

Felix Bungener, *Calvin, sa vie, son oeuvre et ses écrits*, Geneva, 1862.

E. Staehelin, *Johannes Calvin, Leben und ausgewählte Schriften*, 2 Vols., Elberfeld, 1863.

F. W. Kampschulte, *Johann Calvin, seine Kirche und sein Staat in Genf*, Leipzig, 1869 and 1899.

Paul Wernle, *Johannes Calvin*, akademischer Vortrag, Basel, 1909.

————, *Calvin und Basel*, Tuebingen, 1909.

Rudolf Grob, *Briefe ueber Calvin*, Zurich, 1918.

Adolph Zahn, *Die letzten Lebensjahre von Johannes Calvin*, Stuttgart, 1898.

Heinrich Hoffmann, *Johannes Calvin*, Frauenfeld, [n.d.]

August Lang, *Johannes Calvin*, Leipzig, 1909.

F. Puaux, *Vie de Calvin*, Strassbourg, 1864.

A. Sayous, *Calvin*, Geneva, 1839.

August Lang, *Zwingli und Calvin*, Bielefeld, 1913.

Fritz Barth, *Calvin und Servet*, Berne, 1909.

R. Staehelin, "Calvin," in *Realenzyklopaedie für Protestantische Theologie und Kirche.*

J. H. Merle d'Aubigné, *Histoire de la Réformation au temps de Calvin*, 8 Vols., Paris, 1863-1878.

Florimond de Raemond, *Histoire de la naissance, progrez et décadence de l'hérésie de ce siècle,* Paris and Rouen, 1605-1647.

P. Charpenne, *Histoire de la Réforme et des Réformateurs de Genève,* Paris, 1861.

E. Bloesch, *Geschichte der Schweizerisch-Reformierten Kirchen,* 2 Vols., Berne, 1898.

Karl Bauer, *Valérand Poullain,* Elberfeld, 1927.

Rudolf Grob, *Die Praedestinationslehre Calvins und ihre Bedeutung für unsere Zeit,* Lecture delivered at the Cathedral Church of Zurich, May 9, 1917. (MS.)

J. Bohatec, W. Hollweg, W. Kolfhaus, J. Neuenhaus, H. Strahtmann, Th. Werdermann, *Calvinstudien,* Festschrift zum 400, Geburtstage Johann Calvins, Leipzig, 1909.

Adolph Zahn, *Studien über Johannes Calvin,* Gütersloh, 1894.

Udo Smidt, *Calvins Bezeugung der Ehre Gottes,* Berlin, 1927.

J. Haarbeck, *Die Lehre von der Heiligung nach Johannes Calvin,* Neukirchen, 1918.

Louis Goumaz, *La doctrine du salut d'après les commentaires de Jean Calvin,* Lausanne and Paris, 1917.

C. Schmidt, *Wilhelm Farel und Peter Viret,* Elberfeld, 1860.

Ernst Troeltsch, *Die Soziallehren der christlichen Kirchen und Gruppen,* Tuebingen, 1912.

Alfred Erichson, *Bibliographia Calviniana,* Berlin, 1900.

Other sources are noted in the footnotes.

Index

Hezekiah, King, 42
Huguenots, French, 28, 40, 50, 134-137

Inquisition, Roman, 40, 51, 114, 133, 146
Institutes, Calvin's, 18, 23, 28-30, 36, 38, 44, 46, 50, 54, 55, 64, 68, 69, 90, 94, 99, 111, 113, 119, 131, 146

Jeremiah, The Prophet, 18
Jesuits, The, 15, 40, 144

Kampschulte, F. W., 17, 83, 84, 93, 106, 107
Knox, John, 142

Lambert, Jean, 74, 135
a Lascos, John, 146
Libertines, The, 25, 35, 58-59, 96, 102, 107, 119, 121, 124, 126, 127, 128, 130, 131, 133, 135, 136, 139
Lord's Supper, The, 24, 51-52, 54, 59, 60-61, 65-68, 76, 89, 122-124, 141-142, 146, 147
Loyola, Iñigo, 15, 34, 39
Luther, Martin, 16, 17, 23, 26, 27, 29, 32, 40, 67-68, 70, 77, 88, 124, 139, 146, 152
Lutheran Church, 32, 68, 130, 137, 139, 146

Manlich, Matthieu, 56
Marot of Ferrara, 38, 39-40
Martin, Henry, 34
"Martyrologue," Crespin, 26
Mary, "Bloody," 130, 146
Melanchthon, Philip, 25, 37, 68, 69-70, 72, 89, 112, 130, 132, 146
Mercier of Paris, 143
Micah, The Prophet, 42
Michelangelo, 39
Michelet, Jules, 34, 131
Mimard, 51, 53, 54
Morata, Olympia, 105
Moses, 30
Myconius of Basel, 28, 64

Navarre, Queen of, 21-22, 28
New Thinkers, The, 27
Noyon, 24

Oekolampad of Basel, 25, 28, 45, 64, 67, 68, 86
Olivetan, Peter, 16, 38, 69
Oporin of Basel, 63
Ordinances, 89, 141
Ory, The Inquisitor, 40

173